Born to SHOP

HONG KONG

Third Edition

Born to SHOP

HONG KONG

Third Edition

SUZY GERSHMAN
and
JUDITH THOMAS

Introduction by
DIANE FREIS

BANTAM BOOKS

NEW YORK · TORONTO · LONDON
SYDNEY · AUCKLAND

BORN TO SHOP: HONG KONG
A Bantam Book / August 1986
Bantam Second Edition / February 1988
Bantam Third Edition / February 1990

Produced by Ink Projects.

Library of Congress Cataloging-in-Publication Data

Gershman, Suzy.
  Born to shop. Hong Kong / Suzy Gershman and Judith Thomas.
—3rd ed.
      p.   cm.
  ISBN 0-553-34803-5
  1. Shopping—Hong Kong—Guide-books. 2. Hong Kong—
Description and travel—Guide-books. I. Thomas, Judith (Judith
Evans)
II. Title.
TX337.H85G47 1990   380.1'45'000255125—dc20   89-28120
                                                                            CIP

Published simultaneously in the United States and Canada

PRINTED IN THE UNITED STATES OF AMERICA

FG   0 9 8 7 6 5 4 3 2 1

The BORN TO SHOP Team:

reported by:
Judith Thomas
Jill Parsons
editor: Jill Parsons
executive editor: Toni Burbank
assistant to executive editor: Linda Gross
cover art: Dave Calver
book design: Lynne Arany
copy editor: Archie Hobson
proofreader: Lorie Young
maps: David Lindroth

TO LIBBY HALLIDAY PALIN
one of our best finds ever

Editorial Note

The currency used in Hong Kong is the Hong Kong dollar, which is also signified by a dollar sign. All prices quoted in this book are in U.S. dollars unless otherwise noted. Although every effort was made to ensure the accuracy of prices appearing in this book, it should be kept in mind that with inflation and a fluctuating rate of exchange, prices will vary. Dollar estimations of prices were made based on the following rate of exchange: $1 (U.S.) = $7.8 (H.K.).

Acknowledgments

This book continues to be dedicated to our friend and colleague Libby Palin, who first introduced us to the inner workings of Hong Kong. Through her network of friends we were able to get started on an adventure that is still unfolding.

Our working relationship with the Hong Kong Tourist Association has grown with each revision. Karisa Yuen-Ha Lui and Steven Wong, in the Hong Kong office, have been our eyes and ears for all three editions. They have anticipated our toughest questions and always come through with answers. We thank them from the bottom of our shopping bags. Our grateful thanks go also to Eugene Sullivan. In the New York office Mary J. Testa-Bakht has been a tireless colleague, providing us with tips on resources around the world. Thanks also to Terry Fu in New York for his shopping tips.

Morris Simoncelli, at Japan Air Lines, has been a great believer in our book. We don't think that there's a finer airline flying to Hong Kong than JAL.

C & H International continues to get us the best airfares around the world. Many thanks to Lillian Fong and Patsy Ho for helping us to save.

The Ramada Renaissance Hotel has become our Kowloon shopping headquarters. We thank Andrew Hepburn and Susan Field for making our stay so comfortable. In the United States, a big thank-you to Judy Crawford and her team.

At Hilton International Hotels, thanks to Kerry Green Zobor, and in Hong Kong, to Gillian Stevens.

x ▼ ACKNOWLEDGMENTS

Special thanks to Diane Freis, who wrote the introduction to this book and is one of our best friends in Hong Kong and Kowloon.

Finally, thanks to our kids (Lauren, Ross, and Aaron), who love to see their names in print.

CONTENTS

Preface

Welcome to the revised, reorganized, and re-written *Born to Shop: Hong Kong* (Third Edition). We've returned to our favorite shopping city and checked every listing. The best, and our favorites, have stayed. We've added some terrific new listings and redone the designer sections. Now you can find sections on your favorite Continental, American, and Asian designers as well as a brand-new section on up-and-coming designers and Hong Kong's own Local Talents. We've discovered even more shops where your dollar will go the furthest, whether you're shopping for local arts and crafts or important jewelry.

We've concentrated on the changing factory-outlet scene, and have listed stores we think have quality merchandise. We no longer rattle off every designer-name outfit that we see in an outlet, because they move around too fast, but we do let you in on the stores we consider true outlets.

There's a whole new section on neighbor-hoods to help you find your way around. Although many of the big-name stores have several shops throughout Hong Kong and Kowloon, we have only listed one or two of their most convenient locations. Check the new index in the back of the book to see at a glance which stores are in the neighborhoods you'll be shopping in. This way you won't miss one of them.

Since our first trip to Hong Kong five years ago the pace has become even more frantic. Shops open and close at an amazing rate, but we still show you how to find the best deals in shopping, hotels, and even airfares. As with all our books, some basic rules apply:

▼ No store can purchase a listing in this book or any book we write; we accept no advertising or paid announcements of any kind.

▼ Most of the stores never know we have "officially" visited them, no matter how many times we return.

▼ While our inside sources help to put us on the right track, we do visit each of their recommendations to see for ourselves.

▼ All opinions expressed are solely our own. We are very opinionated and outspokenly honest. Many guidebooks do not editorialize to the extent that we do.

▼ We do update the book regularly, but if you catch a change, please drop a card to *Born to Shop*, Bantam Books, 666 Fifth Avenue, 25th Floor, New York NY 10103.

▼ The turnover of stores is very high in Hong Kong; many don't go out of business but simply move to other locations. We have done our best, but please realize that—especially in Hong Kong—anything goes.

It is also our policy to mention brand names of goods we've seen in a store, but we cannot promise you that these same designer goods will be available in a certain store when you go there. "Now you see it, now you don't" is common practice in Hong Kong.

Suzy Gershman and Judith Thomas

Introduction

Welcome to Hong Kong, the crossroads of the world. All of the best things in life are here for your pleasure, and usually at bargain prices. It's just a case of knowing where to look. No local guide could take you on a better tour than Suzy Gershman and Judith Thomas do here.

Hong Kong is the world's best shopping center. There are world-class shopping malls. There are big-name boutiques that populate downtown Central. But that isn't really what brings the millions of tourists flocking here year after year.

They come for the bargains.

Every commodity in the world is here in Hong Kong; shoppers never have to travel far to find bargains. The best part of all is the fact that if one shop doesn't have what you want, the next one will . . . or the next.

Of course, half the fun of shopping in Hong Kong is bargaining. Everyone knows the price is negotiable, and it's a poor sport who doesn't go in prepared to argue.

Both Suzy and Judith are experts in finding the best bargains in town. They know this town better than many of the locals. I live here, but when they come to town and we sit down to visit, I invariably ask them for the latest secrets.

You may not develop an overnight love affair with Hong Kong as I did, but I promise you'll love the shopping. And isn't that why most tourists come?

Diane Freis

I ▾ THE BUSINESS IS BUSINESS

Welcome to Hong Kong

Hong Kong is synonymous with freedom for many Chinese and Americans alike. There is a free port, and a freely flourishing capitalistic economy. If you have been to Hong Kong before, you will notice that the pace has quickened. The deals are happening faster and the money is flowing more freely. Merchants in Hong Kong are living for today more than ever before.

The city of Hong Kong itself remains a magnificent conglomeration of skyscrapers and boat people, street markets and designer boutiques. Hong Kong is a shopping mecca, a true blend of two worlds. Most of the people dress Western style; there are more Rolls-Royces per square foot (excuse us, meter) than anywhere else on earth. Yet 98% of the population is Chinese; the People's Republic will take over the colony in 1997, and many of the people who live here are poor. Factories complain about labor shortages, yet the streets are overflowing with merchandise of every variety.

Tourism is the third largest business in Hong Kong, with shopping leading the way in dollars spent. The city is alive night and day. It is hard not to get caught up in the fervor, the deals, the excitement.

The Lay of the Land

When we refer to Hong Kong what we are talking about is the island itself, of course, but also Kowloon, the New Territories, and a few hundred islands. For the purposes of definition, we consider it all Hong Kong. In 1997 the British have to return both the island of Hong Kong and the New Territories to mainland China. In less than a decade, all that we refer to as Hong Kong will be considered part of the People's Republic of China.

Shopping in Hong Kong is concentrated heavily in two areas, Central and Tsimshatsui. Both are considered neighborhoods, or districts, part of the larger Hong Kong and Kowloon. Central is very upscale, civilized, businesslike, and modern. Tsimshatsui is older, more gritty, and more active in a frenetic way. There is more fashion in Central, but there are more deals to be had in Tsimshatsui. Factory outlets are outside of the main shopping areas, in towns like Lai Chi Kok and Kwun Tong. These are all part of the Kowloon peninsula.

The wealthy folk live on the Peak, which is the mountaintop on Hong Kong Island, or around Repulse Bay, out toward Stanley, or in the tony Harbour City condos, which are in Tsimshatsui, in Kowloon. The poor live in crowded apartment buildings in Mong Kok or on sampans in Aberdeen's typhoon shelter. But the tourists can be found exploring almost every neighborhood of Kowloon and Hong Kong Island.

The Free Port of Hong Kong

Hong Kong did not become a shopper's mecca over a long span of time or because of the industrialization of the world. It was *created* to be a shopping paradise, for very real economic reasons. "Hong Kong isn't a city, it's a shopping mart," one observant soul said back in the late 1800s. Hong Kong is a capitalist's dream: There is duty on only five commodities, and no duty on outgoing goods.

There is little government interference; the system is a textbook example of laissez-faire. If you think you can get away with it, the place to try is in Hong Kong. People come to Hong Kong to make their fortunes, and always have. Don't be surprised if you catch what we call Hong Kong Fever once you're in town a few days—you get a mad, passionate urge to go into business because suddenly everything looks so easy and millions of dollars in profits seem so possible. If you have any intellectual interest in the study of capitalism, Hong Kong is the place to go to school.

Because Hong Kong is a free port, goods come in without taxation. For example, take your basic Chanel suit. Made in France, the suit costs *x francs* (or dollars) in France. When it's shipped to the United States, the price goes up because of shipping costs, and because the U.S. government levies high taxes against items that are competitive with U.S.-made goods. Since you can be very happy in an American-made suit, the duty on the Chanel suit is about 33%. Very steep! Send that same suit to Hong Kong and you have only shipping costs—there is no 33% duty whatsoever. This does not mean that Chanel suits are a bargain in Hong Kong (they aren't—but for other reasons). This is just to explain to you how the system works.

The free-port part becomes especially important for goods made by other countries in the Pacific Basin—Japan and mainland China. There are very high duties on Japanese goods in the United States, and Japan is a rather expensive country, but Japanese-made bargains abound in Hong Kong. The same is true of goods from South Korea and Thailand. The markets are especially good places to shop for inexpensive clothing from Seoul.

A Short History of Hong Kong Trade

I f you've read or seen *Shōgun* or *Tai-Pan*, you're going to be one step ahead of us on this, but here goes. The Hong Kong area has always been a hotbed of commerce because China silk came out of either Canton or Shanghai. Let's step back in time to the middle 1600s. You remember the Portuguese and their "black ship"? The black ship brought goods from Europe in exchange for silk from China. This was a great business, and the Portuguese wanted it all to themselves. So did the British, the Spaniards, the French, and, later, the Americans.

The only problem was, the big British ships couldn't get into the shallow waters of Macao (the Portuguese port), which is somewhat closer to Canton. But they soon happily discovered that the perfect port was on the island of Hong Kong. So for no other reason than deep water, Hong Kong became the "in" place. Queen Victoria howled with laughter when in 1842 Hong Kong was given to the British as a prize of war.

It was really a laughing matter. You see, not only were silks and woolens being traded, there also was a thriving business in opium. The first Opium War ended with the British winning and getting Hong Kong, in perpetuity. The second and third times they won, they got the rights to Kowloon and then certain mainland territories for ninety-nine years. Back then, ninety-nine years sounded like a darn long time. However, in June of 1997, that ninety-nine–year lease is up, and those territories will go back to China on July 1.

The True Meaning of Duty-free

As a "free port," Hong Kong does whatever it wants and usually gets away with it. A free port is different from a duty-free port. And just because the British do not charge levies on goods coming in or going out does not mean that you don't pay duty on them when you bring them home. But you get a bit of a head start on a bargain this way.

So Hong Kong is both a free port and a duty-free port, two different factors that work together to make a bargain a real bargain.

We are all familiar with the so-called duty-free shops in airports and on tourist shopping streets in most major cities of the world. Most of these shops aren't duty-free; they use that expression as a come-on. But that's another point. How different is Hong Kong from one of these shops? That is the real question. Our answer: Not very.

The basic prices of regular retail goods are very much in keeping with the prices of goods in any of the duty-free shops in airports or boutiques around the world, so that you're really talking only of a discount between 10% and 20%—not worth the flight. But we're all too smart to shop in duty-free airport shops regularly, aren't we? So we realize that there's more to shopping in Hong Kong than meets the eye.

On top of that, there are several shops in Hong Kong that claim to be duty-free. In fact, there's one that is so big and so huge and so obvious that when you are in Kowloon you can't help but see it and think that you must try this place. Relax. Duty-free shop prices in Hong Kong are basically no different from anyone else's prices—fancy sign or no.

When a Buy Is a Good-bye

A true-blue shopper has been known to lose her head now and again. And no place on earth is more conducive to losing one's head than Hong Kong. You see so many great "bargains" that you end up buying many items just because the price is so cheap, not because you even need or want them. When you get home, you realize that you've tied up a fair amount of money in rather silly purchases. We've made so many mistakes, in fact, that we've had to have a long and careful talk with ourselves to come up with an out-of-town shopping philosophy that lays down the ground rules.

Shopping in a foreign country is much more romantic than shopping at home, there's no question about it. And, face it, most people go to Hong Kong just to shop. Even nonshoppers admit that they prefer to shop when away from home; they, too, love Hong Kong. But if you make a mistake while shopping in another American city, you can usually return the merchandise and get a credit with just a small amount of hassle. On a foreign trip, returns can be a major problem and usually aren't worth the effort. So, to keep mistakes to a minimum, we have our own rules of the game:

▼ Take a careful and thorough survey of your closet (including china and linen) and your children's closets before you leave town. Know what you've got so you can know what you need. While you don't have to need something in order to buy it, knowing that you need it (and will be saving money by buying it abroad) will help your conscience a lot.

▼ If you *need* an item of clothing to complete an ensemble, bring a piece of the outfit with you. (At the very least, very carefully cut a small swatch of fabric from the inside of the hem or a seam.)

▼ If you are planning on having an item made to fill a hole in your wardrobe, bring the other parts of the ensemble with you. If you expect to be 100% satisfied with anything you have custom-made in Hong Kong, you have to put 100% effort into your side of the deal. Show your tailor the suit that the blouse is supposed to go with.

▼ Figure the price accurately. Carry a calculator and do your figuring at the American Express rate, not the bank rate.

▼ Figure in the duty. Each person is allowed $400 duty-free. If you are traveling with your family, figure out your family total. Children, even infants, still get the $400 allowance. If you have more than $400 worth of merchandise, you pay a flat 10% on the next $1,000; after that you pay according to various duty rates.

▼ Will you have to schlepp the item all over the world with you? If it takes up a lot of suitcase room, if it's heavy, if it's cumbersome, if it's breakable and at risk every time you pack and unpack or check your suitcase, if it has to be handheld—it might not be worth the cheap price tag. Estimate your time, trouble, and level of tolerance per item. Sure, it may be inexpensive, but if it's an ordeal to bring it home, is it really a good buy?

▼ Likewise, if you have to insure and ship it, is it still a bargain? How will you feel if the item never makes it to your door?

▼ Do your research on prices at home first. We spent several hours choosing and shipping lamps from a factory-outlet source only to discover an American discounter who, once the price of the shipping was taken into account, charged the same price.

▼ We are ambivalent about the value of counterfeit merchandise and cannot advise you whether to buy it or to walk away from it. If you suspect an item to be a fake, you must evaluate if this is a good buy or a good-bye. Remember that fakes most certainly do not have the quality of craftsmanship that originals have. You may also be asked to forfeit the item at U.S. Customs or pay duty on the value of the real object. But you may have a lot of fun with your fakes.

▼ Our rule of thumb on a good buy is that 50% (or more) off the U.S. price is a valuable saving. We think that a saving of less than 20% is marginal, is not worth the effort (of course, it depends on the item and how it will come back into the country with you, etc.), and is usually not a good buy. If the saving is 20% to 50%, we judge according to personal desire and the ratio of the previous points. If the saving is 50% or better, we usually buy several and whoop with joy. That's a good buy!

▼ Remember, excess is the name of the game in Hong Kong. It's easy to go overboard. Learn to say good-bye to a bad buy before you set foot on Anglo-Chinese soil.

Be Prepared

U nless you are used to traveling in the Far East, you will find Hong Kong extremely different from anything you've ever seen before. Depending on how sheltered your life has been, you may even go into culture shock. We won't preach about politics or the poor, but we do suggest that you be mentally prepared for what you are about to experience. There are a few particularly important cultural details:

▼ Chinese street vendors and retailers may be rude to Anglos. We try not to generalize about a thing like this, but you'll soon discover it is a common thread of conversation among tourists and expats alike. In shops—particularly big-name shops—the sales help is usually nice or nicer.

▼ The system is greased by "tea money"—tip everyone and anyone if you want favors, information, or even a smile. While a service charge is often added to a restaurant tab, leave a few cents extra.

▼ As a tourist, you will never get the cheapest price possible, so forget it.

▼ Because of the British tradition, the Chinese queue for taxis, buses, etc. Do not butt in line.

▼ Many Chinese are Buddhists. You may see shrines or religious ornaments beside store doors or apartments.

2 ▾ DETAILS

Information Please

How to, where to, and what to, are the questions everyone asks when planning a trip to Hong Kong. No other Asian city has the choices Hong Kong offers in hotels, transportation, and shopping. As a result, just planning the trip can be a nightmare. Everyone has his favorite places to recommend. Listen to them all, then make your own lists. We have compiled ours from listening to scads of expats, locals, and experts and then seeing for ourselves.

Hong Kong is an easy city to negotiate once you know the system. Spend some time with maps before you go and you will hit the streets running. Don't be afraid of the language barrier.... There isn't any. Most Chinese living in Hong Kong understand English, either written or spoken. We have never had a problem. Carry your hotel's card with you, with addresses in Chinese and English in case you end up in the New Territories or at outlying factory outlets and need directions home. Outside of the main shopping districts, there may be fewer people who speak or understand English, but there are plenty of folks who are willing to try to help you out.

The times we've had trouble getting a point across or giving directions we found that simply writing out your question or the address is helpful for the person you are talking to. Often, it's not that they don't understand English but are just having difficulty understanding your accent.

Booking Hong Kong/1

Most Hong Kong guidebooks are the standard texts containing information on where to stay, what to eat, and which sights to see. Take your choice. Our favorites are those put out by the Hong Kong Tourist Association. You can pick up a packet full of brochures published by the HKTA as you exit passport control at Hong Kong International Airport. If you visit HKTA's main counter at Jardine House, 1 Connaught Place, 35th floor, you can pick up a more complete selection. HKTA publishes three pamphlets that we consider a must: *The Official Guide to Shopping, Eating Out and Services in Hong Kong* gives you shop addresses of every HKTA member shop by area and by category. While they do not recommend one shop over another, they at least have elicited a promise from their member shops to be honest. If they are not, you have the HKTA on your side. Look for their listings of factory outlets that are members of the association. Addresses are given in both English and Chinese. The *Official Hong Kong Guide* is published monthly and contains general information about the city. The HKTA also publishes a weekly newspaper. It contains news of events and shows, along with the usual ads for shops.

A magazine that we rely on is the *A-O-A Map Directory*. It is handed out free at the airport and the HKTA offices. Maps show both building and street locations. Since so many addresses include the building name, street, and area, it makes finding an address simple. For example, if you are looking for the Gucci shop in the Landmark on Des Voeux Road in Central, simply locate Des Voeux Road in Central on the map and find the Landmark building. You then know the cross streets and surrounding points of reference.

Delta Dragon Publications has expanded its line of local guidebooks and publishes *Hong Kong Factory Bargains* and *Hong Kong Yin & Yang*. *Hong Kong Factory Bargains* is updated yearly and contains many factory-shop listings. If you are planning to be in the city for an extended period of time or are simply determined to hit all of the factory outlets (no matter how exhausting this may be), this is a useful book to have. Addresses are given in Chinese and English. *Hong Kong Yin & Yang* is a general guidebook.

Booking Hong Kong/2

Many tour companies and large hotel chains offer shopping packages for Hong Kong, but if you want to put together your own, we recommend some of our favorite shopping hotels that will put you in the heart of the action. Some are fancier than others. They are all convenient to the MTR (Hong Kong's subway system).

Some secrets that might make booking your hotel easier:

▼ Ask the hotels first if they are offering weekend or five-day rates. Almost all hotels discount rooms during the off season (January). When there is not a lot of business in town, rates come down. Hong Kong has so many conventions, and so much tourism, that it is tough to predict when business might be slow; but it doesn't hurt to try.

▼ The Hong Kong Tourist Association publishes a brochure called *Hong Kong Hotel Guide*. Write to their head office in Chicago for a copy (HKTA, Suite 2400, 333 North Michigan Avenue, Chicago IL 60601). This publication provides a comprehensive list of all the possibilities, including addresses, phone numbers, room rates, fax numbers, and services offered.

▼ Check the big chains for promotional rates. Often you can prepay in U.S. dollars and save on price fluctuations. Consider putting together your own group, and booking yourself as a tour package. Every hotel has a special department to deal with groups, and offers incentives.

▼ We rate hotels as inexpensive (under $100 per night), moderate ($100–$200 per night), and expensive (over $200 per night). All rates include government tax (5%) and hotel service charge (10%). We have listed our hotels together by area, on Hong Kong Island or in Kowloon. There are benefits to staying on either side of the harbor. If you have business in Central, you will probably want to be on the island. If you are here on holiday, and want easy access to the factory outlets, stay in Kowloon.

Shopping Hotels of Hong Kong

Central

HONG KONG HILTON: One of our favorite hotels, the Hilton is located just a few blocks away from great shopping at the Landmark, Prince's Building, Swire House, and the Pedder Building. It has its own extensive shopping arcade where you can get your suits made, buy all your jewelry, souvenirs, and shirts, and have a manicure without ever leaving the hotel. The service staff is very knowledgeable about where to find the unusual in Hong Kong. There is even an outdoor swimming pool, and a family plan so that children under sixteen stay free in their parents' room. One of the Hilton International hotels. Reservations: (800) 445-8667. Moderate.

HONG KONG HILTON, 2 Queen's Road, Central, Hong Kong

▼

HONG KONG MARRIOTT: One of the newest additions to the Hong Kong hotel race, the Marriott is not only gorgeous, it is also connected directly to one of the chicest shopping arcades in town. Completed in 1989, the twenty-seven–story tower has 564 guest rooms, an outdoor pool, fitness rooms, water views, and The Mall/Pacific Place underneath. It is located on a hill just east of the main Central shopping district, midway between the Hong Kong Convention Center and the Landmark. It is easy to reach via the Admiralty MTR. Since this is the Marriott's flagship hotel in Asia, it is guaranteed to be first-rate all the way. Reservations: (800) 228-9290. Expensive.

HONG KONG MARRIOTT, Pacific Place, 88 Queensway, Central, Hong Kong

▼

MANDARIN ORIENTAL, HONG KONG: The Mandarin is one of Hong Kong's old luxury hotels. A favorite of tour packagers, this recently renovated hotel is well located near the Star Ferry, and has a great shopping arcade. Many big names have boutiques on the mezzanine shopping level. Reservations: (800) 663-0787. Expensive.

MANDARIN ORIENTAL, HONG KONG, 5 Connaught Road, Central, Hong Kong

Kowloon

RAMADA RENAISSANCE HOTEL: The Ramada Renaissance is well located for all the action in Kowloon. It is directly opposite the sprawling Harbour City complex, a five-minute walk to the Tsimshatsui MTR stop or the Star Ferry, and a two-second walk to the heart of Kowloon shopping. The hotel is brand-new, spanking clean, and has larger-than-usual rooms. There are gourmet restaurants and an attached shopping arcade (Sun Plaza). The hotel is especially well designed for the businessperson, with speaker-equipped telephones and personal-computer outlets in all rooms. The Business Center has fax machines, laptops with software, and VCRs for rent. They offer a fitness center and a large indoor swimming pool. The Ramada Renaissance was recently sold to the owners of the New World Hotels, but Ramada will continue to manage the property. Reservations: (800) 228-2828. Moderate.

RAMADA RENAISSANCE HOTEL, 8 Peking Road, Tsimshatsui, Kowloon

▼

THE REGENT: Still considered to be one of the most spectacular locations in Hong Kong, the Regent occupies the tip of Kowloon Peninsula, and the views from the lobby bar at night are nothing short of spectacular. There is a hotel shopping arcade that is good, and the New World Centre is right next door. The rest of Kowloon is at your doorstep. We stay here just for the view. This is top-of-the-line luxury. Reservations: (800) 545-4000. Expensive.

THE REGENT, Salisbury Road, Tsimshatsui, Kowloon

▼

HYATT REGENCY HONG KONG: The epitome of a shopping hotel. The lobby is directly above the shopping arcade. The arcade has been renovated and now houses some very chic designer shops. The hotel is a popular tour group choice because of its convenient location and price. There are 706 rooms, all with shopping views. Reservations: (800) 338-9000. Moderate.

HYATT REGENCY HONG KONG, 67 Nathan Road, Tsimshatsui, Kowloon

▼

THE PENINSULA: The ultimate shopping/luxury hotel in Kowloon is the Peninsula. Its lobby has seen more business deals and contract negotiations than any other spot in Kowloon. The shopping arcade boasts some of the biggest names, including Chanel, Cartier, and Louis Vuitton. You can't ask for a better location. Reservations: (800) 223-6800. Expensive.

THE PENINSULA, Salisbury Road, Tsimshatsui, Kowloon

▼

OMNI THE HONG KONG HOTEL: Harbour City has three hotels built in and around its office and shopping complex; we like this one the best. It is the closest to Ocean Terminal and has a mezzanine that is devoted to antiques shops. The lobby design is modern chic, and the rooms overlook either the harbor or the shopping. Reservations: (800) 448-8355. Inexpensive.

OMNI THE HONG KONG HOTEL, Harbour City, 2 Canton Road, Tsimshatsui, Kowloon

Getting There

When it comes to booking your plane tickets, have we got news for you. You can do it the regular way, or you can get a deal. We love to fly Japan Air Lines, and find that their service is tops. JAL flies out of New York, Los Angeles, Chicago, and San Francisco, as well as fifty-six other cities in thirty-three countries. Their package tours and special fares make them unbeatable. Tours are offered in conjunction with Hemphill Harris Travel Corporation, TBI (a division of Japan Travel Bureau), Pacific Bestour, and Visitours. There are ninety-seven different programs combining the best of countries in Asia and the Pacific. Most tour packages include airfare, land travel, and food, and cost less if you had put the package together yourself. Start with a phone call to a Japan Air Lines office for specific information, and they will refer you to a local representative. In the continental United States call (800) 525-3663. Or, in New York call (212) 838-4400; in Chicago (312) 565-7000; in San Francisco (415) 982-8141.

Flights to Hong Kong, especially from the East Coast, are packed. One of the reasons for this is that there are wholesalers who buy blocks of tickets, knowing they will be able to resell them to travel agents and tour groups. Because they buy in bulk, they get a better price. These ticket brokers pass the savings on to their customers. Our friend Libby, who travels frequently back and forth to Hong Kong, introduced us to Lillian at C & H Travel. Lillian and her comrades are ticket brokers for many airlines to many destinations. We have used C & H to book tickets to Hong Kong and Europe, and find that their prices are hard to beat. You can book any class of service; Lillian will tell you the airline and time when you can get the best deal. The seats are legitimate. They have nothing to do with coupons or other questionable practices. Call her and tell her we sent you. Her number in Los Angeles is (213) 387-2288. Lillian will also assemble tours into China or other Asian destinations. Be sure to ask. It is usually cheaper to book a package, which includes room, breakfast, and all taxes, than to just purchase the airfare.

There are over sixty major tour wholesalers who book Hong Kong tours. They normally do not deal directly with the public but offer their services to the travel industry. The tourist does best to contact a local travel agency and ask for brochures on Hong Kong tour packages. If you are not sure how to go about arranging your tour, you can write to some of the bigger wholesalers and ask them to recommend an agency in your area. Some of the larger ones include:

AMERICAN EXPRESS CO., 300 Pinnacle Way, Norcross GA 30719. Telephone: (800) 241-1700

CARAVAN TOURS, 401 North Michigan Avenue, Chicago IL 60611. Telephone: (800) 621-8338, ext. 111

GLOBUS-GATEWAY/COSMOS, 150 South Los Robles Avenue, Pasadena CA 91101. Telephone: (800) 556-5454

INTER PACIFIC TOURS, 111 East 15th Street, New York NY 10003. Telephone: (800) 468-5000

MAUPINTOUR, 1515 St. Andrews Drive, Lawrence KS 65044. Telephone: (800) 255-4266

NET TOURS, 150 Powell Street #307, San Francisco CA 94102. Telephone: (800) 227-5464; in California: (800) 792-0747

TBI, 45 Rockefeller Plaza #633, New York NY 10111. Telephone: (800) 223-0266

Don't overlook international carriers as a good source of information and packages. Note that direct service does not mean that the airplane does not stop; it simply means that you will be booked straight through. Some West Coast flights do not stop; others do.

More and more people are choosing to tour Asia on a cruise ship. Royal Viking Line, Holland America Line, Cunard, and Norwegian America Line all offer cruises stopping in Hong Kong. Ships tie up at Ocean Terminal on the Kowloon Peninsula. You couldn't have a better shopping location.

Getting Around

Even though everywhere you look in Hong Kong you will see signs in Chinese, and everywhere you walk you will hear people speaking Chinese, you will have no trouble getting around. Often the people speaking Chinese also speak, read, or understand English, and the signs that you can't read at first probably have the information somewhere in English—just smaller. Hong Kong has been a British colony for so long that English is a second language. Most cab drivers speak and understand English. Always travel with a map, in case you need to point to where you want to go, or if you are merely wandering around and simply want to get your bearings.

Mass transportation in Hong Kong is superb. Most rides on the MTR take under twenty minutes. Crossing the harbor by car or cab during rush hour is hardest, but doing it on the Star Ferry or the MTR is a breeze. If you intend to sightsee, pick up the HKTA brochure *Places of Interest by Public Transportation* to get exact directions and bus routes throughout Hong Kong Island and Kowloon. There are many ways to get around.

AIRPORT TRANSPORTATION: Getting to your hotel from Kai Tak International Airport can be accomplished via bus or taxi. The airport bus provides access to many major hotels. Fares run about $6 (H.K.) to Tsimshatsui hotels and $8 (H.K.) to Hong Kong Island hotels. Take bus A1 for Tsimshatsui, A2 for Central and Wanchai, and A3 for Causeway Bay. Buses run every fifteen minutes from 7 A.M. until 11 P.M. Check to make certain that your hotel is on the list. You can call 3-7454466 to get exact details.

Some hotels will send a special car or bus to pick you up. The Ramada Renaissance has a fleet of Jaguars. A driver will meet you outside of Customs and help you with your luggage. This is an extra fee, but after a long flight the service is worth it. Limousine prices run about $140– $200 (H.K.). Taxi stands are near the arrival lounge. A large sign will give you approximate fares to different areas of Hong Kong and Kowloon. If you are confused, look for the transportation desk across from the arrival doors. The staff there will help you find the best means of transportation to your hotel. Don't forget to stop by the HKTA desk to pick up their free brochures on the city.

MTR: The Mass Transit Railway (MTR) makes going anyplace in Hong Kong a delight. Look for the symbol ⊀, which marks the MTR station. Three lines connect the New Territories to industrial Kwun Tong to business Central to shopping Tsimshatsui to the residential eastern part of the island. New stations are being added, and a new tunnel has recently connected Kwun Tong directly to Quarry Bay.

The longest trip takes less than sixty minutes, and tickets are figured on a per-trip basis. You can buy your ticket at the station vending machines by looking for your destination and punching in the price code. You will need exact change, which you can get from a change machine nearby. There are also ticket windows where you can buy multiple tickets. If you are visiting Hong Kong from overseas, the best value is a $20 (H.K.) tourist MTR ticket, which can be obtained from any HKTA office, MTR station, select Hang Seng Banks, or MTR Travel Services Centres. You must buy your ticket within two weeks of your arrival and show your passport at the time you purchase it. With this ticket you can ride for $20 (H.K.) worth of travel on the MTR and get your last ride anywhere in the system even if you do not have enough value left.

If you are unclear about how the system works, pick up a copy of the MTR guidebook at any station ticket office, or telephone 3-7500170, which is the MTR Passenger Enquiry Hotline.

Remember to keep your ticket after you enter the turnstile, because you will have to reinsert it to exit. If you get off at the wrong stop and owe more money, the machine will let you know.

The MTR runs between 6 A.M. and 1 A.M. If you need to get somewhere earlier or later, take a taxi.

BUSES: Hong Kong's bus routes can also get you to just about anywhere you might want to go. Most of the buses are double-deckers and provide a great way to see the city as you ride. China Motor Bus runs the Hong Kong Island cream-and-blue buses, and Kowloon Motor Bus operates the cream-and-red ones. Bus stops are marked with a large disc on a pole containing the numbers of buses that stop there. You need exact change to take the buses, which can be a pain if you don't know where you are going or how much it costs. Always carry extra change and simply point to your destination on a map. The bus drivers are friendly and will help. If they are too busy, a fellow rider will fill in. The most expensive bus ride is $7 (H.K.). Buses operate from 6 A.M. until midnight daily. The main bus terminals are in Central: below Exchange Square and next to the Macao Ferry Pier on Connaught Road; in front of Wanchai Ferry Pier; and in front of the North Point Ferry Pier. If you're traveling from Kowloon, the main bus terminals are in front of the Star Ferry, Jordan Ferry, and Tai Kok Tsui Ferry terminals. Signs are in English and Chinese. The HKTA publishes a brochure giving bus routes. For more information you can call China Motor Bus (5-658556) or Kowloon Motor Bus (3-7454466).

MINIBUSES AND MAXICABS: These sixteen-seat vehicles travel some of the same routes as the double-decker buses. They are not as easy to use unless you already know your way around. The red-and-yellow ones are called Minibuses. To get one to stop, yell *"Yau lok!"* You pay as you get off, depending on the distance you have traveled. The green-and-yellow buses, called Maxicabs, follow more distinct routes. You can take these to the Peak, Ocean Park, Aberdeen, and other tourist locations. You pay a fixed price based on destination as you get on. Main terminals are beside the Star Ferry terminal in Hong Kong (for Ocean Park) or beside City Hall (for the Peak).

TAXIS: Finding a taxi in Hong Kong is like finding one in any major city (except L.A.)— just raise your hand. If the taxi is free, it will have a raised flag, or the sign on top will be lit. As you enter the taxi, the meter will start, with an immediate charge of $6.50 (H.K.). From then on the charge is $.80 (H.K.) per quarter kilometer. Taking the Cross-Harbour Tunnel will cost an extra $10 (H.K.) for the cab to return; crossing costs $10 (H.K.), making the total additional fees $20 (H.K.). There are surcharges for luggage ($2 H.K. per piece), waiting time, and radio calls. If a taxi is in Central and has a sign saying "Kowloon" it means that the driver wants a fare going back to Kowloon and will not charge the extra $10 (H.K.) tunnel fee. Shift changes occur at 4 P.M., and it is sometimes hard to find a cab. If a taxi doesn't stop for you on a busy road, it is probably because he is not allowed to. Look for a nearby taxi stand where you can pick up a cab. Hotels are always good places to find a taxi. Even if you are not staying at that particular hotel, the doorman will help you and appreciate your tip. Taxis in the New Territories and on the island of Lantau have slightly cheaper fares.

TRAINS: The Kowloon-Canton railway system services the areas between Hung Hom and the Chinese border, where you can change trains and continue into the People's Republic of China, and on to the USSR and London. There are two main service routes: the daily express for those going to the People's Republic, and the commuter train for those who wish to sightsee or commute. The final stop is at Lo Wu, and you must have a visa to continue from there.

FERRIES: The most famous of all Hong Kong ferries is the Star Ferry, with service from Kowloon to Central and back. The eight-minute ride is one of the most scenic in the world. You can see the splendor of Hong Kong Island's architecture and the sprawl of Kowloon's shore. The green-and-white ferries have been connecting the island to the peninsula since 1898.

Fares are still very affordable. First class (upper deck) is $1.00 (H.K.) and tourist class (lower deck) $.60 (H.K.). The difference is minimal except at rush hour, when the upper deck is less crowded. The Central/Tsimshatsui service runs from 6:30 A.M. to 11:30 P.M. There is also a ferry connecting Tsimshatsui with Wanchai and the new convention facilities. This service operates between 7:30 A.M. and 11 P.M. Other ferries connect Hong Kong with various outlying islands. The terminal is west of the Star Ferry terminal at the Outlying Districts Service Pier. Buy a round-trip ticket to save time and allow yourself to relax. The HKTA has a schedule of ferry service, or you can call the Yaumatei Ferry Company at 5-423081.

TRAMS: Watch out crossing the streets of Central, or you are likely to be run over by a tram. Island trams have been operating for more than eighty-five years, running from the far western Kennedy Town to Shau Kei Wan in the east. They travel in a straight line except for a detour around Happy Valley. Fares are $.60 (H.K.) for adults and $.20 (H.K.) for children. Pay as you exit. Many trams do not go the full distance east to west, so note destination signs before getting on. Antique trams are available for tours and charters, as are the regular ones.

The Peak Tram has been in operation for more than 100 years. It is a must for any visitor to Hong Kong—unless you are afraid of heights. You can catch the tram behind the Hilton Hotel, on Garden Road. A free shuttle bus will take you from the Star Ferry or Central MTR station (Chater Garden exit) to the Peak Tram terminal. The tram runs to the Peak every ten minutes starting at 7 A.M. and ending at midnight. The trip takes eight minutes. At the top you hike around to various viewing points, or peek in on some of the expensive mansions and high rises. The best time to make this trip is just before dusk; you can see the island scenery on the trip up, walk around and watch the spectacular sunset, then ride down as all the city lights are twinkling. The tram costs $10 (H.K.) round-trip or $6 (H.K.) one-way for adults and $4 (H.K.) round-trip for children.

RICKSHAWS: The few remaining rickshaws are lined up just outside of the Star Ferry terminal on Hong Kong Island. No new rickshaw licenses have been granted since 1972, and the gentlemen who still hold their licenses have been pulling rickshaws for some years. Rarely, if ever, do people actually go for a ride around Central. Most people just want to have their pictures taken. The cost for a ride or picture is negotiable. Pictures should cost around $10–$20 (H.K.), and a ride around the block $50 (H.K.). If business is slow you can negotiate a better deal. Prices are not fixed or regulated.

CAR: Avis, Budget, and Hertz have offices in Hong Kong if you want to drive yourself. You must be eighteen or older and hold a valid driver's license or international driver's permit. We think that driving around Hong Kong is more work than pleasure. Hotels offer a car and driver for an hourly rate, which varies depending on the hotel and car. Check the concierge desk before committing to either.

HYDROFOIL AND JETFOIL: Those traveling to Macao will want to know about the hydrofoil and jetfoil service, which runs every hour between 7 A.M. and 1:00 A.M. from the Macao Ferry Pier in the west end of the Central District. The trip take a little under an hour, with jetfoils being slightly faster than hydrofoils. Since Macao is a Portuguese colony, you must bring your passport.

Snack and Shop

I t's quite easy to get a snack in Hong Kong. It's simply a question of how adventurous you are. One of us doesn't hesitate to eat from street stands; the other needs white linen. The salads in a good hotel restaurant should be fine. We don't drink the water in quantity.

Experiment as much as you wish. We offer a few suggestions for fun, inexpensive, colorful stops that won't take much time and are convenient to most of your shopping trips. If you're out shopping at the factory outlets in the outlying areas you may want to bring along a picnic lunch, or at least something to drink. There are a few fast-food and local shops mixed in among the factory buildings, but the less adventurous traveler will probably be happier with a packed lunch.

ITALIAN TOMATO TOKYO: We know this sounds like the wrong shop in the wrong town, but trust us.... Located directly across Canton Road from Harbour City, this fast-food restaurant is part of the Mitsukoshi department store. The Silvercord Building is to the right as you exit. Italian Tomato offers both Chinese and Italian fast food. We like the pizza, the spaghetti, or the noodles, although you can get much fancier meals as well. The decor is crisp and clean; service is fast and prices are inexpensive.

ITALIAN TOMATO TOKYO, Sun Plaza Arcade, Canton Road, Tsimshatsui, Kowloon

▼

THE FOUNTAINSIDE: If you are shopping in Central you definitely don't want to stop long. The Landmark has two café-restaurants that are pleasant and offer a good chance to refresh yourself and people-watch. We like the Fountainside on the main level for its quick service and good espresso. The mezzanine-level restaurant, La Terraza, is slightly more formal. Either is good for a cool drink or a quick salad. Afternoon tea is also available at both.

THE FOUNTAINSIDE, The Landmark, Des Voeux Road, Central, Hong Kong

▼

SUN TUNG LOK SHARKS FIN RESTAU-RANT: You can't leave Hong Kong without *dim sum* and then some shark's fin soup. This is our favorite spot for both, located at the far end of the Harbour City complex, in the Ocean Galleries. The atmosphere is noisy and the restaurant is always crowded. It will take a couple of trips to taste all the varieties of seafood offered, and have *dim sum* too.

SUN TUNG LOK SHARKS FIN RESTAURANT, Ocean Galleries, 25–27 Canton Road, Tsimshatsui, Kowloon

▼

FOOD STREET: If you are in Causeway Bay and in need of a quick bite, there is no easier place to stop than along Food Street. This pedestrian arcade is lined with predominantly Chinese restaurants. Entry to Food Street is from either Gloucester Road or Kingston Street, one block west of Victoria Park.

FOOD STREET, Gloucester Road, Causeway Bay, Hong Kong

Hours

Shops open late and stay open late. The majority of specialty stores open at 9:30 A.M. and close at 6:30 P.M. However, these are just general guidelines; depending on the area, there are stores opening as late as 10 or 11 A.M. and closing as late as 11 P.M. Most shops in the main shopping areas of Tsimshatsui and Causeway Bay are open seven days a week. Those in Central close on Sunday.

Major public holidays are honored in many shops. Everything closes on Chinese New Year. Do not plan to be in Hong Kong and do any shopping at this time. The stores that remain open charge a premium. The stores where you want to shop will all be closed.

Store hours are affected by the following public holidays: January 1 (New Year's Day); January/February (Chinese New Year); March/April (Good Friday, Easter Sunday and Monday); June (Dragon Boat Festival); August 25 (Liberation Day); December 25 (Christmas); and December 26 (Boxing Day). On public holidays banks and offices close, and there is a higher risk of shops closing as well. Factory outlets will definitely not be open. Many holiday dates change from year to year. For specific dates contact the HKTA before you plan your trip.

If you are planning a tour of the factory outlets remember that lunch hour is anywhere from noon to 2 P.M., although 1 P.M. to 2 P.M. is most common. Outlet shops will close for one hour along with the factory. You might as well plan to have lunch then too.

Department-store hours differ from store to store. The larger ones, like Lane Crawford and Chinese Arts & Crafts, maintain regular business hours, 10 A.M. to 5 or 6 P.M. The Japanese department stores in Causeway Bay open between 10 and 10:30 A.M. and close between 9 and 9:30 P.M. They have alternating closing days, however, that can be confusing. Call before going.

U.S. Prices vs. Hong Kong Prices

I f it is "Made in Hong Kong" is it cheaper in Hong Kong? The answer to this is yes—and no. A shirt manufactured in Hong Kong and sold in Hong Kong is going to cost less than the same shirt sold in New York. First of all, in Hong Kong there is no shipping; and second, there is no duty. However, the big-name designers don't care. Manufacturing has become so sophisticated that goods can be cut in China, assembled in Hong Kong, and finished in France. So where were they made? In this case, the label will say "Made in France"—it sounds better! Major manufacturers assemble and ship from many parts of the world. The Pacific Basin is serviced from Hong Kong, Europe from Italy, and the United States from the Dominican Republic. Prices are often the same throughout the world. It has nothing to do with cost.

There is one other caveat about those famous words "Made in Hong Kong." Just because an item is made there does not mean you will find it in local stores or outlets. Many garments are shipped direct to the overseas stores, with only dust left behind in the warehouse. We have looked high and low for The Limited factories, to no avail. But a sweater will turn up here and there. Forenza lookalikes show up at O.P.; but alas, no factory. A lot of the merchandise that is "Made in Hong Kong" is not sold in Hong Kong.

Comparable items sold in both Hong Kong and the United States are also comparable in price. On our last trip, we bought a designer silk blouse on sale in Los Angeles. We got to Hong Kong, hoping to pick up some more pieces, only to find the same blouse, and everything else, but not on sale. The real bargains in Hong Kong are not on items that you can find on sale at home, but on unique, made–in–Hong Kong items, outlet items, custom-crafted items, and look-alikes.

European-made Bargains

There are few European-made bargains in Hong Kong. OK, there may be several if you run into a big sale period. But for the most part, it is wrong to assume that Hong Kong prices are cheaper than U.S. prices on expensive European-made designer goods.

On good merchandise not made in Hong Kong, prices can go either way. On most European designer goods, the prices in Hong Kong are equal to or slightly cheaper than in the United States, but not nearly so cheap as in Europe. The big designer names are *licensed* to Hong Kong business moguls, who can charge whatever they want. Hence you'll visit the Joyce Boutique and discover that Joyce carries every big European name you've ever loved—or she owns a separate store (Fendi, Krizia, etc.). Joyce's prices are very, very high. Joyce is getting very rich. You may be saving nothing—free port or no, duty-free or no—absolutely nothing by shopping in this store. (Since Joyce is somewhat erratic in her pricing, check the individual designer listings for price comparisons—Joyce's Kenzo is a better bargain than her Bottega Veneta.)

We happen to like Joyce Boutique and always visit it (there are a few) when we are in town—especially the Landmark location. We know many women who escape to Joyce because it is "their kind of store." We always warn them that the markups are high. We also suggest that they fly to Joyce specifically for one of the two sales—June and December.

If you want to save money on European-made goods, your best opportunity to do so is during a sale. Sales in Hong Kong are a little bit earlier than in Europe—the summer sales are in June, not July or August; the Christmas sales are in December.

Big point: If you see merchandise that you always thought was made in Europe, and it's very inexpensive in Hong Kong, you may be thinking that we are crazy and don't know what we are talking about. We are not, and we do. Goods that are labeled "Made in Anyplace" but are dirt cheap are made in Hong Kong (or Macao or South Korea), even though the labels suggest otherwise. All the inexpensive "Lacoste" shirts we bought in Hong Kong had "*Fabriqué en France*" labels.

Hong Kong on Sale

Hong Kong has two traditional sale periods, the end of August and shortly before Chinese New Year (January-February).

Aside from European merchandise, everything else goes on sale during this same period. What you'll find is a lot of no-name merchandise that didn't interest you when it cost $50 (U.S.) but is looking a lot better when it's marked down to $30.

The best thing about the sales in Hong Kong is that this is your best time to get regular retail merchandise at its lowest price. The real bargains in Hong Kong are not in retail stores; the real bargains in Hong Kong may not be in perfect condition. So if you insist on brand-new, clean, undamaged goods, you should feel safe buying them on sale. If you have teens or are on a limited clothing budget, shop Hong Kong during the sale periods. Check the *South China Morning Post* ads for special sale announcements.

Remember, the best buys in Hong Kong are not in retail shops—so, to us, whether you are there for a sale period or not is meaningless.

Typhoon Retailing

During the summer (from May to September), Hong Kong falls prey to typhoons. To protect the population best, the Royal Observatory now ranks the typhoons in numerical order, going up from 1 to 10. While each number has some significance in terms of the velocity of the wind, we will translate this to you only in terms of shopping habits.

No. 3 typhoon: The Star Ferry might stop running.

No. 8 typhoon: All stores are supposed to close; everyone is supposed to go home or seek shelter. Offices will not be open during a No. 8. *However,* hotel stores will stay open and may even jack up their prices.

Tourists are told to stay inside the hotel during a No. 8. The hotels circulate a brochure telling you what to do: Close the drapes, stay away from the windows, etc. You can stay in your room all day reading the latest Judith Krantz novel, or you can drink Singapore Slings at the bar. Or you could do what any normal person would do: Go shopping. If you stay indoors, you'll find every shop in the hotel is doing a booming business. We were even offered special typhoon prices.

Seconds Stores

We all make mistakes, so it's easy enough to understand that Hong Kong manufacturers make mistakes as well. If a thousand units go down an assembly line, one of them will not be perfect enough to pass inspection. Yet the manufacturer rarely can afford to toss out the baby with the bathwater. Instead, he collects all those slightly imperfect items and sells them to a store that doesn't mind slightly faulty merchandise.

In the industry, this merchandise is called seconds, irregulars, or imperfects. The stores that sell seconds fall into many different categories.

▼ Some are owned by the manufacturer himself. Baccarat owns its own seconds shop, as does Marimekko. Even Ralph Lauren and Calvin Klein have their own outlet shops.

▼ Sometimes department stores have bargain rooms that specialize in seconds or imperfects (as at Filene's of Boston), while elsewhere in the store the merchandise is absolutely perfect.

▼ Sometimes the imperfect goods are sold to a retailer whose primary business is in this kind of merchandise.

▼ Seconds and imperfects or irregulars are also often unloaded on small-time businessmen who may sell through their own outlets, or sell on street corners, at flea markets, at subway exits, or wherever they can get away with it. (Always expect merchandise sold in these places to be imperfect or even counterfeit; give it the twice-over carefully.)

Depending on the brand, the "inferior" merchandise may not have anything wrong with it. Particularly with name goods, the quality controls are so incredibly strict that when a unit does not pass inspection, it still may *appear* to be perfect. Possibly only the maker could find the defect.

"Damages" almost always have something wrong with them—but often it's fixable, or something that doesn't upset you considering how good the bargain is.

Here are some of the flaws that may send a unit to the seconds or damages bin; watch for them in your inspection of lower-priced name goods:

▼ dye lot that does not match other dye lots
▼ stripes that are not printed straight or do not match at seams
▼ prints that are off-register
▼ bubbles in glass or plastic
▼ uneven finish
▼ nonmatched pattern at seams
▼ zipper set in poorly or broken zipper
▼ puckered stitching
▼ belt loops that don't match

Remember, seconds are not sale merchandise that hasn't sold; they are stepchildren. Most stores will not admit that they sell seconds. While there are a lot of seconds available in Hong Kong, they are seldom sold through regular retail outlets or seconds stores. Some seconds are sold in factory outlets, but factory outlets have now become such a big business that they usually sell overruns. Street vendors and markets sell seconds.

If you are shopping in a seconds resource or a factory outlet, remember to check for damages or slight imperfections. Some imperfections are more than slight.

Family Secrets

The biggest secrets in retailing are the ones that are usually reserved for members of the owner's family, employees, and their trusted friends. We have a few of these listings in the book, but all too often you cannot gain entry without a letter of introduction, a phone call, or being accompanied by a member of the family.

Generally speaking, the larger the manufacturing firm, the better the chances that they offer their employees a discount on the goods they produce. The discount will be the least expensive price ever paid for that merchandise. If you have a friend who has a friend who knows someone, etc., they may be able to buy an item for you. If you have family or friends with factories in Hong Kong, the family secrets they have will get you the best discounts possible.

For the most part, the stranger or the tour guide who sends you to a certain shop and tells you that this place is a family secret is getting a kickback from the source, and the only secret is "how much." The price of the kickback has been added to the price of your goods. You are overpaying and getting ripped off. Unless you are dealing with personal friends or well-connected friends of friends, do not expect to get in on anything the rest of the world can't get in on.

The family secrets we discovered while in Hong Kong are revealed to you in this book. Nothing is more important to the Chinese than family or secrets. And don't you ever forget it.

Factory-Outlet Shopping

Since manufacturing is the business Hong Kong is in, it didn't take the business honchos long to figure out a brilliant piece of merchandising—factory outlets. Factory outlets have become so popular in Hong Kong that they are an established part of the retail structure. In fact, there are about half a dozen local publications that report on the goings-in, out, and on of the factory-outlet trade.

The factory-outlet business is one that borders on a scam. While there is nothing illegal about it at all, the business is a license to mark up. A huge number of tourists of all nationalities are being ripped off in these factory outlets simply because the factory outlets aren't true factory outlets. They have been created for the tourist business.

The prices in factory outlets are not wholesale, and may indeed be the same as regular retail. Often a street price will be cheaper than a factory-outlet price.

It works this way: Americans (and others as well) love the words "factory outlet"—they mean bargain to them, they mean wholesale, they mean value for the dollar. And they mean cheap. Manufacturers realized that if they had a way to reach tourists (and also Anglo locals— known as expats), they could become middlemen and make a profit. When they saw how well the gig was working, they went into the business of being a factory outlet and raised prices.

Some manufacturers have done so well in the factory-outlet business that they now produce their goods solely for their tourist and local clients—they don't even export! While most of the outlets listed in the various guides are fun to visit, many of them are rip-offs. Or, to put it more kindly, are in business just to be in business. We have several factory outlets listed and will give you the lowdown on them in the listings section. We do not have every one—they come and go quickly, and we found a high percentage of them a waste of time. If you find you are interested in outlets beyond the extent that we have outlined them in the section called "Factory Outlets" (see page 153), check out the Hong Kong Tourist Association's mimeographed listing of current factory outlets. Their list is totally nondiscriminatory— they don't tell you anything about the stores, they just give you names, addresses, and phone numbers and tell you what the places sell. You can pick up this list (it's free) at the Hong Kong Tourist Association office. We have liked about 75% of the places on their sheets and think that's pretty good.

We think that Hong Kong's factory outlets are a lot of fun—certainly more fun than the shopping centers—but we pick our outlets with extreme care so that we do not get ripped off. If you're in Hong Kong for a couple of days only, your time is precious—think about it before you go off on a long trek to the New Territories just for one resource.

Deals and Scams

Hong Kong is the city of deals and scams. The people who succeed here are the sharks. This is not a place for the naïve, the nice, or the neurotic.

In Hong Kong, as Cole Porter might say, *anything goes.*

Most of the good stuff in Hong Kong is available only through connections, or to people who know how the system works. When you shop in Hong Kong, you are playing in the big leagues. Just when you think you know how to swim, you get thrown in with the sharks.

It is very easy to get taken. You can be eaten alive and not even know it.

At a superficial glance, everything in Hong Kong seems cheap; everything seems like a great deal. When you look more carefully, you see that European-designer merchandise sold in boutiques is outrageously expensive and the brand-name, quality merchandise you crave is nowhere to be seen.

When you look again, everything starts to look alike and you get very confused. What is the difference between the pearls that cost $8 a strand and the ones that cost $100 a strand, which seem to be identical? Can this sweater with the label you have never heard of truly be the designer sweater you think it is? Will the polo shirts fall apart in the washing machine? Do you really get what you pay for, or does the trickiest person get to be the richest person? If market value is the price the market will bear, are you being taken? You may experience utter panic on the streets of Hong Kong as your mind reels and your heart beats faster.

Finally you realize that this is fun. It is a game—how much can you absorb and learn about the system so that you can turn it to your own advantage? We're here to pass on to you everything we know, but you will invariably go through all the other stages first. Then you will come to trust us when we tell you that in Hong Kong, deals and scams are a way of life. You can enjoy them and relish the game, or you can make yourself nuts. The choice is yours.

Private Labels

Private labels are the opposite of designer labels but are now becoming competitive and exciting. Almost all big American department stores have private labels, many of which are made in Hong Kong. The private-label business is one of direct contracting.

The manufacturer who owns a license has to charge a higher price for his designer goods than his regular merchandise because he is paying out a piece of the action to the designer. He can make that exact same merchandise and sell it without the label or the logo and charge much less. He can put his own company name in it for some product recognition and brand following, or he can sew a department-store label in it and let the store take the responsibility for convincing the public that the item is of good quality. More and more department stores are going into the private-label business, connecting their fine reputations with the quality of the merchandise they have contracted for.

The famous British chain Marks & Spencer has made its name on the quality of its private-label goods. You don't have to go to London to stock up but can buy its private label (St. Michael) in Hong Kong. We are inclined to trust any private-label goods we like from Marks & Spencer because the firm is known for its devotion to quality.

Marks & Spencer quality has become the standard for the most in private label and has come to mean:

▼ the best ingredients in food, with freshness dates on goods
▼ care tags on all garments
▼ dye lots that match
▼ polyfilament thread, because it is the strongest kind available
▼ exact color match of zipper
▼ no puckering in stitching

When you inspect private-label merchandise, pretend you work for Marks & Spencer and use this checklist as your own certification of the quality of what you are buying. Stanley Market is filled with private-label merchandise.

Shipping

We have done a good bit of shipping from Hong Kong and have good news to report: It's easy and it's safe. Even better news: It's relatively inexpensive. Whether the item is as cumbersome as a giant Foo dog, as small as a few ginger jars, or as fragile as dinner plates, you can arrange to ship it home. All it takes is a little time and a little more money.

Remember that Hong Kong is an island and that shipping is a way of life—as it has been there for centuries. The British are used to bringing things in from overseas. People with money who live in Hong Kong automatically expect to pay the price of shipping something in—especially items of Western design. Importing is a way of life for expats; exporting is a way of life for big businesses. Shipping in and out of Hong Kong is therefore very easy.

If you anticipate buying an item that needs shipping, do your homework before you leave the United States. You may need a family member to claim the item at Customs if you will still be out of the country, or you may even need a Customs agent (see page 45). You will also want to know enough about shipping costs to be able to make a smart decision about the added cost of your purchase. To make shipping pay, the item—with the additional cost of shipping, duty, and insurance (and Customs agent, etc., if need be)—still should cost *less* than it would at home, or should be so totally unavailable at home that any price makes it a worthwhile purchase. If it's truly unavailable (and isn't an antique or a one-of-a-kind art item) at home, ask yourself why. There may be a good reason—such as it's illegal to bring such an item into the country! If you are indeed looking for a certain type of thing, be very familiar with American prices. If it's an item of furniture, even an antique, can a decorator get it for you with a 20% rather than 40% markup? Have you checked out all the savings angles first? Are you certain the item is genuine and is worth the price of the shipping? There are many furniture fakes in Hong Kong.

There are basically two types of shipping: surface and air. (Air can be broken down two ways: unaccompanied baggage and regular air freight.)

Surface mail (usually by ship in a transpacific transaction) is the cheapest. Surface mail may mean through the regular mail channels—that is, a small package of perfume would be sent through parcel post—or it may require your filling an entire shipping container or at least paying the price of an entire container. Surface mail may take three months; we find two is the norm. If you are doing heavy-duty shipping, look in the back of the *South China Morning Post* for shippers wanting to fill containers.

If you're shipping by container but can't fill a container, you might want to save even more money by using groupage services. Your goods will be held until a shipping container is filled. The container will then go to the United States, to one of only four ports of entry (Los Angeles, New York, San Francisco, or New Orleans), where you can meet the container at the dock, be there when your items are unpacked, and then pay the duties due. A full container is 1,760 cubic feet of space (or 8 feet, 6 inches by 8 feet, 6 inches by 20 feet long) and will not be delivered to your door (no matter how much you smile). A full container to New York City costs about $2,500 (without insurance). Packing is usually priced apart from shipping, so if you are not shipping chairs and need lots of packing, the container could cost you another $2,000.

Air freight is several times more expensive than surface, but gives you the assurance of a quick delivery. We can't think of anything that would have to be flown to us in the States; if it were so delicate and so important as to need to be flown, it might indeed need an international courier, who is a person who hand-carries the item for you (often this is done with pieces of art or valuable papers). There are also overnight air package services, much like Federal Express, that deliver within a day or two. This area is growing just the way overnight U.S. services expanded in the past three years, so check out the latest possibilities. Crossing the dateline can make "overnight" deliveries seem longer or shorter.

If you want to price a few local freight offices, we have used these, or have been referred by friends who have used them with great success:

Unaccompanied Baggage Ltd.
Counter 330, Departure Hall
Hong Kong International Airport, Kowloon
3-7698275

Pan Pacific Services Ltd.
80–82 Morrison Hill Road, 2nd floor
Wanchai, Hong Kong
5-744844

Michelle Int'l Transport Co. Ltd.
Room 1002, 20 Connaught Road West
Western District, Hong Kong
5-487617

Unaccompanied baggage may be sent home whenever you want—you take it with your luggage to the airline desk and make the arrangements there. If your returning baggage has no new possessions in it, tag it "Returning American Goods" so the Customs people know what it is. (They will still open it if they want to.)

Shipping prices to the United States from Hong Kong are much more reasonable than shipping from the United States to Hong Kong. Unaccompanied baggage usually is the same price either way.

It is important to note that textiles (including sweaters) *cannot* be shipped, due to the heavy import duties. Carry them, or pay the price!

Shop Ships and More

You can have items shipped directly from shops for you. Many Hong Kong stores, especially tailors, will ship your purchases to the United States for you. Most people we know who have done this are surprised when their goods arrive by UPS. Ask about the shop's shipping policies before you decide to ship—some stores will charge you for their trouble (a flat fee), then the actual shipping rate, and then an insurance fee.

Try to pay for the purchase with a credit card; that way if it never arrives you'll have an easier time getting a credit or a refund. Be sure to ask when the store will be able to ship out the goods. We planned to send home some perfume so as not to have to lug it around for a month's worth of touring. The shopkeeper told us she was so backed up on her shipping that it would take her at least six weeks to mail our order. Then it would take several weeks or months for the package to arrive by surface mail. We took it with us.

If you want to save a little money, and if the item is of manageable size, consider shipping it yourself. Get the materials from a stationery store and go to the local post office. The Hong Kong Postal Service is amazingly efficient. Make sure you meet local requirements—they may not allow certain kinds of tape, etc. We suggest twine and filament packing tape. Hand-print the labels and on the package itself, so if they separate you still have a chance to get the package.

The U.S. Postal Service automatically sends all incoming foreign-mail shipments to Customs for examination. If no duty is being charged, the package goes back to the post office and will be delivered to you. If duty is required, the Customs officer attaches a yellow slip to your package, and your mail carrier will collect the money due when the package is delivered to you. If you feel the duty charge is inappropriate, you may file a protest, or you don't have to accept the package. If you don't accept it, you have thirty days to file your objection so the shipment can be detained until the matter is settled.

If you are caught between these two methods, ask your concierge to ship it for you. He will bill your room from the actual postage and supplies; you are expected to tip him for his trouble. Also, we're suspicious snobs and trust only concierges at first-rate deluxe hotels. We advise you to do the same.

Be sure to keep all paperwork. If you use a freight office, keep the bill of lading. If the shop sends your package, keep all receipts.

Ask about the policy for breakage from any shop that ships for you.

Know the zip code where you are shipping to in the United States.

Remember that you can ship unsolicited gifts valued up to $50 duty-free.

Insurance

Insurance usually is sold per package by your shipper. Do not assume that it is included in the price of delivery, because it isn't. There are several different types of insurance and deductibles or all-risk (with no deductible); you'll have to make a personal choice based on the value of what you are shipping. Remember to include the price of the shipping when figuring the value of the item for insurance purposes. If you bought a desk for $1,000 and it costs $500 to ship it home, the value for insurance purposes is

$1,500. If you have the replacement-cost type of insurance, you should probably double the price, since that is approximately what it would cost you to replace the item in the United States. If you're counting on your credit card's purchase protection plan (see page 57), remember that it only covers the replacement cost of the item and doesn't include the cost of shipping the item.

U.S. Customs and Duties

Have you ever noticed that when you get off the plane in a foreign city, you more or less breeze through Customs? Yet when you return to the United States, you may go through a rather involved system that may or may not include inspection of your luggage and a barrage of questions, some of them personal or even insulting. Well, if it makes you feel any better, all nationals go through more or less the same procedures when they return to their own countries. In fact, in recent years, the United States has been changing its welcoming ceremonies to the red light/green light system, an imitation of the European system that's been in operation for years.

To make your reentry into the United States as smooth as possible, follow these tips:

▼ Know the rules and stick to them!
▼ Don't try to smuggle anything.
▼ Be polite and cooperative (until the point when they ask you to strip, anyway. . . .)

Remember:

▼ You are currently allowed to bring in $400 worth of merchandise per person, duty-free. Before you leave the United States, verify this amount with one of the U.S. Customs offices.

Each member of the family is entitled to the deduction; this includes infants (but not pets).

▼ You pay a flat 10% duty on the next $1,000 worth of merchandise. This is extremely simple and is worth doing. We're talking about the very small sum of $100 to make life easy—and crime-free.

▼ Duties thereafter are based on a product-type basis. (Hefty levies on hand embroidery!)

▼ The head of the family can make a joint declaration for all family members. The "head of the family" need not be male. Whoever is the head of the family, however, should take the responsibility for answering any questions the Customs officers may ask. Answer questions honestly, firmly, and politely. Have receipts ready and make sure they match the information on the landing card. Don't be forced into a story that won't wash under questioning. If you tell a little lie, you'll be labeled as a fibber and they'll tear your luggage apart.

▼ You count into your $400 per person everything you obtain while abroad—this includes toothpaste (if you bring the unfinished tube back with you), gifts, items bought in duty-free shops, gifts for others, the items that other people asked you to bring home for them, and—get this—even alterations.

▼ Have the Customs registration slips for your personally owned goods in your wallet or easily available. If you wear a Cartier watch, for example, whether it was bought in the United States or in Europe ten years ago, should you be questioned about it, produce the registration slip. If you cannot prove that you took a foreign-made item out of the country with you, you may be forced to pay duty on it!

▼ The unsolicited gifts you mailed from abroad do not count in the $400-per-person rate. If the value of the gift is more than $50, you pay duty when the package comes into the country. Remember, it's only one unsolicited gift per person.

▼ Do not attempt to bring in any illegal food items—dairy products, meats, fruits, or vegetables. Liquor-filled chocolates are a no-no for some reason, but coffee is OK. Generally speaking, if it's alive, it's *verboten*. We don't need to tell you it's tacky to bring in drugs and narcotics.

▼ Antiques must be at least 100 years old to be duty-free. Provenance papers will help. Any bona fide work of art is duty-free whether it was painted fifty years ago or just yesterday; the artist need not be famous.

▼ Dress for success. People who look like hippies get stopped at Customs more than average folks. Women who look like a million dollars, who are dragging their fur coats, who have first-class baggage tags on their luggage, and who carry Gucci handbags but declare they have bought nothing are equally suspicious.

▼ Other items may be duty-free. Also talk to the Customs office about the Generalized System of Preferences (GSP), which allows many items (some quite surprising) to be admitted to this country duty-free to help the economy of the nation from which they come. Hong Kong is a GSP area—you'll marvel at the gems that can come in duty-free ... like gems, for instance (unset stones are duty-free).

▼ The amount of cigarettes and liquor you can bring back duty-free is under government regulation. Usually, if you arrive by common carrier, you may bring in duty-free one liter of alcoholic beverages. You may bring in an additional five liters on which you must pay duty—at $10.50 per gallon on distilled spirits—so obviously you don't want to go over your allowance unless you are carrying some invaluable wine or champagne. If you drive across borders, the regulations may vary—but it's unlikely you will drive home from

Hong Kong. (If you do, please write and tell all.)

You may also bring back 100 cigars and one carton of cigarettes without import duty, but there will be state and local taxes on the smokes. You cannot trade your cigar-cigarette-liquor quota against your $400 personal allowance, so that even if all you bought while abroad was ten gallons of champagne (to bathe in, no doubt), you probably will not have paid $400 but will still have to pay duty and taxes. Also please note that you must be twenty-one or over to get the liquor allowance, but you may be any age for the puffables—thus an infant gets the same tobacco allowance as an adult. No cigars from Cuba, please.

▼ Some no-nos are governed on a statewide basis, so check your Customs officials at your planned port of entry. A few tips:

1. Elephant ivory is a no-no. You used to be able to import African, but no Asian ivory. Now both are illegal.

2. Tortoiseshell is a no-no no matter where it comes from (unless, that is, it comes from a plastic tortoise).

▼ If you are planning on taking your personal computer with you (to keep track of your budget, perhaps), make sure you register it before taking it out of the country. If you buy a computer abroad, you must declare it when you come in.

3 ▾ MONEY MATTERS

Paying Up

Whether you use cash, traveler's check, or credit card, you are probably paying for your purchase in a currency different from American dollars. For the most part, we recommend using a credit card—especially in fancy stores. Plastic is easy to use, provides you with a record of your purchases (for Customs as well as for your books), and makes returns a lot easier. Credit-card companies, because they are often associated with banks, may give the best exchange rates. The price you pay, as posted in dollars, is translated on the day of your purchase. Let's say the Hong Kong dollar is trading at $7.80 to $1 (U.S.). Your hotel may only offer an exchange rate of $7.50 when you convert your money. American Express will probably give you a higher rate of exchange.

The bad news about credit cards is that you can overspend easily, and you may come home to a stack of bills. But one extra benefit of a credit card is that you often get delayed billing, so that you may have a month or two to raise some petty cash.

If possible, travel with more than one credit card. Some stores will only take MasterCard or Visa. Others will accept only American Express. Some prefer one to the other, but will accept either. Very often you can negotiate a discount for not using plastic at all. If the shopkeeper does not recognize your credit card, be sure to identify it as a MasterCard or whatever it is. The new bank cards all look so different that more than once we have had a stumped store owner examining our credit cards trying to figure out what they were.

Before you go on your trip be sure that you understand your credit-card company's policy on lost or stolen cards, and inquire about their buyer's protection plan. Most credit cards have certain rules relating to lost or stolen cards, and to purchases that are not good. (See page 56).

Traveler's checks are a must—for safety's sake. Shop around a bit; compare the various companies that issue checks, and make sure your checks are insured against loss or theft. While we like and use American Express traveler's checks, they are not the only game in town. Ask around. At different times of the year, during special promotions, American Express checks may be offered free of a service charge by the banks. This is a good time to stock up. If you are a very good customer, your bank should offer this service to you, anyway. Call and ask. Thomas Cook provides traveler's checks free, and in foreign currencies. This is a big plus when changing checks at hotels or shops, because you will have a guaranteed rate of exchange. However, you must buy the checks through a bank, Deak-Perera, or another currency broker who may not give you the same rate of exchange as the American Express office abroad. Don't forget the American Express machines that are appearing in more and more airports and at American Express travel offices in most major cities. You can use your card to get cash or traveler's checks in either U.S. dollars or foreign currencies.

Currency Exchange

As we've already mentioned, currency exchange rates vary tremendously. The rate announced in the paper (the *South China Morning Post*) every day is the official bank exchange rate, and does not apply to tourists. Even by trading your money at a bank, you will not get the same rate of exchange that's announced in the papers.

▼ You will get a better rate of exchange for a traveler's check than for cash, because there is less paperwork involved for banks, hotels, etc.

▼ Hotels generally give the least favorable rate of exchange, but we find some flexibility here. You are limited by where you are staying, however. Many hotels will not change traveler's checks for nonpatrons. Hotel shops will often negotiate on the rate of exchange. It is important to know that day's bank rate before you start shopping. When in doubt, use your calculator to double-check the multiplication.

▼ Don't change money (or a lot of it, anyway) at airport vendors, because they will have the worst rates in town. Yes, higher than your hotel.

▼ If you want to change Hong Kong dollars back to U.S. dollars when you leave, remember that you will pay a higher rate for them. You are now "buying" dollars rather than "selling" them. Therefore, never change more money than you think you will need, unless you are planning to stockpile for another trip.

▼ Have some foreign currency on hand for arrivals. After a lengthy transpacific flight, you will not want to have to stand in line at some airport booth to get your cab fare. You'll pay a very high rate of exchange and you'll be wasting your precious shopping time. Your home bank or local currency exchange office can sell you small amounts of foreign currency. No matter how much of a premium you pay for this money, the convenience will be worth it. We ask for $50 worth of currency for each country we are visiting. This will pay for the taxi to the hotel, tips, and the immediate necessities until you decide where to change the rest of your money.

▼ Keep track of what you pay for your currency. If you are going to several countries or must make several money-changing trips to the cashier, write the sums down. When you get home and wonder what you did with all the money you used to have, it will be easier to trace your cash. When you are budgeting, adjust to the rate you paid for the money, not the rate you read in the newspaper. Do not be embarrassed if you are confused by rates and various denominations. Learn as much as you can, and ask for help. Take time to count your change and understand what has been placed in your hand. The people you are dealing with already know you are a tourist, so feel satisfied that you understand each financial transaction.

▼ Determine mental comparative rates for quick price reactions. Know the conversion rate for $50 and $100 so that in an instant you can make a judgment. Then, if you're still interested in an item, slow down and figure out the accurate price. Do not make the mistake of equating Hong Kong and U.S. dollars, even as a quick mental fix. You'll be sorry later.

▼ When you check your credit-card slip before leaving the store, make sure to circle the "H.K." in front of the "$" sign. Since both currencies use the "$" symbol, you want to make very certain that your credit-card company does not bill you in U.S. dollars. When

your credit-card bill arrives, double-check once
again.

Bargaining as a Way of Life

When you walk into a store in New
York, Paris, or London, you ask the
price of an item, whip out your credit
card or cash, and say "Thank you very
much." No bargaining; no haggling. Not so in
Hong Kong, where life is based on bargaining.
Hong Kong society revolves around the art of
the bargain. You want to buy an apple at the
corner stand? Buy two and offer a little less
than double; you will probably be successful.

There are a few places where the British
customs have prevailed. Bargaining does not
take place on buses, in the MTR, or in taxis
(unless you are going for a long drive, or are
hiring the car for a day). Otherwise just about
everything is negotiable. Hotel rooms are a flat
rate—unless you are with a group or are a
travel agent and receive a discount. Airlines
offer bargain prices to get you to travel at
off-peak times. Store sales offer bargains to get
rid of old stock.

Nowhere is bargaining more important, however, than in the various markets (see page
95). Here, it is open season on tourists and
you are expected to bargain fiercely to get the
best deal. Unless you come from a similar
background you will very likely become exhausted and give up. Once you give up, it's
guaranteed that you have just gotten the bad
end of the bargain. In fierce bargaining you
will know that you are getting near the fair
price when the shopowner becomes less gra-
cious and more grudgingly quiet.

If you are hoping to bargain successfully we
have a few tips for you to follow:

▼ Do not try to bargain while wearing expensive jewelry or clothing. We always go to the market in jeans and a T-shirt, or old slacks and a nondescript sweater.

▼ If you are bargaining for an expensive item like a carpet, camera, or piece of jewelry, have some background knowledge. If you can find a fault with the product and emphasize that you are doing the merchant a favor by relieving him of inferior goods, you will be in a stronger bargaining position.

▼ Never chat with the shopkeeper, argue, or show that you are passionately interested in the item. The more businesslike and disinterested you appear to be, the less quickly the merchant will think that the cash is in his pocket.

▼ Always try to bargain alone. If you are with your spouse or friend, take the white hat/black hat positions. If you are the one looking at the item, have your friend talk about how he/she saw the same thing in New York and it was less money, better looking, and easier to buy.

▼ Ask to see the inside of the item (watch, camera, or electronic device). Most shopkeepers won't want to bother. If they do, look like you know what you are examining and make clucking noises as if something is wrong. If the shopkeeper says "What?" just shrug knowingly. The trick is to be on the offensive, not the defensive.

▼ Keep repeating your position and do not waver. This is a tried-and-true assertiveness-training tactic; it works. You must have a lot of time available to bargain well. Wearing down the opponent is the key to success.

▼ As a last resort in bargaining, walk away. But don't ever walk away from something you can't live without. If you're just bluffing the shopkeeper will know, and you will lose ground in the bargaining. If you are serious about walking away, the shopkeeper will more than likely offer you a final deal, with the understanding that if you do walk away the price will not go that low again. Don't be too surprised if the price the shopkeeper offers you as you start away is much lower than where the bargaining had broken off. If the item is so special that you can't live without it, pay that price. If not, then be prepared to do without.

Returns, Repairs, and Rip-offs

The problem with returns, repairs, and rip-offs is that they take more time than cash to fix, and your time is what's valuable. Try not to buy merchandise abroad that you think may have to be returned. However, should you have a problem, see to it at once. Send a fax or telex rather than a letter (too slow) or phone call (no record of your complaint). Notify your credit-card company so that your bill is adjusted and the charge is held.

When you return the item, send it by registered mail to ensure that you have the signature of the person who received it. You will have to do a Customs declaration anyway, if the package is of any bulk. Let the store manager or owner know when you expect it to arrive. If the problem is serious, contact the Hong Kong Tourist Association and send them carbon copies of your corespondence. They are the authorized, government-sponsored body of the tourism industry in Hong Kong, and they have a special section set up just to deal with customer inquiries or complaints. Call 5-244191 (Fax: 852-5-810 4877; Telex: 74720 HX), and ask for the Membership Department of the HKTA. If you wish to write, the address is: Hong Kong Tourist Association,

Jardine House, 1 Connaught Place, Central, Hong Kong. They will intercede on your behalf if the store is a member of their association (most are). If the store is not a member, they will pass the complaint over to the Consumer Council, a division of the city government. Hong Kong is very consumer-oriented, and does not want dissatisfied tourists. If you have a legitimate complaint, don't hesitate to pursue it.

Sometimes with better-quality merchandise you can exchange it in an American store. This is highly unusual, since many stores are franchise operations, but it is worth a try before you start negotiating halfway around the world. If you are making a return, you must have your sales slip to prove what you paid. Don't expect a cash refund, and be happy if you get a store credit.

American outlets should repair Asian-bought European merchandise, provided it's genuine. There may or may not be a fee for this; it may be negotiable. The bigger problem is whether your "international guarantee" will be honored in the United States. Before you leave the store, check to make sure that your guarantee contains a complete description of the item, including model and serial number, plus purchase date, name and address of the shop, and official stamp. If you are buying a name-brand watch or electronic device, be sure that the store is an authorized representative. Guarantees that do not have all these items are not worth the paper they are written on. Be sure that you are not receiving a local guarantee or retailer guarantee instead of a worldwide/international guarantee. If you have been misled, first contact the head office of the store, then send your paperwork to the HKTA and your credit-card company to notify them of your dispute. You must do all of this in writing.

The last resort is, in fact, your credit card. The American Express Card offers Purchase

Protection℠. This plan, automatic with every card, assures you of extra insurance coverage for the first ninety days from the purchase date if the item you bought (with your card) is lost, stolen, or accidentally damaged. Remember to save all receipts. You must prove the purchase date and the fact that you used your American Express Card, although you can always call Amex for your "record of charge." American Express also offers Buyer's Assurance℠. This plan extends the warranty of any purchase up to one extra year.

All credit-card companies have similar programs; check with each one individually to find out the rules before you go. Some companies ask you to sign up for the program; some plans are only for customers with "gold" cards. Call the main number for your bankcard and ask.

Two Last Calculating Thoughts

1. Even if you have a Ph.D. in mathematics from MIT, we suggest you keep a calculator in your purse or pocket at all times. Furthermore, it should be the kind that uses batteries. Solar calculators are very cute, but your purse is dark inside, and many shops are, too. There's nothing worse than trying to do a hard bit of negotiating when your calculator won't calculate. If you use your calculator frequently, or your children like to play with it, buy new batteries before you leave on the trip.

2. The departure tax from Hong Kong is one of the steepest in the world. It must be paid in Hong Kong dollars at the time you check in at the airline counter. Credit cards, checks, and traveler's checks are not accepted. Put

the money away in a safe place and don't touch it. Children have to pay too. At last notice the rate was $100 (H.K.) for adults and $50 (H.K.) for children.

4▾ SHOPPING TIPS

A Word About Neighborhoods

When we refer to Hong Kong we include the island of Hong Kong, the peninsula of Kowloon, the New Territories, and outlying islands. When people give you an address for a shop "in Hong Kong," you'll soon realize that addresses here are a combination of street, neighborhood, and city. An address like 121 Ice House Street, Central, Hong Kong, would be on Hong Kong Island, in the city of Hong Kong, in the Central District. An address reading 6 Nathan Road, Tsimshatsui, Kowloon, would be on Kowloon Peninsula, in the district of Tsimshatsui.

The British colony of Hong Kong could, in fact, be divided into three distinct parts. The island of Hong Kong is 29 square miles in size, with the city of Hong Kong stretching east and west along the north shore, across the Fragrant Harbour, *Heung Gong*, from the mainland peninsula. The main city on the peninsula side is Kowloon, which encompasses 4¼ square miles of densely populated residential, commercial, and industrial land. North of Kowloon is the area known as the New Territories, which is the largest land mass in the colony, beginning at Boundary Street and going to the border of the People's Republic of China, Guangdong Province. The land referred to as the New Territories includes the 234 islands that surround Hong Kong Island. Many are tops of volcanoes and not habitable. Lantau island is the largest, followed by Lamma and Cheung Chau; all three are linked to the mainland by ferry.

As far as quality shopping is concerned,

Hong Kong and Kowloon are the star areas. Although the New Territories are developing very quickly, and many factories are relocating there—due to the land availability and cheaper rents—Hong Kong and Kowloon still contain 95% of the shops.

Each city is further broken down into neighborhoods, each with distinct personalities. However, due in part to the population density, people talk about neighborhoods like Central, Wanchai, Causeway Bay, and Tsimshatsui as if they were cities, not neighborhoods. To find your way around, it is important to make the distinction, however.

Because we list shops by category rather than by area, we have added a directory in the back (see page 000) to help you locate shops within an area. If you plan to spend the day in Central, check our index for a list of shops in that area. You'll want to plan each shopping day in Hong Kong carefully to get the most out of each neighborhood.

Hong Kong Island Neighborhoods

The island of Hong Kong is very hilly, with development concentrated along the shoreline closest to Kowloon and Victoria Harbour. The central part of the island is home to many wealthy families who have secluded estates on the mountain or live in lavish apartment buildings overlooking the bay. Real estate prices here equal those in Beverly Hills or New York City. If you have a chance, take a tram to the Peak for a spectacular overview of Hong Kong.

Hong Kong Island

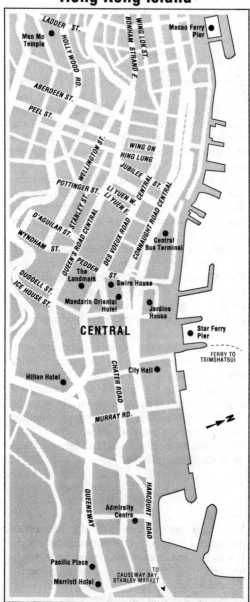

Central

Hong Kong's financial core is located in Central. The Star Ferry terminal is located in Central. The Landmark is located in Central. Almost all of the big-name designers have their main boutiques in Central. It is the core, the hub, and the banking center of Hong Kong. The Central District extends north and south from the harbor to Upper Albert Road, and east and west from the Supreme Court building to just before the Macao Ferry Pier.

Shopping in Central can be glitzy or earthy. The Landmark houses over 100 shops on five floors, surrounding a huge central atrium. European designers either have their shops here or across the street in Swire House, the Prince's Building, or the Mandarin Oriental Hotel. Farther west, between Queen's Road and Des Voeux Road, are the shopping lanes, Li Yuen East and Li Yuen West, where you can find good buys on purses, notions, casual clothing, and Chinese goods. If you have a strong stomach, visit Central Market, the trading area for fruit, vegetables, and meat. Still farther west, on the border of the Western District, is Wing On Street, also known as Cloth Alley, where you can pick up Chinese silk and silk cord for a good price. Walk up the steep steps at Pottinger Street to reach Hollywood Road and the antiques shops. Also be sure to explore Wyndham Street and D'Aguilar Street for unusual shopping finds.

Western

Western is more Chinese in flavor than any of the other Hong Kong Island neighborhoods. It was the first area to be settled by the British, who did not stay long, moving east to Central and Kowloon and leaving Western for the Chinese immigrants who came in great numbers after 1848. It has remained truly Chinese ever since.

Going west from Central, the area begins shortly after Central Market, at Possession Street, and continues to Kennedy Town. It includes the famous Man Wa Lane, where you can purchase your own personalized chop (see page 220), the Shun Tak Centre above the Macao Ferry Terminal, the evening Poor Man's Nightclub, and Wing Lok Street, which is full of Chinese herbalists. The farther west you wander, the more exotic the area becomes, until you finally feel that you have left the "big" city with its towering skyscrapers and descended into traditional China. You will find "bird restaurants" where bird lovers bring their pets to have tea and compare notes, jade carvers, snake shops, handicrafts shops, and rope factories galore. The University of Hong Kong is in this area, as is the Man Mo Temple. Across from the Man Mo Temple on Hollywood Road be sure to visit Ladder Street, which leads to Cat Street and the Thieves Market, where you can buy anything from old bicycle wheels to jade.

Wanchai

Heading east from Central, you will encounter the well-known "Suzy Wong" district of Wanchai. Back in the 1950s and 1960s this was the red-light district, frequented by sailors on leave and wealthy businessmen looking for diversion. Those days are long past, and although Wanchai's reputation lives on, all that remains are a few bars and fewer girls. Big business has slowly been encroaching and changing the face of the neighborhood. Today's most risqué nightlife comprises discos, hostess clubs, Chinese ballrooms, and topless bars.

Wanchai's latest claim to fame is the new Hong Kong Convention and Exhibition Centre (HKCEC) with its twin hotel towers. The New World Harbour View Hotel and Grand Hyatt Hong Kong Hotel have 852 and 573 rooms respectively. The complex has 18,000 square meters of exhibition space in two halls, twenty-six meeting rooms, and two theaters. Nearby are the new Arts Centre and Academy for Performing Arts. The Star Ferry provides direct access from Kowloon Peninsula as it travels from Tsimshatsui to Wanchai Pier.

Old Wanchai has been pushed back from the waterfront, and will continue to be developed. If you want to see some of the original architecture and shops, prowl Queen's Road East and the lanes connecting it to Johnston Road.

Causeway Bay

The second-best shopping district on Hong Kong Island is Causeway Bay. It is bordered by Victoria Park on the east and Canal Road on the west. Its northern boundary is the harbor, while the southern is Leighton Road. Part of the bay has been filled in and is now home to the Royal Hong Kong Yacht Club. One of the most colorful parts of Causeway Bay is its typhoon shelter, where sampans and yachts moor side by side. You can have dinner on a sampan while cruising the harbor.

The main shopping in Causeway Bay centers around four Japanese department stores: Sogo, Daimaru, Matsuzakaya, and Mitsukoshi. Behind them is one of our favorite shopping lanes, Jardine's Bazaar, which is alive with action from early morning into the night. Many of the shops in Causeway Bay stay open until 10 P.M. due to the street action. A few blocks over from the Excelsior Hotel, at right angles to Victoria Park, is Food Street, a small pedestrian mall filled with nothing but restaurants.

Happy Valley

Happy Valley is situated directly behind Causeway Bay and is well known for its racetrack, amusement park, and shoe shops. Horse-racing season lasts from September to June, and during this time thousands of fans stream in and out of the area. Aw Boon Haw Gardens on Tai Hang Road is Hong Kong's version of a funhouse. It is 150,000 square feet of statues set in a Chinese park that is gaudy and wild—something you will not forget.

We have heard both good and bad tales of shoe shopping in Happy Valley. Some of our Chinese friends swear by the shops along Leighton Road. We have never been too excited by them. And if you have big American feet (size 8 or larger) you shouldn't even plan on doing too much shoe shopping in Hong Kong.

North Point/Quarry Bay

With the expansion of the MTR to the end of the island and the opening of the second crossharbor tunnel connecting Kwun Tong to Quarry Bay, shopping in North Point and Quarry Bay has begun to perk up. The once moderate Cityplaza shopping center has become a major mall with Part II containing a Uny department store, an ice-skating rink, a kids' fantasy arcade, and chic shops. The Japanese department store Jusco has opened around the corner in the Kornhill Shopping Complex. As you travel farther east the area becomes largely residential, and interesting only if you are on a complete island tour and determined to not miss a thing.

Stanley/Repulse Bay/Ocean Park

Only Stanley Market is worth visiting for shopping (see page 97), but it is worth this trip to "the other side of the island" to see the most beautiful part of Hong Kong Island. Repulse Bay is developing as one of the major recreation and beach areas of the island, with new hotels and expanded facilities. It is exceedingly crowded on the weekends, but delightfully quiet midweek. You can visit Stanley village, shop, and get in a little time at the beach all in one easy trip.

Ocean Park, opened in 1977, is farther across the island, toward Aberdeen. It is 170 acres of beautifully developed parkland. There are two parts, lowland and highland, connected by a cable-car ride that will take your breath away. The amusement park section, Water World, opened in 1984, boasts the longest roller coaster in the world. You can easily spend a day or more just seeing the park. Souvenir T-shirts are a great buy here.

Kowloon Neighborhoods

The peninsula of Kowloon was ceded to the British during the Opium Wars, in one of three treaties that created the Royal Crown Colony of Hong Kong. We think it was the best gift Britain ever received.

Kowloon is packed with shops, hotels, excitement, and bargains. You can shop its more than 4 square miles for days and still feel that you haven't even made a dent.

Like Hong Kong Island, Kowloon is the sum of many distinct neighborhoods.

Kowloon Peninsula

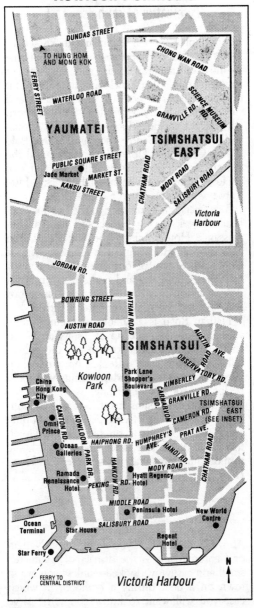

Tsimshatsui / Tsimshatsui East

The tip of Kowloon Peninsula is known as Tsimshatsui and Tsimshatsui East. It is home to most of the fine hotels, and the heart of serious shopping in Kowloon. At the very tip of Tsimshatsui are the Star Ferry Terminal and the Harbour City Complex. This western harborfront includes Ocean Terminal, Ocean Galleries, Ocean Centre, the Omni Marco Polo Hotel, Omni The Hong Kong Hotel, and the Omni Prince Hotel. It has miles and miles of enclosed shopping with no sight of sky. Jules Verne would have loved it.

Tsimshatsui is also home to the famous Peninsula Hotel, Regent Hotel, and Ramada Renaissance Hotel. Exiting the Star Ferry, you pass by Star House and the Chinese Arts & Crafts Store, one of our favorite sources for mainland China arts and crafts. As you travel down Canton Road you'll pass the Silvercord Building and the Asia Computer Centre.

Nathan Road is a famous shopping boulevard that starts at the tip of Tsimshatsui and continues into what is known as "the golden mile." Nathan Road offers shop after shop after shop of anything and everything you could be looking for in Hong Kong.

Heading into Tsimshatsui East you encounter the New World Centre, a giant shopping arcade that connects to the New World Hotel, the Peninsula Centre, and Mody Road, home to more fur stores than anywhere else in Hong Kong.

Yaumatei

Above Tsimshatsui, if you go north on Nathan or Canton roads, is the district of Yaumatei, small and easily overlooked—unless you are in town on a boat during a typhoon, in which case you will want to know about the large typhoon shelter, which houses a community of boat people similar to the one in Aberdeen. The most famous shopping site in the area is the well-known Jade Market at Kansu and Battery streets. Here you can shop from 10 A.M. until 4 P.M. (although many shops close about 2:30 P.M.) going from stall to stall negotiating for all the jade that you might fancy (see page 102).

At night you will want to visit the Temple Street Market. As you push your way through the shoulder-to-shoulder crowds you'll have the chance to buy from the carts, have your fortune told, or enjoy an open-air meal. (See page 101).

Hung Hom/Kwun Tong/Sham Shui Po/Mong Kok

Factories, factories, factories, and outlets are what we love about the outlying neighborhoods of Kowloon. Mong Kok is reputed to be the most crowded part of Hong Kong. We figure more people, more bargains. For details about factory-outlet shopping see Chapter 7. Hung Hom is the most famous of the factory areas because of Kaiser Estates, once a down-and-dirty block of manufacturing buildings, now a combination of glitzy factory shops, jewelry showrooms, and real factories. If you are in town on a tour, this is where you will be brought. *But be warned:* Bargains may be better elsewhere.

The New Territories

The New Territories stretch on beyond Kowloon to the border of the People's Republic of China. They begin around Boundary Street in Kowloon, although there is much dispute as to the real border. At the far end of the New Territories is the Sung Dynasty Village, a re-creation of an ancient Chinese village. Tsuen Wan is the fastest-growing city in the area. Major shopping centers, hotels, and housing are being opened here. The MTR's last stop is in Tsuen Wan.

The Building System

Most of us are used to finding stores on street level, with fancy glass storefronts and large numbers identifying their address. There are many such stores in Hong Kong, but many more are operated out of office buildings. You will arrive at an address to see only a cement building. Before you think that the address is wrong, go into the lobby and look at the directory. The store or business will probably be listed with a floor and room number next to it. You may think that this isn't worth the trouble, but we have found some of our best buys in shops that were the hardest to find.

Because of this practice of "office shopping," the addresses in Hong Kong usually refer to a particular building. When getting the address of a particular shop, instead of being told that it is at 17 Hankow Street, you are likely to be told that it is in the Sands Building. Luckily, many maps are marked with the actual buildings and their addresses. Cab drivers are so used to the system that you can usually give them the name of the building and they will take you right there.

If you are not using one of our tours to plan your shopping expedition, work carefully with a map so that you determine all the shops in one building at one time. Remember that it is not unusual for a business to have a shop on each side of the harbor—so decide if you are going to be in Hong Kong or Kowloon before you make plans.

The Beijing Rule of Shopping

T he Beijing Rule of Shopping is the Asian version of our Moscow Rule of Shopping; it has nothing to do with shopping in Moscow and only a little to do with shopping in Beijing.

Now: The average shopper, in pursuit of the ideal bargain, does not buy an item he wants on first seeing it, not being convinced that he won't find it elsewhere for less money. This is human nature. A shopper wants to see everything available, then return for the purchase of choice. This is a normal thought process, especially in Hong Kong, where every merchant seems to have exactly the same merchandise. If you live in Beijing, however, you know that you must buy something the minute you see it, because if you hesitate it will be gone. Hence the name of our international law.

When you are on a trip, you probably will not have time to compare prices and then return to a certain shop. You will never be able to backtrack cities—and if you could, the item might be gone by the time you got back. What to do? The same thing they do in Beijing: Buy it when you see it, with the understanding that you may never see it again. But since you are not shopping in Beijing and you may see it again, weigh these questions carefully before you go ahead:

1. Is this a touristy type of item that I am bound to find all over town? Are there scads

of shops selling this kind of stuff, or is this something few other vendors seem to have?

2. Is this an item I can't live without, even if I am overpaying?

3. Is this a reputable shop, and can I trust what they tell me about the quality of this merchandise and the availability of such items?

4. Is the quality of this particular item so spectacular that it is unlikely it could be matched anywhere else or at this price?

If you have good reason to buy it when you see it in Hong Kong, do so. But also remember some of the caveats that apply specifically to shopping in Asia.

The Beijing Rule of Shopping breaks down totally if you are an antiques or bric-a-brac shopper, since you never know if you can find another of an old or used item, if it would be in the same condition, or if the price would be higher or lower. It's very hard to price collectibles, so consider doing a lot of shopping for an item before you buy anything. This is easy in Hong Kong, where there are a zillion markets that sell much the same type of merchandise in the collectibles area. (This includes the entire Hollywood Road area.) At a certain point, you just have to buy what you love and not worry about the price. Understand that you always will get taken; it's just a matter of for how much.

If you are shopping for cameras, watches, or high-ticket electronics, you must go through a very elaborate bargaining process before you ever get to the price you might pay if you were going to buy. This makes comparison shopping very difficult. Vendors know how to make it even more difficult by putting the screws to you. For example, you want a camera. You have done your homework and know that the camera you want costs $275 from 47th Street

Photo in New York. You decide to go to a few shops in Hong Kong to find out how the prices are running and what's available before you make the big purchase. You walk into Shop A, which you have chosen at random, since there are several million such shops within shouting distance. The marked price on the camera is $300. You begin to bargain, because you know that $275 is the U.S. price. You finally get the price down to $250. You think this is a pretty good price, but you want to try some other shops. You thank the vendor and say you want to think about it. He says, "If you buy it right now, I'll make it $225. No one else would take this loss, but I've spent all this time with you already, and my time is valuable. If you come back later, the price will be $250." Now you are in hot water. Is this a con job to get you to commit, or must you take advantage of a great bargain when it comes your way and get on with living life? Well, we can't decide this one for you, because there are many values at stake here—which include the fun of the chase, your time, and the camera. But part of the Beijing Rule of Shopping is the understanding that a bargained price may come around only once. (On the other hand, it may come around several times. . . .)

Because of the preponderance of seconds merchandise and tourists, there is a high turnover in markets and with pushcart vendors. If you see an item you adore in a street resource, buy it. You may never see it again . . . unless you see it again. (That's Zen.)

Shopping Services

Hong Kong, being the shopping mecca it is, has more than its share of shopping "experts." You can ask anyone on the street "Where can I get . . . ," and you will be led to the *best* shop. Rarely will the best shops match up. Open the paper and you will see "Shopping tours of the factory outlets . . . best deals." Invariably you will be hustled to Kaiser Estates and into a jewelry manufacturer's showroom. Much referral business in Hong Kong results in the tour operator or guide receiving a commission, usually 10% of the cost of the item you are buying. The manufacturer simply tacks this 10% on to the cost of the items he is selling. Many guided tours to the "best bargains in Hong Kong" operate on this basis. A taxi to Kaiser Estates would be cheaper.

We have never recommended shopping services or tours, for just this reason. We love the thrill of discovering a bargain on our own. We love the adventure of trekking to Kwun Tong in search of an out-of-the-way factory outlet. But we also realize that not everyone has Indiana Jones in his soul. We also realize that some people don't have much time. They are in Hong Kong on business, with four hours of free time and a shopping list two pages long. For these people we recommend Temptations Shopping Consultants.

Temptations, as their fans call them, is a group of expatriate American and British ladies, married to businessmen stationed in Hong Kong. They have kids, and busy lives, but shopping is their job. They are our kind of gals.

Temptations is an upfront kind of business. You pay them a flat hourly fee for their time, their connections, and their experience. They provide a limousine and lunch and take you shopping. Any commission that a shop might offer them is passed on to you. So if a merchant is offering them a 10% discount on the merchandise you pay at least 10% less for that item. They'll even step in and do some additional bargaining in order to assure you of getting the best deal possible. They are straightforward and direct, and do their best to find whatever you are looking for. In order to use their service most effectively you should be prepared to give them some ideas about your personal style and preferences, sizes, etc. They come highly recommended by a local friend who knows everything about everybody ... sort of the Elsa Maxwell of Hong Kong.

Temptations is most useful for the shopper looking for important items like fur, jewelry, and antiques. Hiring the services costs $280 (minimum) for four hours and includes a chauffeur-driven Mercedes limousine, a shopping consultant, and lunch. The cost remains the same for two people but goes up for three and more. It is best to call their U.S. office to get the full details. One of the original owners has repatriated to Macon, Georgia, and can be reached by calling (912) 742-2425 or writing Temptations Shopping Consultants, 1231 Jefferson Terrace, Macon GA 31201. If you are in Hong Kong and wish to reach the offices directly, call (852) 5-226237 (Fax: (852) 5-845-5960). Their address in Hong Kong is Temptations Asia Ltd., General Post Office Box 10935, Hong Kong.

Who Ya Gonna Trust?

Trust being such a desirable commodity (since it's also so elusive), the system has provided for those of us who are concerned and don't know who to trust in Hong Kong.

1. The Chinese System of Trust: The Chinese know that you can't trust anyone except family. As a result, nepotism reigns supreme. Rich people in Hong Kong (whether Anglo or Chinese) do their business within a small cadre of those they trust—most of whom

are interrelated. On high-ticket items, they never take risks on outsiders or unknown vendors.

2. The HKTA System of Trust: The HKTA is the Hong Kong Tourist Association. They are a heavy-duty presence in Hong Kong and are uniformly referred to as the HKTA. Because rip-offs are so common in Hong Kong, the HKTA put together a merchants' association. They make merchants swear to be honest when they join. In exchange, the merchants get a little red Chinese-junk sticker (it's about 6–8 inches high) to put in their window, signifying that they are approved by the HKTA and therefore honest. This is nice in theory; but let's face it, honesty can't be policed. If you have a problem, call the HKTA. They have set up a special shopper's hotline for consumers with questions or complaints. Call the main number (5-244191) and ask for the Membership Department. If the shop is not a member of the association, the HKTA will pass on the complaint to the Government's Consumer Council. If you have an inquiry, call and ask for the Shopper's Hotline. While most red-junk shops are honest, a red junk in the window is not a graven-in-stone promise that you aren't being taken. However, the HKTA does care.

3. The Lily System of Trust: We developed this one ourselves, and it is a derivation of 1 and 2. We got the skinny on a good bit of Hong Kong's retailing from a woman named Lily, who comes from one of the grand old Hong Kong British families (she's third generation Hong Kong). Lily ran off and married the son of a Chinese warlord when she was sixteen, and then left him when she was twenty-five. She now lives in grand style in a villa nestled into the Peak. As a result of her background, she is related to the wealthiest of the British and the Chinese families,

and knows everyone who's "in." If Lily recommends a source, it's usually trustworthy. If yet another connection in Hong Kong—from the same circle—recommends the same source, even better. Many of the stores in this book, specifically the outlets, have been recommended to us by Lily, by her friends, or both.

Frauds and Fakes

Many types of merchandise are hard to duplicate. Serious fakes take the same equipment and operation as serious originals. It is harder to make an imitation ruby than not. If a ruby were offered to us on the street in Hong Kong, we would consider it real but hot, rather than fake. On the other hand, no one has ever offered us a ruby—so there you are.

People who sell imitations have to be connected to a master operation that supplies the merchandise. The imitation-watch business works this way: Say you want an imitation Cartier watch. You aren't going to walk into Cartier in the Peninsula Hotel and ask them where to buy an imitation. You'll pick a small operation in Kowloon and wander in and ask for an imitation. The owner will deny any knowledge. You insist on an imitation. Finally he brings out a Rolex copy that says Rolland on it. You say, "No, I want the Cartier that says Cartier, or the Rolex that says Rolex, not Rolland." He pretends not to understand you, and finally, in frustration, you leave. If you want a better chance of success, you say to the vendor, "My friend (name or description, as appropriate) from home told me she bought a great Cartier watch here. It was an imitation, but it said Cartier on it. Do you have any more of those watches? I'd like to buy several." The shopkeeper will either deny that he was the one or will disappear into the back room and "find" what you are looking for.

More imitations are being sold out of the established shops than in, however. There is one strip of shops along the "Golden Mile" on Nathan Road that is like an arcade. The shopkeepers are selling real goods from their storefronts, but they also have a picture book of real watches on the counter. You point to the picture of the watch you want and negotiate the price; then someone disappears out the back door and reappears with the copy. You have paid and are out of there before any passerby could even blink an eye. The same is true of markets. Nothing is displayed in the open, and you must convince the watch merchant that you are not a police officer before he will deal with you. The counterfeit goods are hidden in car trunks somewhere in the back parking lot. Because they are in high demand with tourists, imitation status watches have also gone up in price. We remember friends bringing them home for $10, and no one thinking anything was wrong. Now, everyone knows it is illegal, and more people seem to want them, and the prices have soared. We found that prices on the street in New York were actually cheaper, although Los Angeles prices were not. If you live in Oklahoma, you might not have such comparison shopping available.

Most of the merchandise entering the United States comes in without names. A look-alike Chanel watch will be exported to Los Angeles, with no name on the face. The trademark is done locally, thus avoiding Customs. We really think the whole practice is seedy, not to mention illegal, and don't believe that these people should be supported in business. *Buyer beware:* Know what you are buying and what risks you are taking.

In some areas, like antiques, fakes are made and passed off as real to an unsuspecting buyer. Unless you have your Ph.D. in Ancient Chinese art, you can hardly distinguish a good antique from a great fake. In this area you should only buy through a reputable dealer or auction house. Don't just walk into a Hollywood Road shop and expect to find the best items. What's left is being sold privately through a dealer or through an auction. (See page 222 for details.)

High-priced Imitations

While the market in cheap copies of designer goods seems to have dried up in Hong Kong, it is still the place to go to have the expensive imitations of even more expensive merchandise made for you. We like the story of our friend Mr. X (whose name we cannot tell you because it happens to be a household word). Needless to say, Mr. X's family is unreasonably wealthy. Prior to her birthday one year, Mrs. X gave her husband an ad she had torn out of *Vogue*—she had seen a bauble from Harry Winston that she thought would be nice.

On her birthday, Mrs. X received from her husband the ad—stapled to an envelope containing two plane tickets to Hong Kong. The X family flew to Hong Kong, went to Trio Pearls, and showed them the ad. The piece was copied for Mrs. X. Mr. X paid for the trip and the piece of jewelry, and still saved money.

You can get excellent reproductions of furnishings and jewelry in Hong Kong for large savings—if you are the kind of person who spends a lot in these categories to begin with. You can also do well with items like furs and china service for ten dozen. No one commissions a fake antique, but you can have a great time saving money with fabulous "fakes" of the very real kind. Really good fakes cost a lot and are passed off as serious art.

Tailors also pride themselves on making copies of high-priced designs. If you want an Ungaro original but can't pay the price, bring the fabric and pattern to Hong Kong with you, and a tailor will make the ensemble for you at a fraction of the Paris price. Comparison-shop carefully before commissioning a "designer" outfit. Some tailors are very conservative and will not have the kind of flair necessary to pull off a high-fashion look.

Scams

Hong Kong is the original Scam City. If you think you are street smart, you can still learn a trick or two in Hong Kong. If you know you are naïve, get smart now.

The wise man asks, "How can you tell if you are being cheated in Hong Kong?"

The philosopher answers, "How can you tell how much you are being cheated in Hong Kong?"

We list only shops we have done business with, and, we hope, any retail establishment listed in this book would never consider seriously cheating you. But we don't guarantee it, and it doesn't hurt to be on the ball. Markets and street vendors are much more likely to con you than established retail outlets.

▼ Feel the goods and carefully inspect any item wrapped in plastic. For example: You go to a store and see the sample silk blouse and decide to buy it. As you are paying, a seemingly identical silk blouse, perfectly wrapped in sealed plastic, is put in your shopping bag. You're no dummy, so you say, "Is that the same blouse?" You even check the size. You are assured that everything is correct and you have just been given a factory-perfect blouse that is clean—unlike the much-handled sample you chose. You smile with contentment. Fool. Open the plastic. There is a good chance that the blouse you have been given is exactly like the sample in every way—except that the silk is of an inferior quality. Feel the goods. Not everyone will cheat you. But many will try.

▼ Pick the skins for shoes or leathergoods that are being custom-made, and make it clear that you expect the skins you pick to be the skins in your garment. Have them marked with your initials. If you go for a fitting, before the linings are added, check your skins to make certain they are the same.

▼ Jade is very difficult to buy. Real jade should be cool to the touch when you lick your finger first. Most plastic is not cold, although we understand that some fake jade is. A true test requires scientific measurement of hardness, specific density, and light refraction. Good luck, sailor.

▼ Never trust anyone, no matter how much you think you can trust him. Never underestimate the possibility of a scam. Murphy's Law of Hong Kong: If you can be taken, you will be.

5▼MYSTERIES OF HONG KONG

An Alphabetical Guide

ANTIQUES: An antique is any item of art, furniture, or craft work that is over 100 years old. The problem is proving it. There is no governing body in Hong Kong that "officially" proclaims an item to be over 100 years of age. There are many agencies that look and sound official, and have official papers, stamps, and seals, but none of them are government sanctioned. In Hong Kong, anything goes. This is very frustrating for the consumer who is trying to determine a fair value for a piece of art.

True antiques are a hot commodity, and unscrupulous dealers take advantage of that need by issuing authenticity papers for goods that are not old. To make matters worse, Hong Kong does not require its dealers to put prices on their goods. Depending on the dealer's mood, or assessment of your pocketbook, the ginger jar you love could cost $150 for you and $100 for me.

Only you can determine if you feel like you're getting a good deal. Pick a reputable dealer, and ask a lot of questions about the piece, its period, etc. If the dealer doesn't know, and doesn't offer to find out, he probably is not a true antiques expert. Get as much in writing as possible. Even if it means nothing, it is proof that you have been defrauded if later you find out your Ming vase was made in Kowloon, circa 1989. Your invoice should contain what you are buying, age of item (including dynasty, year), where it was made, and any flaws or repairs done to the piece.

CAMERAS: There is a camera glut in Hong Kong. Knowing where and what to buy requires a little work on your part. Start by doing research at home as to what equipment you need. Do NOT allow a Hong Kong camera salesman to tell you what he thinks you should buy, or what is a good deal. Once you feel comfortable that you know what you are looking for, visit at least three shops and compare prices. We have discovered that prices can vary by as little as $10 and as much as $200 before negotiations begin. Be sure that you ascertain that the price for the camera includes a worldwide guarantee. You can get the same camera without the guarantee, and the price will be considerably less. The first time you have the camera fixed and get the bill you'll realize why it was such a bargain.

As soon as you start serious negotiations, examine the camera very carefully. It should still be in its original box, complete with styrofoam that packs it tightly. Remember that camera boxes can be repacked. Check to make sure yours was not. Look at the guarantee to verify that it is a worldwide guarantee and is authentic. There must be a stamp from the importing agent on the registration card. The dealer will add his stamp upon conclusion of the sale. If you are really careful you will call the importing agent and verify the sale. Check the serial numbers on the camera and lens with those on the registration card to make sure that they match. Take out the guarantee before the camera is repacked and ask to have it repacked in front of you. No bait and switch will happen this way. Ask to have the following information included in the store receipt: name and model of camera; serial numbers of parts; price of each item; date of purchase; itemized cost of purchase with total sum at the bottom; and form of payment you are using.

CARPETS: As the Persian carpet market has dried up, the popularity of Chinese carpets, both new and old, has escalated. China still has a labor pool of young girls who will work for very little money and sit for long periods of time tying knots. Carpets come in traditional designs or can be special-ordered. Price depends on knots per square inch, fiber content, complexity of design, how many colors are used, and city or region of origin. Any of the Chinese Arts & Crafts Stores is a good place to look at carpets and get familiarized with different styles and price ranges. You can visit the Tai Ping Carpet showroom in Central and then make an appointment to visit the factory in Kowloon (see page 229) to watch work in progress.

When considering the material of the rug, consider its use. Silk rugs are magnificent and impractical. If you are going to use the carpet in a low-traffic area or as a wall hanging, great. Silk threads are usually woven as the warp (vertical) threads and either silk or cotton as the weft (horizontal). The pile, nonetheless, will be pure silk. Wool rugs are more durable.

Chinese rugs come in every imaginable combination of colors. No one combination is more valuable than the next. Some older carpets have been colored with pure vegetable dyes; more modern ones use sturdier synthetics in combination with vegetable dyes. Avoid carpets that were made with aniline dyes, since these are unstable. To test for aniline dye, spit on a white handkerchief and then rub the cloth gently over the colors. If only a little color comes off you are safe. If the carpet has been dyed with aniline dyes, you will get a lot of color. These dyes were used on older rugs that were crafted at the beginning of the century.

CERAMICS AND PORCELAIN: Ceramic and porcelain wares available in Hong Kong fall into three categories: British imports, new Chinese, and old Chinese. For current British china resources see pages 218-220. New Chinese pottery and porcelain is in high demand. Although much of the base material is being imported from Japan and finished in Hong Kong, it is still considered Chinese. Two factories, Overjoy and Ah Chow, will take orders directly. Otherwise you would do as well to shop Hollywood Road and the big Chinese Arts & Crafts emporiums.

Porcelain is distinguished from pottery in that it uses china clay to form the paste. Modern designs are less elaborate than those used during the height of porcelain design in the Ming Dynasty (A.D. 1368–1644) but the old techniques are slowly being revived. Blue-and-white ware is still the most popular and can be found at the various Chinese government stores, including Chinese Arts & Crafts.

CHINESE NEW YEAR: The most important festival of the year, the Chinese New Year, falls on a different day in each of our years due to the lunar calendar. It is usually in the latter part of January. Every year is identified with an animal that gives character to those born under it. According to legend, when Buddha asked all of the animals to come to him, only twelve showed up. As a result he named the years after them. The animal signs are those of the Rat, Ox, Tiger, Rabbit, Dragon, Snake, Horse, Ram, Monkey, Cockerel, Dog, and Pig.

During the Chinese (Lunar) New Year, most stores will close. For a few days preceding the festivities, it is not unusual to find prices artificially raised in many local shops, as shopkeepers take advantage of the fact that the Chinese like to buy new clothing for the new year.

CHINESE SCROLLS: Part art and part communication, Chinese scrolls are decorative pieces of parchment paper, attached at both ends to round pieces of wood, against which they are rolled, containing calligraphy and art relating to history, a story, a poem, a lesson, or a message. Some scrolls are mostly art, with little calligraphy, but others are just the opposite. Being able to identify the author, or artist, makes the scroll more valuable, but it is usually not possible. Chinese scrolls make beautiful wall hangings, and are popular collector's pieces.

CLOISONNÉ: The art of cloisonné involves fitting decorative enamel between thin metal strips on a metal surface. The surface is then fired under just the right temperatures and the finish is glazed to a sheen. It sounds simple, but the handwork involved in laying the metal strips to form a complicated design, and then laying in the paint so that it does not run, is time-consuming and delicate, and takes training and patience to perform. Works by the very finest artists bring in large sums of money. But it is also possible to get a small vase for about $20. You can also find rings, bracelets, and earrings for good prices at most of the markets.

COMPUTERS: All the famous brands, makes, and models of computer can be found in Hong Kong, but you had better be computer literate to know if you are getting a better deal than you could get back home. Be sure to check the power capacity, voltage requirements, guarantees, and serial numbers of every piece you buy. Clones are also available, and at very good prices. However, "Buyer Beware" applies doubly in this category.

EMBROIDERY: The art of stitching decorations onto another fabric by hand or machine is known as embroidery. Stitches can be combined to make abstract or realistic shapes, sometimes of enormous complexity. Embroidered goods sold in Hong Kong include bed linens, chair cushions, tablecloths, napkins, runners, place mats, coasters, blouses, children's clothing, and robes. Traditionally embroidery has been handsewn. However, today there are machines that do most of the work. Embroidery threads are made from the finest silk to the heaviest yarn. One popular form of embroidered work sold in Hong Kong is whitework, or white-on-white embroidery. Most of it is done by machine, but the workmanship is very good. Hand-embroidered goods are hard to find today, and very expensive.

FUR: As one of the world's largest fur manufacturers, Hong Kong offers good buys on coats and jackets of midrange quality. There are hundreds of factories turning out massmarket coats, with a few factories geared to the high end. Since pelts are sold at international auctions, the savings come in the labor, not the material. Buy fur coats with great care. Ask to see the skins inside the lining, and know your quality. If buying a mink, remember that the female skins are considered to be the best because they are lighter, smaller, and silkier; the coat will require more skins, and therefore be more expensive. When examining the skins check to see that they have been fully let out. This means that they have been cut in strips and sewn back together in widths of not more than ⅜ inch. Fully let out skins are silkier and softer. There should be no skimping on the underarms or around the neck. If you are having a coat custom-made, select your own skins with the help of the retailer. Mark your skins with your name to ensure those are the ones used. Have at least two fittings, and make changes if necessary. Most of all, be careful to get all your skins. Even one saved is a profit for the furrier.

FURNITURE: Chinese antique furniture is based on purity of form, with decorative and interpretive patterns carved into the sides or backs. Many designs date back to the Shang period, to the early 17th century B.C.

Many of the older pieces of authentic Chinese furniture have been left to rot in warehouses, or are sitting in disrepair in the backs of shops. It takes an experienced eye to spot them.

Antique furniture is a hot collector's item. Dealers and collectors alike are scouring the shops and auction houses. It is better to find an unfinished piece and oversee its restoration, however, than to find one that has already been restored. If it has been, find out who did the work and what was done. Some unknowing dealers bleach the fine woods and ruin their value. Others put a polyurethane-like gloss on the pieces and make them unnaturally shiny.

If your taste doesn't run to the older pieces, the more modern furniture designs are also beautiful. The most popular pieces are made from rosewood, which is becoming harder to find, thus more expensive than other woods. If you are buying a rosewood piece it is smart to have it verified by an expert and not just take the word of the dealer.

If you do decide to buy, decide beforehand how you will get the piece home. If you are shipping it through the shop, verify the quality of their shipper and insurance. If you are shipping it yourself, call a shipper and get details before you begin to negotiate the price of the piece. You may be able to offset the cost of shipping by the amount of discount you receive.

HAPPY COAT: One of the hottest-selling tourist items is the happy coat, or jacket with a stand-up mandarin collar, usually made of embroidered silk with decorative flowers, animals, and birds. Happy coats can be extravagant and luxurious or simple and plain. They make great housecoats and are good souvenirs of Hong Kong. Many shops sell them already wrapped and ready to go.

IVORY: *We have a word of warning:* Articles made from elephant ivory will not be allowed into the United States. It is not smart to try to run them and get caught.

Carvers in Hong Kong are currently using dentin from walrus, hippopotamuses, boars, and whales as ivory. If you want to make sure you are not buying elephant ivory, look for a network of fine lines that is visible to the naked eye. If the piece you are buying is made of bone, there will not be any visible grain or luster. Bone also weighs less than ivory. Imitation ivory is made of plastic, but can be colored to look quite good. However, it is a softer material than real ivory, and less dense. Many *netsuke* that you find in the markets are made of bone dust or plastic.

There are very few antique ivory pieces left in Hong Kong. If someone claims to be selling you one, be very wary.

JADE: The term *jade* is used to signify two different stones, jadeite and nephrite. The written character for jade signifies purity, nobility, and beauty. Jade has been revered in China for 5,000 years, and is available in many forms. It is considered by some to be a magical stone, protecting the health of one who wears it. The scholar always carried a piece of jade in his pocket for health and wisdom. Jade is also reported to pull the impurities out of the body.

Jadeite and nephrite have different chemical properties. Jadeite tends to be more translucent and nephrite more opaque. For this reason, jadeite is often considered to be more valuable.

Jadeite comes in many colors, including lavender, yellow, black, orange, red, pink, white, and many shades of green. Nephrite comes in varying shades of green only. The value of both is determined by translucence, quality of carving, and color. Assume that a carving that is too inexpensive is not jade. "Jade" factories work in soapstone or other less valuable stones. The Jade Market (see page 102) is a fun adventure and a good way to look at lots of "fake" and real jade. Test your eye before you buy. If you are determined to buy a piece of genuine jade, we suggest that you use a trusted jeweler or other reputable source (such as the Chinese Arts & Crafts Stores or the jade boutique in the Lane Crawford department store); you'll pay more than you might in a market or a small jewelry shop, but you'll be paying for peace of mind.

NETSUKE: A *netsuke* is a Japanese-style carving, usually small, of an ornamental figure. *Netsuke* were originally designed to enable the kimono wearer, who has no pockets, to carry a small case looped over the belt. The *netsuke* was fastened to the kimono belt with a short cord. The quality of the carving indicated the importance of the wearer. Most old *netsuke* are carved out of ivory, which is now illegal to import into the United States. New *netsuke* figures are being made in Hong Kong, carved out of bone or plastic. They are stained or colored to look old, but don't quite achieve the patina or grace of aged ivory. The current rage in Hong Kong is *netsuke* of erotic figures. The carvings are somewhat coarse and usually made from bone, stained or watercolored for that old look.

OPALS: Hong Kong is considered the opal-cutting capital of Asia. Dealers buy opals, which are mined mainly in Australia, in their rough state and bring them to their factories in Hong Kong. There they are judged for quality and then cut either for wholesale export or for local jewelry. Black opals are the rarest, and therefore the most expensive. White opals are the most available; they are not actually white but varying shades of sparkling color. The opal has minuscule spheres of cristobalite layered inside; this causes the light to refract and the gem to look iridescent. The more cristobalite, the more "fire." An opal can contain up to 30% water, which makes it very difficult to cut. Dishonest dealers will sell sliced stones, called doublets or triplets depending upon the number of slices of stone layered together. If the salesman will not show you the back of the stone, suspect that it is layered. There are several opal "factories" in Hong Kong. These shops offer tourists the chance to watch the craftsmen at work cutting opal, and offer opal jewelry for sale at "factory" prices. It's an interesting and informative tour to take, but we couldn't vouch for the quality of any opal you might buy from a factory. Again, it's best to trust a reputable jeweler if you wish to buy a quality stone.

PAPERCUTS: An art form still practiced in China, papercuts are handpainted and handcut drawings of butterflies, animals, birds, flowers, and human figures. Often they are mounted on cards; sometimes they are sold in packs of six, delicately wrapped in tissue. We buy them in quantity and use them as decorations on our own cards and stationery. Stanley Market has shops selling papercuts.

PEARLS: The first thing to know about pearls is that the best ones come from Japan. If you are looking for a serious set of pearls, find a dealer who will show you the Japanese government inspection certification that is necessary for every legally exported pearl. Many pearls cross the border without this, and for a reason.

Pearls are usually sold loosely strung and are weighed by the *momme*. Each *momme* is equal to 3.75 grams. The size of the pearls is measured in millimeters. Size 3s are small, like caviar, and 10s are large, like mothballs. The average buyer is looking for something between 6 and 7 millimeters. The price usually doubles every ½mm after 6. Therefore, if a 6mm pearl is $10, a 6½mm pearl would be $20, a 7mm $40, and so on. When the size of the pearl gets very high, prices often triple and quadruple with each ½mm.

Most pearls you will encounter are cultured.

The pearl grower introduces a small piece of mussel shell into the oyster, and then hopes that Mother Nature will do her stuff. The annoyed oyster coats the "intruder" with nacre, the lustrous substance that creates the pearl. The layers of nacre determine the luster and size. It takes about five years for an oyster to create a pearl. The oysters are protected from predators in wire baskets in carefully controlled oyster beds.

There are five basic varieties of pearls: freshwater, South Seas, *akoya*, black, and *mabe*. **FRESHWATER PEARLS** are also known as Biwa pearls, and are the little Rice Krispies–shaped pearls that come in shades of pink, lavender, cream, tangerine, blue, and blue-green. Many of the pearls larger than 10mm are known as **SOUTH SEAS PEARLS.** They are produced in the South Seas, where the water is warmer and the oysters larger. The silver-lipped oyster produces large, magnificent silver pearls. The large golden-colored pearls are produced by the golden-lipped oyster. The pearls you are probably most familiar with are known as **AKOYA PEARLS.** These range from 2mm to 10mm in size. The shapes are more round than not, and the colors range from shades of cream to pink. A few of these pearls have a bluish tone. The rarest pearl is the **BLACK PEARL,** which is actually a deep blue or blue-green. This gem is produced by the black-lipped oyster of the waters surrounding Tahiti and Okinawa. Sizes range from 8mm to 15mm. Putting together a perfectly matched set is difficult and costly. **MABE PEARLS** (pronounced maw-bay) have flat backs and are considered "blister" pearls because of the way they are attached to the shell. They are distinguished by their silvery bluish tone and rainbow luster.

Pearls are judged by their luster, nacre, color, shape, and surface quality. The more perfect the pearl in all respects, the more valuable.

SILK: The art of weaving silk originated some 4,000 years ago in China. Since that time it has spread throughout Asia and the world. China, however, still remains the largest exporter of cloth and garments. Hong Kong receives most of its silk fabric directly from China. Fabric shops in the markets sell rolls of silk for reasonable prices. Try Wing On Street (Cloth Alley) or Li Yuen East and West. Embroidered silk fabric is also very popular, and can be found in the Chinese Arts & Crafts Stores around the city. Silk is graded according to evenness of weave, strength, color clarity, and elasticity. Be sure, when buying silk, that it is real. Many wonderful copies are on the market today. Real silk thread burns like human hair and leaves a fine ash. Synthetic silk curls or melts as it burns. If you are not sure, remove a thread and light a match.

SNUFF BOTTLES: A favorite collector's item, snuff bottles come in porcelain, glass, stone, metal, bamboo, bronze, and jade. The glass bottles with a carved overlay are rare and magnificent. There are schools of snuff bottles that are especially valuable to collect. You can find more ordinary examples in any of the markets.

TEA: The Museum of Tea Ware in Flagstaff House, Cotton Tree Drive, Central, Hong Kong, is a good place to start an exploration into the mysteries of tea. Teahouses are popular in Hong Kong. Don't be surprised to see many people at the tables accompanied by their birds.

Varieties of Chinese tea are almost unlimited. Tea has been grown in China for over 2,000 years, and reflects the climate and soil where it is grown, much as European and American wines do. There are three categories of tea: green or unfermented tea, red or fermented tea, and semi-fermented tea. It is customary to drink Chinese tea black, with no milk, sugar, or lemon. Cups do not have a handle but often do have a fitted lid to keep the contents hot and to strain the leaves as you sip. Since Hong Kong is a British colony, you may also find many hotel lobbies and restaurants that serve an English high tea (a great opportunity to rest your feet and gear up for a few more hours of shopping).

YIXING POTTERY TEAPOTS: Tea utensils are a popular item to purchase in Hong Kong, with Yixing pottery teapots being one of the most popular and expensive. They are made from unglazed purple clay and are potted by hand to achieve different forms of balance. They often resemble leaves, trees, or animals. Proportion is achieved by changing the balance of the base, top, and handle. Yixing teapots are always signed by the artist who made them, and the more famous artists' teapots sell for over $1,000 (U.S.).

6 ▾ TO MARKET, TO MARKET

Market Heaven

Hong Kong is market heaven. There are fruit and vegetable markets, general merchandise markets, jade markets, thieves', ladies', and men's markets. There are market lanes and market areas. There is even a market city.

Markets are a way of life in Hong Kong, and we love them. But they are a very real slice of life. They are not pretty or fancy. If you have a squeamish stomach, avoid the food markets that sell live chickens or ducks and slaughter them on the spot. Many visitors who have only seen chicken wrapped in cellophane find this distasteful. But it is the way of life in Hong Kong. Open-air food markets like Jardine's Bazaar are a little easier to take than indoor ones, like Central Market, where the sights and smells are intense. Merchandise markets are busy and hectic. There are no spacious aisles or racks of organized clothing. Some markets exist only for certain hours of the day or night. At a preappointed time, people appear from nowhere, pushing carts laden with merchandise. They set up shop along the street, selling their goods until the crowds start to dissipate, at which time they disappear into the night. It is fun to get to a market like Ladies' Market before the unofficial opening time to watch it set up.

Markets have their own rules, just like stores. If you want to be successful at bargaining and come home with good buys, we offer a few suggestions:

▼ Dress simply. The richer you look, the higher the starting price. Most goods on carts do not have price tags. If you have an engagement ring that broadcasts RICH AMERICAN, turn it around, or leave it in the hotel safe. We like to wear blue jeans and T-shirts to the market. We still look like visitors, but no one can tell what our budget is.

▼ Check with your hotel concierge about the neighborhood where the market is located. It may not be considered safe for a woman to go there alone, or after dark. We don't want to sound chauvinistic or paranoid, but crime in market areas can be higher than in tourist areas—especially at the night markets.

▼ Carry the local currency and have a lot of change with you. Most market shops or stalls do not take credit cards. It's also difficult to bargain and then offer a large bill and ask for change. As a bargaining point, be able to say you only have so much cash on hand.

▼ Branded merchandise sold on the street can be hot, counterfeit, or of inferior quality.

▼ Sizes may not be true to the tags.

▼ Go early if you want the best selection. Go late if you want to make the best deals.

▼ Never trust anyone who does business from the street to mail anything for you.

▼ Don't give your hotel address to anyone who wants to bring you some other samples the next day.

▼ Make sure you are buying something you can legally bring back to the States. Don't buy ivory; all varieties are illegal to import. Don't buy tortoiseshell; it will be impounded by Customs.

▼ Don't pay the asking price unless you want to give the vendor the privilege of telling all his friends what a chump you are.

Most markets have no specific street address, but are known by a set of streets that intersect the beginning or the middle of the market area. The majority of cab drivers know where the markets are by name. However, it is always a good precaution to have your concierge write the name of the market and location in Chinese before you leave. You probably won't need it, but it can't hurt. Buses, trolleys, and the MTR usually service the markets as well. Your concierge can give you exact directions from your hotel. Take a hotel business card with you, so you'll have the address in Chinese in case you need directions back home.

STANLEY MARKET
Stanley Main Street, Stanley Village, Hong Kong

Stanley Market is world-renowned. Any tourist coming to Hong Kong knows about Stanley. Shopping legends abound about fabulous bargains on designer clothing. After all the buildup, we find the reality a bit disappointing. Since honesty is the name of our game, we are going to tell you the truth about Stanley Market.

Don't get us wrong. We love Stanley Market. It is located in a beautiful part of Hong Kong Island. There are more tourist goods here than anywhere else. You have concentrated shopping for just about anything you might want to buy. It's fun, it's clean, and it's festive; but you will pay retail for the privilege.

Stanley Market's success has led to the bargain hunter's defeat. Stanley used to be a secret find. No longer. Now that everyone comes here expecting to find deals, shopkeepers are taking advantage of a good situation. It is capitalism at its best . . . or worst. The shops even take credit cards, which is a sure sign of high prices. Always bargain for a discount if you have enough money to pay in cash.

We find our best buys in the market as we venture off the main shopping streets. There are side and back alleys where the less-established market people sit with their boxes and bags. We have always found one or two artists doing handpainted T-shirts and stationery stores selling silk-screened art cards. These are things that you won't find in most stores in town. We also load up on the fabric jewelry pouches that are half the price of the ones you find at China Arts & Crafts. Imitations abound here. Wool sweaters are a good buy as long as you are not looking for *Vogue* styling. We have purchased everyday ones for $30–$40. More intricate handknitted styles are more expensive. The last time we were there the "hot" item was Fila. The time before that it was Polo. The names change, but the emphasis on designer logos remains. The most important thing to remember is that this is a market, and the merchandise turns over at a fast pace.

People in the know often tell you not to go to Stanley Market on the weekend. We beg to differ. We have been to Stanley on weekends and on weekdays. On weekdays it is virtually empty; but weekends—even during tourist season—are not the nightmare we had been led to believe they are. It *is* crowded on weekends; but let's face it, China is crowded, weekend or not. There is nothing you can't handle at the market on weekends unless you are in a wheelchair or are totally claustrophobic, in which case we do suggest going during the week. If you are in Stanley on an especially lovely day, don't forget that you can walk to Stanley Beach from the market. This is especially fun on weekends and during the Dragon Boat trial races. During the summer there are lifeguards on duty and refreshment stands where you can cool off. If you are really looking for a beach resort, Repulse Bay is just around the bend, closer to town. You can get there by bus or taxi.

We usually travel to Stanley by bus (No. 6 or No. 260) and return (with all our purchases) by taxi. The bus leaves from the Central Bus Terminus or in front of the Star Ferry terminal, and takes about forty-five minutes in moderate traffic. The fare is $3.50 (H.K.) and $6.40 (H.K.) respectively. You will need exact change. If you are traveling to Causeway Bay, bus No. 63 will pick you up at Tung Lo Wan Road. That fare is $3.50 (H.K.), but there is no service on Sunday and holidays. The taxi fare will run you approximately $15 (U.S.). Fares are rising quickly, so budget for it to be even more than this. On the way home, you can pick up a taxi in front of Watson's, in Stanley's main square.

You can start your tour of Stanley Market at Watson's and use it as a landmark in case you get separated from friends or family. (They also have rest rooms.) From Watson's, walk straight down Stanley New Street toward the water and when you reach the main street of the market, choose left or right. We usually go left first, and explore the main market street, then the alleys that lead up the hill. The restaurants are located in this area. If you are really in a hurry there are fast-food stands in the market as well. When you retrace your steps along the main street and continue on the other side of Stanley New Street, you will have a beautiful view of the beach and can stop to take pictures. You can take a right on Stanley Market Road and circle around back to Watson's and the taxi stand afterwards. The main street is where you can expect to find your more substantial purchases. These shops are housed in buildings, and have been in the same location for years. Many of them take credit cards and traveler's checks. If not, there are two banks on Main Street. We find it easier to bargain with cash. Some of the items you can expect to find are cashmere and wool sweaters ($20–$150); happy coats ($12–$20); linen pillow covers, guest towels, napkins, and tablecloths ($5–$200); men's shirts ($7–$20); silk underwear sets ($10–$20); cloisonné beads ($15); leather and suede coats, pants, and jackets ($150–$200); jewelry pouches ($5–$10); handpainted combs ($1); handpainted papercut stationery ($5 for a set of five); chops (see page 220) with your name carved in Chinese characters ($25); and T-shirts ($5–$25). Nowhere else in Hong Kong will you find such a concentration of good take-home souvenirs.

If you haven't bought too much to carry and are taking the bus home, the stop is across the main road at the top of the market. Ask for directions. You can get off at Admiralty to connect to the MTR. Market hours are seven days a week, 10 A.M. to 7 P.M.

LADIES' MARKET (MONG KOK MARKET)
Argyle Street and Nathan Road, Mong Kok, Kowloon

One of our most closely guarded shopping secrets is the Ladies' Market. It is one of our two favorites for "expect anything" finds. It is called Ladies' Market because the majority of the merchandise is ... for ladies. There are men's goods as well, but ladies' wares predominate. The area where the market happens is in the middle of a high-density residential neighborhood. There are regular shops along the street by day; but come dusk, hundreds of carts appear to take places in front of them. Some of these are elaborate setups, others are very simple. This is considered to be an established market where you should not encounter stolen goods. Nevertheless, we always examine the merchandise very carefully, especially if there is a designer's name attached.

The market is in action from noon to midnight, although we really recommend coming during the early evening. This is when the place is in full swing and you will be the safest. Keep your wallet or purse secured while you are in the market. Although Hong Kong is known for its safety, pickpockets love the markets.

The market sets up a short distance away from the Mong Kok MTR station. The streets have the feeling of a carnival, with lots of people parading by the stands, stopping to examine shirts, socks, sewing sets, buttons, and bras. There are some toys and sunglasses, but mostly lots of trinkets, shirts, socks, and everyday goods. Getting there is easy on the MTR. Take the train from Central, Admiralty, or Tsimshatsui to Mong Kok. Exit in the direction of Sincere Department Store. Cross Sai Yeung Choi and turn right on Tung Choi. This is where the market begins. Walk on Tung Choi until it dead-ends into Dundas. If you turn right and cross Sai Yeung Choi again you will be on Nathan Road. Mong Kok station will be to your right, and Yaumatei to your left. There will be more action on the other side of the station as well, toward Mong Kok Street.

TEMPLE STREET MARKET (KOWLOON NIGHT MARKET/ THIEVES' MARKET)
Temple Street and Jordan Road, Kowloon

This market has just as many names as personalities. It has been growing over the years, due to the popularity of the street scene that happens around it as much as to the merchandise. It is rumored that much of the merchandise found here has been stolen or is counterfeit. We can't confirm or deny this fact but just say, Be aware. On any given night you will find an endless variety of everyday shirts, socks, jewelry, homeware, and children's clothing. We got a great deal on a suitcase for $25. There are lots of items that cost $2. The market is extremely crowded, with people pushing and shoving to get past. If you are nervous in crowds, don't go. Don't carry a lot of cash. Dress down; don't carry a purse. And just enjoy the action.

We especially like the cultural scene that happens on some of the back streets. You can peek into the mah-jongg parlors and listen to the clacking of the tiles and the hollering of the players; you can get your fortune told; you can watch as the amateur opera singers perform famous Chinese operas; you can watch magicians do their tricks, be treated by an acupuncturist or acupressurist, or watch a dentist plying his trade at curbside.

Getting to this market is very simple. Take the MTR to the Jordan Road station. Exit toward Yue Hwa Department Store. At the exit turn right and walk three blocks to Temple Street. Take a right again on Temple Street; you will see the market begin. Follow the market as it goes in a U back to where you started. Hours are from 8 P.M. to midnight.

JADE MARKET
Kansu and Battery streets, Yaumatei, Kowloon

The Jade Market is a day market where you will find your best buys on those little green (or violet or pink) stones that everyone will expect you to bring home. The scene varies according to the day, time, and season. One time we went, it was so crowded we could hardly squeeze our way in to look; another time, we were the only ones there. We can't guarantee what you will find, but we do know that you won't be disappointed if you are looking for variety and a chance to hone your bargaining skills.

The market is located in an enclosed area that used to be a playground at Kansu and Battery streets. An outside market takes place around the enclosed one at Reclamation Street. Here you will find "unofficial" stone dealers, clothing salesmen, and just about everything else. Across Reclamation Street is the large Yaumatei Food Market.

The Jade Market is an official market organized by the Hong Kong and Kowloon Jade Merchants Workers' and Hawkers' Union Association. Each merchant inside the fence is licensed to sell jade, and should display his license above his stall. It is a good idea when buying to note the number next to your purchase, just in case you have a problem later on and the jade turns out to be plastic.

If you are hoping to buy quality jade, there are a few things to check. Make sure that the color is pure and strong. There should be no hint of black (unless the jade is black) or yellow. If the color is translucent, that is a good sign of value. Make sure that the color is as even as possible. A carving will have variations, but a jade circle should not. Also, check for fault lines. A good piece of jade will not have them. If any of the above faults appear in the piece of jade you are buying, bargain accordingly. (See page 89 for more information on jade.)

As you walk into the market, stop and get your bearings. The area is laid out in rows of carts, back to back in the middle and around the perimeter. We like to do one walk through before we get serious. There is more for sale than just jade, so keep your eyes open for other good buys. One year we bought lapis beads, and another time inexpensive colored-stone necklaces. The jade merchants have very similar merchandise; it's just a matter of how much you want to spend and which one will make you the best deal. We go from cart to cart asking the price on the same item. As soon as the merchants get the gist of what we are doing the price starts coming down. This only works if the market is not crowded. On a crowded day, we usually follow a Chinese person around and watch how he or she conducts business. Most often, the asking price is written on a piece of paper; then the buyer's bargaining price is written after it; and so on. If your eyesight is good enough you can get an idea of what the item is worth, and then bargain the same way. The dealers have a special way of negotiating that is quite interesting. The one making the offer will shake hands under a newspaper with the one selling. At the same time, he will indicate with his fingers what he is offering. The seller will then reply in kind, using his fingers. No one can see what the negotiations represent. As soon as they remove their hands from under the paper the negotiations have been concluded. Bargaining is part of the system even among the traders. If you are not willing to bargain here, don't buy. You will get the same, if not a better, price in the Chinese Arts & Crafts Stores, paying retail. The merchants in the Jade Market expect to lower their price by 20% to 40% depending on your bargaining skill and their need. We have always had our best luck by pulling out a single bill and saying, "This is all we have left." If the shopkeeper says no, we walk away and try again elsewhere. This method has never failed us yet. If you want to make the best deal, and are planning to buy a lot, stick with one vender.

If you are a serious collector, there is another "unofficial market" that takes place around the corner on Canton Road. Canton Road crosses Kansu Street one block after Battery, toward the harbor. Walk away from Kansu Street until you see the retail jade sellers' shops. In front of them you will see groups of men quietly dealing stones. Stand back and watch the method, which is very secretive. If you didn't know, you would think that they were simply having a conversation. You need to know your jade to deal here.

To get to the "official" jade market, take the MTR to Jordan Road and walk toward Yue Hwa Department Store. Take a left and then another left to get onto Nathan Road. Walk five blocks toward the underpass and then take another left onto Kansu Street. You will see the market ahead of you, two blocks farther down.

Market hours are 10 A.M.–4 P.M., although many of the vendors close up shop at 2 P.M. Go early rather than late.

POOR MAN'S NIGHTCLUB
(MACAO FERRY)
Macao Ferry Pier, Connaught Road, Sheung Wan, Hong Kong

The Poor Man's Nightclub is an outdoor market close to the Macao Ferry Depot building. This is a market mostly for the locals. There are lots of outdoor tables, food stands, and lights. The merchandise sold here tends to be on the serious-junk-and-trinket side. There are watches, jeans, pens, shoes, T-shirts, tapes, and hair ornaments. Sometimes you will find the watches with the "real" names, more often not. The atmosphere is lively, and if you are looking for an evening's entertainment, with no expectations of making a fabulous find, you will enjoy it here

To get to the market either take the MTR on the Central side of Sheung Wan and walk toward the harbor or take the trolley down Connaught Road and get off when you see the lights of the market. This is not a heavily traveled area at night except for the market, and we feel better on the trolley or in a cab. Market hours are 8 P.M.–midnight.

JARDINE'S BAZAAR
Causeway Bay, Hong Kong

If you stay in Causeway Bay, you have a foot up on the rest of the world when it comes to Jardine's Bazaar, Jardine's Lookout (a hillside residential area), and the web of streets between the two. This is what we came to China for. The first half of the market is full of fruit, vegetables, and other foodstuffs. At midpoint Jardine's becomes a dry-goods market and sells many of the same items you will find at the Poor Man's Nightclub. Jardine's is also in a home-sewing neighborhood, so you may enjoy wandering around looking at fabrics and notions.

One of our favorite evenings is a night visit to Causeway Bay: Visit Jardine's, Sogo, and

Mitsukoshi, and have dinner at the Shanghai Restaurant over Mitsukoshi.

CENTRAL MARKET
Queen's Road, Central, Hong Kong

The major food and produce markets for Hong Kong Island are located in specific areas. Central Market serves the area of Central. As you get even remotely close to Central Market on a sunny summer day, you will know where you are. The air will smell pungent and ripe. Central Market is located in a three-story warehouse, and the ventilation is not terrific. As a result the odors waft onto the surrounding sidewalks. The market sells every variety of fresh produce and meat that you might imagine. There are three levels of gleaming vegetables and fruit, clucking chickens, and quacking ducks in cages waiting to be picked for dinner. We can only take a few minutes in here, before we want to rescue all the caged animals. We do think that the market is fascinating, however, if you want a glimpse of the real Hong Kong life-style.

WESTERN MARKET
Des Voeux Road West, Sheung Wan, Hong Kong

The Western District's version of Central Market is due for some exciting changes. Plans are to turn it into Hong Kong's version of Covent Garden. The 83-year-old market will become a cultural bazaar featuring musicians, cafés, and, best of all, shops. The previous occupants are being moved to a new market in Sheung Wan.

KOWLOON CITY MARKET
Lion Rock Road, Kowloon

This one is a bit far out, but is especially entertaining because this is where the young locals like to hang out. Merchandise is a little more with-it; there's more fun in the air. This is one of the few markets where you'll find china sold. There are lots of blue jeans, factory-outlet rejects, and fashions from young Japanese and Chinese designers. This market only operates during the day. We like going after lunch to make sure that it is hopping.

CAT STREET MARKET
Central, Hong Kong

Cat Street Market is alternatively known as the Thieves' Market or Ladder Street Market. Originally, many of the goods set out on the blankets were hot off a truck, and the sellers could gather them up quickly if the authorities came around. Now the market is more pedestrian, with many of the goods being from homes, but legally so. You will find hubcaps, refrigerator doors, old radios, and toilets, along with antiques and jade. The shops behind and around the market specialize in formal antiques and have some wonderful pieces. After you pass the Man Mo Temple on Hollywood Road, turn right onto Ladder Street. Down Ladder Street and on Upper Lascar Road, you will see blankets covered with goods. There is an official Cat Street Market Building behind the street vendors, where you can buy furniture and antiques. The market operates during normal business hours.

The Lanes

"The Lanes" is a collective term for a group of small markets set in streets and alleys—usually only one block long. Except for Pottinger Street, which is a stairway filled with booths, the Lanes are built between large buildings. They're sort of the Asian version of the Burlington Arcade in London.

The Lanes are all in Central, and are within walking distance of each other. They are also near many other places in Central, so it's likely you will pass them in your daily travels.

LI YUEN STREET EAST: If you're looking for an inexpensive look-alike designer handbag, Li Yuen Street East is just the place. There are not a lot of inexpensive, high-quality leathergoods available in Hong Kong, and while Li Yuen Street East is not Neiman Marcus, it is the location of choice for locals who need handbags or briefcases. Expect to pay $40–$50 for a nice leather handbag of the current style. If you look hard, inside the shops that are behind the stalls lining the streets, you can even find a nice Chanel, Fendi, or Hermès copy. They won't have the CC's or the FF's, but the styling and design will be exact. Li Yuen Street East is also famous for its knitting shops, fabric stores, notions, and padded brassieres.

LI YUEN STREET WEST: Perhaps you want one of those satin quilted happy coats or vests that you associate with a trip to China. Li Yuen Street West is crammed with them. Be sure to try them on, as the shoulders sometimes run small. Prices at Stanley Market may be better, but not if you bargain. Whatever you didn't see on Li Yuen Street East will be on Li Yuen Street West, and then some of the same.

POTTINGER STREET: After a big lunch, give your leg muscles a workout and make the steep climb up Pottinger Street. There's nothing unusual for sale here—merely notions. However, we buy shoulder pads by the dozen. They are about half the cost. Notions are about 20% cheaper here than in a regular Hong Kong department store. If you buy jade circles for gifts, you can buy polyester or silk cord in rainbow colors in Pottinger Street. Hang the cord through the circle and you have a beautiful necklace. One meter of cord per necklace will be perfect.

D'AGUILAR STREET: This is a useful address if you need to send flowers, but is otherwise not important. D'Aguilar Street is a lane off D'Aguilar Place. It is also called Flower Lane, and is filled with little stalls that sell— you guessed it—flowers. Prices are low—as they are everyplace in Hong Kong. D'Aguilar Street actually reminds us of San Francisco.

MAN WA LANE: If you are looking for fun, Chinese atmosphere, and maybe some business cards in Chinese, don't miss Man Wa Lane. Man Wa Lane is headquarters of the chop business. But whether you are looking for chops or not, you should see this small, neat street, which spans about three blocks and has a few other stalls that sell general merchandise. If you do buy something from one of the shops and have to return for it, make sure you get a piece of paper with the shop address in both English and Chinese. The stalls do not have numbers but symbols, and they're all in Chinese. We tell you from embarrassed experience: You will never find your way back to a given stall unless you have the address in Chinese.

WING ON STREET: Known as Cloth Alley, this street is three blocks west of the Central Market, and is the place to go for the best buys on fabrics. Almost any type of fabric you might want is sold, from lightweight silks to heavy brocades. The market is open during the day.

7▼HONG KONG LISTINGS

Continental Big Names

GIORGIO ARMANI: Giorgio Armani's clothing is nothing short of spectacular—in both price and style. We can't help but look in every city just to see if there is a sale. Joyce has the Armani boutique as part of her empire, and we always stop in to try on a jacket or two. His look is the feminine version of chic menswear. Armani designs out of Milan, and has two less expensive lines, Mani and Emporio. Joyce also owns the Emporio boutique.

GIORGIO ARMANI, The Landmark, Des Voeux Road Central, Central, Hong Kong

EMPORIO ARMANI, New World Tower, 16 Queen's Road, Central

▼

BALLY: Bally has a great line of shoes and sportswear. We buy it in Europe, in the United States, and yes, even in Hong Kong. The shop's interior is the latest in high-tech, neoclassic design. The prices are good, although no steal. Best of all, the shoes are comfortable and easy to walk in—essential for Hong Kong. Bally has many boutiques to choose from, including those found in large department stores.

BALLY

The Peninsula Hotel, Salisbury Road, Tsimshatsui, Kowloon

The Landmark, Gloucester Tower, Des Voeux Road Central, Central, Hong Kong

▼

BOTTEGA VENETA: Bottega Veneta is the *crème de la crème* of leathergoods, even in Hong Kong where leather handbags are produced with abandon. We have seen copies of Chanel that could pass muster, but if you want Bottega, you have to pay the price. The shiny ground-floor boutique in Swire House has a terrific selection. We even found the black woven handbag we had been searching for all over Europe. Alas, the price was so high that we could not justify the purchase. It is cheaper to buy Bottega in Italy or during a good sale at Neiman Marcus.

BOTTEGA VENETA, Swire House (ground floor), Connaught Road Central, Central, Hong Kong

▼

CACHAREL: If you love the soft, elegant look of Jean Cacharel's clothing for children and young adults, you will be very happy here. The main shop in the Landmark is all blond wood, which makes it look more spacious than it is. The clothing is artfully arranged around the perimeter by style. There are lots of selections up to age six. The baby clothing is the best.

CACHAREL
The Landmark, Des Voeux Road Central, Central, Hong Kong
Ocean Centre (Shop 251), Canton Road, Tsimshatsui, Kowloon

▼

CARTIER: Cartier has a number of boutiques in Hong Kong, but our favorite is the one in the Peninsula Hotel. Of course we like any excuse to be in the Peninsula's lobby to stare at the beautifully garbed ladies having tea. We have observed over the years at Cartier that those who go in to buy usually come out smiling. A gold Cartier watch costs $6,000 and up.

Cartier also makes a very nice scarf for under $200, and purses for under $500. Other stores are licensed to sell Cartier goods, so shop around. For the most part prices are similar all over town.

CARTIER

Prince's Building (ground floor), Chater Road, Central, Hong Kong

The Peninsula Hotel, Salisbury Road, Tsimshatsui, Kowloon

▼

CELINE: Celine is very popular in Hong Kong. It is not as showy as Chanel, or as expensive as Hermès, but has a classic look that coordinates with dressier and with casual clothing alike. There are five boutiques located in the main shopping areas of Hong Kong and Kowloon, each with its own mix of pieces. The boutiques in the Sogo and Tokyu department stores are less formal and the merchandise is more casual.

CELINE

The Landmark, Queen's Road, Central, Hong Kong

The Peninsula Hotel, Salisbury Road, Tsimshatsui, Kowloon

▼

CHANEL: We have good news. There are two Chanel boutiques in Hong Kong, and they are not empty. Since Karl Lagerfeld began designing the line, it has literally been walking out of the stores in the United States and Europe. The new Hong Kong boutiques increase your chance of finding something you love.

There are good Chanel look-alike bags in the market, but they do not have the CC logo. Prices are comparable to those in the United States. A nice pair of daytime earrings will cost

$150–$200. Necklaces run $250–$500 depending on their intricacy. The quilted handbags start at $350 and go up. Those who want Chanel don't seem to mind paying the prices.

CHANEL

Prince's Building, Chater Road, Central, Hong Kong

The Peninsula Hotel, Salisbury Road, Tsimshatsui, Kowloon

▼

COURRÈGES: Courrèges boutiques provide simple, white backdrops for the colorful structured clothing that you have to be in good shape to wear. We still think of the '70s when we see the styling, but not everybody does, or they wouldn't be selling so well. The skiwear is especially appealing.

COURRÈGES, The Landmark, Gloucester Tower, Queen's Road, Central, Hong Kong

▼

CHRISTIAN DIOR: Once exclusively a high-end line, Christian Dior now caters to those with good taste but a more modest pocketbook. Everything you might need, from shoes to shirts to perfume and jewelry, is available. We have seen a lot of Christian Dior labels at various factory outlets over the years, and suspect that some of it is made right in Hong Kong. Christian Dior Monsieur caters just to the guys.

CHRISTIAN DIOR

The Landmark, Edinburgh Tower, Queen's Road, Central, Hong Kong

The Peninsula Hotel, Salisbury Road, Tsimshatsui, Kowloon

CHRISTIAN DIOR MONSIEUR

Prince's Building, Chater Road, Central, Hong Kong

ZOE COSTE: We first fell in love with Zoe Coste's jewelry creations in Cannes and Juan-les-Pins, France. Her look is sort of Egyptian/Greek princess. Prices are high, but we love to go in, try on, and pretend. There are Zoe Coste shops in New York, Chicago, Miami, and Houston as well as in Monte Carlo, Geneva, and Paris.

ZOE COSTE
Hyatt Regency Hotel, 67 Nathan Road, Tsimshatsui, Kowloon
Shell House, Queen's Road Central, Central, Hong Kong

▼

DAKS: A newcomer to the Hong Kong fashion scene, Daks is British to the core. If you need those regimental ties, brass-buttoned blazers, or serious walking-pants trousers, Daks will fit the bill. If you are looking for Continental pizzazz, this is not your store.

DAKS
Prince's Building, Ice House Street, Central, Hong Kong
The Peninsula Hotel, Salisbury Road, Central, Hong Kong

▼

ELLESSE: We usually buy our Italian sportswear in Italy, but happen to like this shop because it features casual clothing for men that is not commonly found in sports shops. The store is long and narrow, with slacks, shirts, and sweaters lining both sides. Prices are fair, considering the quality. A cotton bomber jacket sells for under $200. This is not the place to look for tenniswear.

ELLESSE, The Landmark, Edinburgh Tower, Queen's Road, Central, Hong Kong

ESCADA: The Escada boutique is a temple to what money can buy and what good design is all about. From the time you walk in the door you are hit with splashes of color emanating from the floor and rack displays. Choices are overwhelming. Prices are high. This West German line is very popular in the United States and Canada, but we did not see a lot of crossover merchandise. While you are there, take a look at the slightly less expensive Crisca and Laurèl lines.

ESCADA, Wheelock House, Pedder Street, Central, Hong Kong

▼

FENDI: Ouch! When you see the Fendi prices you might consider it cheaper to book a ticket to Italy. We love this line and buy it extensively in Rome, where prices are reasonable. However, Fendi's Hong Kong store, part of the Joyce empire, is no deal. If you are dying for those little FFFFFs, buy a key case.

FENDI, Hankow Centre, Ashley Road, Tsimshatsui, Kowloon

▼

JEAN-PAUL GAULTIER: A great-looking shop combined with great-looking clothing will attract our attention anytime. Gaultier has both in his Prince's Building boutique. The decor is reminiscent of a submarine, with the racks finished in a tarnished green brass veneer, and portholes for lights. The clothing is as wonderful as the decor, although Gaultier is no longer considered so weird by design standards.

JEAN-PAUL GAULTIER
Prince's Building, Ice House Street, Central, Hong Kong
Ocean Centre (Shop 201), Canton Road, Tsimshatsui, Kowloon

GIVENCHY: Audrey Hepburn looks great in Givenchy. We love the shop and can imagine her in all the clothes. In the last few years, the men's clothing has become even more popular. As a matter of fact, the Hong Kong Givenchy boutiques consider the menswear their best-selling line.

GIVENCHY, The Landmark, Gloucester Tower, Des Voeux Road, Central, Hong Kong

GIVENCHY GENTLEMEN PARIS, Ocean Centre (Shop 212), Canton Road, Tsimshatsui, Kowloon

▼

GUCCI: The big Gucci shop in Hong Kong is in a corner of the Landmark. It is not visible from the main atrium, but it does have street windows on Des Voeux Road. We happen to like the scarves, but find all of the GG's on the doors and mirrors amusing. The Peninsula Hotel has a more tasteful boutique, as do several department stores.

GUCCI

The Landmark, Des Voeux Road Central, Central, Hong Kong

The Peninsula Hotel, Salisbury Road, Tsimshatsui, Kowloon

▼

HERMÈS: The main entrance to Hermès, in the Landmark, is on the street, so do not be misled by the little showcase window you see across from Gucci. Walk outside and into the real shop. This is our favorite Hermès outside of Paris. Although the prices are not as good, the selection is very fine indeed. If you are dying for Hermès bath towels, jewelry, belts, purses, ashtrays, bathing suits, sweaters, or scarves, you will be a happy person. You may be able to find the scarf for slightly less in your airline duty-free selections.

HERMÈS

The Landmark, Des Voeux Road Central, Central, Hong Kong

The Peninsula Hotel, Salisbury Road, Tsim-shatsui, Kowloon

▼

KRIZIA: There is no crossover in merchandise between this small, but well-stocked, store and Top Knitters, which carries the Mirrors by Krizia line. Prices on these fun knitwear designs are high, but we can always hope to hit a sale.

KRIZIA, The Landmark, Des Voeux Road Central, Central, Hong Kong

▼

LANVIN: One of the oldest French houses, Lanvin is famous for fashion and for fragrance. My Sin and Arpège have been top brands ever since we could sniff. The classic, conservative clothing has become more popular with the fashionable young in the last few years. Lanvin's shop in the Landmark, located next to the fountain, is all cream-and-black decor. A center circular display holds the handbags and accessories; silk shirts, suits, and other ready-to-wear pieces are displayed along the walls. The choices are conservative; the prices are high. We didn't see any seconds merchandise anywhere in Hong Kong, so don't get your hopes up.

LANVIN

The Landmark, Des Voeux Road Central, Central, Hong Kong

Hyatt Regency Hotel, Nathan Road, Tsim-shatsui, Kowloon

CLAUDE MONTANA: Claude Montana makes the clothes that we diet to wear. You must be tall and thin to look right in them, but when you do, everyone turns around. All his shops are classically simple, and allow the designs to stand on their own. The two shops in Central and Kowloon are no exception.

CLAUDE MONTANA
> The Landmark, Edinburgh Tower, Queen's Road Central, Central, Hong Kong
> Kowloon Hotel, Middle Road, Tsimshatsui, Kowloon

▼

NINA RICCI: Nina Ricci has made a significant dent in Hong Kong retailing by offering great accessories that complement any outfit. Prices are moderate for designer goods. When we were there a pair of sunglasses was $75. Ties cost $50.

NINA RICCI
> The Peninsula Hotel, Salisbury Road, Tsimshatsui, Kowloon
> Regent Hotel, Salisbury Road, Tsimshatsui, Kowloon

▼

JEAN-LOUIS SCHERRER: We don't think this boutique is as elegant as M. Scherrer's clothing warrants. It is located on the 2nd floor of the Landmark and shares its space with Mirrors by Krizia. The prices are expensive, just as they are in Paris.

JEAN-LOUIS SCHERRER, The Landmark, Des Voeux Road Central, Central, Hong Kong

TRUSSARDI: The Italian Trussardi family is becoming a strong presence in the Hong Kong

market. In the years we have been visiting the boutiques here and abroad, we have seen a tremendous growth in both the quality and the quantity of the lines offered. You can now outfit the whole family in regular Trussardi, Trussardi Jeans, or Trussardi Junior. We have always liked the colored leather totes, which will cost you about $140 in Paris and about $100 in Hong Kong.

TRUSSARDI

The Peninsula Hotel, Salisbury Road, Tsimshatsui, Kowloon

Ocean Centre (Shop 230–236), Canton Road, Tsimshatsui, Kowloon

▼

LOUIS VUITTON: Louis Vuitton has a street entrance, while officially being in the Landmark. This particular Vuitton reminds us of a mini–Paris store, with the emphasis on the decor matching the luggage. However, the range of merchandise is petite by comparison. Prices are similar to those in Paris, and better than in the United States in most cases. This store is incredibly popular with tourists and is usually jammed with customers. Know your merchandise before you come. The street-market imitations have been cleared out, so don't expect to beat the system this time.

LOUIS VUITTON

The Landmark, 14 Des Voeux Road Central, Central, Hong Kong

The Peninsula Hotel, Salisbury Road, Tsimshatsui, Kowloon

American Big Names

ESPRIT: The market in casual American clothing has been captured by Esprit. Stores are all over town. Some are big and fancy (Causeway Bay and Tsimshatsui East), others comfortable and fun. We love the clothing, but don't feel that it is any special deal in Hong Kong.

ESPRIT

> 88 Hing Fat Street, Causeway Bay, Hong Kong
> The Landmark, Des Voeux Road Central, Central, Hong Kong
> Auto Plaza, 65 Mody Road, Tsimshatsui East, Kowloon

▼

DIANE FREIS: Diane Freis is, without doubt, the most famous designer in Hong Kong. Originally from California, Freis was on a trip to Hong Kong in the early '70s and decided to stay. She began designing the basic Freis dress—a panoply of three coordinating prints—and sold it through local stores. She was an instant smash with local-ladies-of-wealth, and soon had her own company.

Although she now runs a multimillion-dollar company, her basic design philosophy is still the same, although Freis continues to modify and update her styles. She oversees or personally creates every design that comes out of her factory.

Because Freis lives and works in Hong Kong, she sells a large percentage of her clothes from her boutiques. She does not believe in sales, and just recently was urged to open a factory outlet to handle merchandise from the previous season's line. Since Diane Freis dresses are timeless and travel without a wrinkle (we have put them to the test), we know that even last season's merchandise won't look like last season.

A Diane Freis original sells at Neiman Marcus for from $400 up, but in Hong Kong you can buy them for from $280 up. There is quite a savings, even buying retail. She has opened boutiques in the United States and plans to open more.

One warning: There are Freis imitations sold under other names. Do not be misled. A Diane Freis dress has a label that says so; the others are poor copies. Don't be fooled. There are too many Diane Freis boutiques to list them all, so we give you a selection of the most convenient ones.

DIANE FREIS

Prince's Building, Ice House Street, Central, Hong Kong

Harbour City, Ocean Terminal, and Ocean Galleries, Canton Road, Tsimshatsui, Kowloon

▼

POLO/RALPH LAUREN: We have been tracking Mr. Lauren for years, in hopes of finding a factory outlet. We finally did find one in Puerto Rico, which doesn't help if you are in Hong Kong. Until we find the factory, his shop in Central is the best location to pick up men's, women's, and children's clothing. It is not nearly so complete a selection as you will find in New York or Los Angeles, but what you find is good solid basics. We have found the prices to be slightly better than in the United States, except on sale. There are both Polo/Ralph Lauren boutiques and Ralph Lauren boutiques, but in most cases they are next door to each other.

RALPH LAUREN and POLO/RALPH LAUREN

Central Building, Queen's Road Central, Central, Hong Kong

The Peninsula Hotel, Salisbury Road, Tsimshatsui, Kowloon

Asian Big Names

KENZO: We are really cheating by putting Kenzo Takada under Asian Big Names. Yes, he is Japanese, but more French than anything else. His clothing originates in Paris, and it is wonderful. Kenzo's new store in Swire House carries a good selection of his line. Prices are moderate for a big-name designer. You can buy a dress for $200 and shoes for $100. There are items here for the whole family.

KENZO, Swire House, Connaught Road Central, Central, Hong Kong

▼

TOKIO KUMAGAI: If you are a fan of original Maud Frizon designs, or of any shoes that are wacky and fun, then Tokio Kumagai shoes will make you smile. There are shoes with faces, feathers, and pigtails. Mr. Kumagai has died, but a design staff is carrying out his concepts. We also liked the ties and leather accessories. The men's shoes are made in Italy and look sturdy enough to last for years.

TOKIO KUMAGAI
Swire House, Connaught Road Central, Central, Hong Kong
The Peninsula Hotel, Salisbury Road, Tsimshatsui, Kowloon

▼

MATSUDA: Matsuda is one of our favorite Japanese designers. The clothing is architectural and distinctive. The prices are high, and you may be able to do better at a big sale in the United States. The interior of the store is a work of art and worth stopping by to see.

Some of the clothing you see in Hong Kong will not be in America due to variations in licensing; if you are a Matsuda fan, you might want to stock up. There is a separate men's boutique next to the ladies' on the ground floor (Shops 9 & 10).

MATSUDA

Swire House, Connaught Road Central, Central, Hong Kong

The Peninsula Hotel, Salisbury Road, Tsimshatsui, Kowloon

▼

ISSEY MIYAKE: One of the premier architects of Japanese spare fashion, Miyake appeals to a select few. You have to have a certain flair to wear the designs well. If you're one of these fashionable few, you'll want to head immediately to the Miyake and Plantation shops in Swire House. None of his stores (even in Tokyo) carry a lot of stock, so putting together a wardrobe can be a frustrating job. The Plantation line is less expensive, but by no means cheap.

ISSEY MIYAKE, Swire House, Connaught Road Central, Central, Hong Kong

Local Big Names

Since we first began traveling to Hong Kong, the Hong Kong designers have been increasingly in the international spotlight. Local designers like Kai Yin Lo and Joseph Ho have been moving successfully on to the international scene as well. We find fashions by these hot local designers to be among the best buys in Hong Kong. Their designs will often cost less in Hong Kong than in the United States or Europe. There is usually not any crossover with the merchandise in the U.S. stores. For instance, Diane Freis designs are not done in bulk, and Kai Yin Lo specializes in one-of-a-kind jewelry.

The Hong Kong Trade Development Council sponsors "Fashion Week" every January, during which buyers come to Hong Kong to see what is new in manufacturing and what the hot talent is designing. Many previously unknown designers have had their start this way. Some of them are now well established, and a new crop of "young" designers are following in their footsteps.

Caveat: You may know of a designer with a Chinese name and assume his or her clothes are cheaper in Hong Kong. This is not necessarily true. After all, there are many American or Canadian designers with Asian surnames who may not even manufacture in Hong Kong—for instance, Joanie Char, Flora Kung, and Alfred Sung.

All the locals mentioned design Western-style garments in Western sizes.

PATRICIA CHONG: Chong is a Hong Kong designer who got her U.S. start at Bloomingdale's. You may remember her as the designer who invented the all-tan bathing suit—you could get a tan without having to be in the altogether. Chong designs her own fabrics first, then her fashions. Her company, called Etuex and Co. Ltd., manufacturers day and evening wear, while the Patricia Chong label specializes in all-silk day and evening clothes. Swimwear is designed under the All Tan label.

PATRICIA CHONG, department stores

▼

JOSEPH HO: We discovered Joseph Ho a few years back when he was just beginning to become famous. We bought quite a few pieces from his line because they were so cheap and so well made. Joseph Ho's designs have continued to grow, and, we are sorry to say, so have the prices. The value is still there, because comparable merchandise in the United States is double the price. Joseph Ho's special talent is in taking a perfectly ordinary blouse, sweater, or skirt and embroidering sequins, lace, or other such notions in a tasteful design on the sleeve, yoke, or bodice. Nothing is too much or so fancy that you can't wear it every day. Many silk and cotton shirts are coordinated with skirts that have a matching detail. A silk shirt will cost $200. Joseph Ho has opened many small boutiques, but his main one is still in the Omni The Hong Kong Hotel. He has also opened an outlet in Kaiser Estates that really is an outlet. Run, do not walk, if you like his fashions (see page 170).

JOSEPH HO
> Omni The Hong Kong Hotel, Canton Road, Tsimshatsui, Kowloon
>
> Swire House, Connaught Road Central, Central, Hong Kong

▼

RAGENCE LAM: Ragence Lam attended London's Harrow School of Art and Royal College of Art, after which he came back to Hong Kong long enough to win the first Young Designer Award (1977) from the Hong Kong Trade Development Council. He continued to work out of London until 1980, when he returned to Hong Kong on a full-time basis. He is no longer considered new, but is definitely a local big name. He now operates both a retail and a wholesale business, with a factory in Hong Kong and a beautiful boutique in Central. His reputation is for fabulous, verging on way-out, designs. If you dress to be noticed and want to buy a designer on the way up, make sure you visit the modern and lush boutique. Prices are $200–$500. The shop is simply called Ragence.

RAGENCE LAM, Swire House, Pedder Street, Central, Hong Kong

▼

EDDIE LAU: Lau started in the fashion business at the age of eleven, learning the tailoring trade. By the age of fourteen he owned his own shop. Not satisfied, Lau went to study at the St. Martin School of Art in London, learning style along with technique. He has been designing and manufacturing in Hong Kong for over ten years now, and is one of the top talents in the field. His work is colorful, expensive, and exciting. Recently, Lau began designing a special line, using Chinese silks, that is sold through the Chinese Arts & Crafts Stores. His shop in the Mandarin Hotel is elegant and geared more toward the tourist trade.

EDDIE LAU
   Mandarin Hotel, Chater Road, Central, Hong Kong
   Chinese Arts & Crafts Stores (H.K.) Ltd., 30 Canton Road, Tsimshatsui, Kowloon

▼

JENNY LEWIS: Jenny Lewis is an English designer with a unique talent who has made her fame by combining antique Chinese fabrics, classic silks, and beaded silks in unusual designs. Her more original designs combine English sensibility with Chinese flair. We think her beaded dresses are reminiscent of Fabrice. Be sure to try them on, however; we found the sizing to be strange. Prices for the beaded creations run around $1,000 and up.

JENNY LEWIS, Swire House, Connaught Road Central, Central, Hong Kong

▼

LIM YING YING: This is not the name of the designer, but the name that has become famous for ready-to-wear and private-label goods that are silky and sensuous. The company began in 1977 when George Wing-On Koh and his sister Colleen Chen decided to come up with a ready-to-wear line for the Trade Development Council's show. As they say, the rest is history. Lim Ying Ying has designed and produced lingerie for Bill Tice, Fernando Sanchez, Eve Stillman, and Oscar de la Renta. Ready-to-wear clients have included Morton Myles, Albert Nippon, Lord & Taylor, and Neiman Marcus. That is why you may see these labels in Lim Ying Ying's outlet store (see page 172). The label is sold in the United States on its own.

LIM YING YING, Hang Fung Industrial Building, 1st floor, Phase 2, 2 G Hok Yuen Street, Hung Hom

▼

KAI YIN LO: If you are into the expensive ethnic look, you will love Kai Yin Lo. Her designs are one-of-a-kind accessories—necklaces, earrings, belts, and some gift items. There is little that costs less than $100. Ms. Lo has positioned herself between the serious jewelry market and fun jewelry. Her necklaces and earrings are made with semiprecious stones and gold, thus necessitating a high price. There really is no competition in this style or price range in Hong Kong.

KAI YIN LO

The Peninsula Hotel, Salisbury Road, Tsimshatsui, Kowloon

Mandarin Hotel, Chater Road, Central, Hong Kong

▼

WALTER MA: Lily and her friends raved about Walter Ma, who happens to have a boutique almost next door to Ragence Lam. We admit that after seeing some people try on the fashions, we got hooked too. There are actually two lines, and the boutiques have different names. The Vee line is also designed by Walter Ma, with emphasis on "young." You should have a great figure to wear these outfits.

WALTER MA/VEE BOUTIQUE

Swire House, Pedder Street, Central, Hong Kong

65 Kimberley Road, Tsimshatsui, Kowloon

▼

JUDY MANN: Judy Mann's claim to fame is that she is the first local Chinese designer to have her own perfume. She began designing for Roncelli of Thayer International and moved back to Hong Kong in 1977 to do her own label. Her look concentrates on the young working woman who wants affordable but stylish clothing. She runs Cheetah Management and sells her designs internationally. Her factory outlet is called Cheetah.

JUDY MANN, Hong Kong Designer's Gallery, Paliburg Plaza, 66 Yee Wo Street, Causeway Bay, Hong Kong

CHEETAH, Prat Commercial Building (11th floor), 17–19 Prat Avenue, Tsimshatsui, Kowloon

RENE OZORIO: Ozorio began his career studying abroad. He graduated from the University of Alberta (Canada) with a fine arts degree in 1970, and began designing prints and textiles for overseas firms. In 1984, the Rene Ozorio Design and Production Company was established. Aside from his own collection of classic yet feminine clothing, which relies heavily on his experience in the textile and color fields, he provides select European companies with private-label designs.

RENE OZORIO
> Sogo Department Store, Designer Depot, 555 Hennessy Road, Causeway Bay, Hong Kong
> That's Boutique, Ocean Centre, Canton Road, Tsimshatsui, Kowloon

▼

WILLIAM TANG: The line is called W. Tang, and we love it. Currently sold in the United States and Australia as well as Hong Kong, the clothes are young and hip and a teensy bit for the with-it set, rather than the ladies who lunch. But he also does a lot of private work and is famous for his wedding gowns, so you can see that the man has a lot of range. Educated in Toronto and London, Tang returned to Hong Kong in 1981. He did some designing for Daniel Hechter and YGM Apparel (Hechter is a licensee of theirs), then worked in New York for Alcena. In 1984 he returned home again to make his mark in knitwear. He has gone into partnership with China and is manufacturing a special line in Shenzhen. His clothing is sold in China, Canada, the United States, and Australia.

WILLIAM TANG, Chinese Arts & Crafts Store, Star House, Canton Road, Tsimshatsui, Kowloon

▼

BEN YEUNG: Ben Yeung is not so up-and-coming as he is well known on a mass-market level. A graduate of UCLA, Yeung studied and designed in Europe. In 1981 he established Benny's Fashion and Design Centre Ltd. to sell to the European and Hong Kong markets. Since that time he has established offices in London, Paris, and Milan where the Cigale and Ben Yeung label is being sold.

BEN YEUNG, Hong Kong Designer's Gallery, Paliburg Plaza, 66 Yee Wo Street, Causeway Bay, Hong Kong

Up-and-coming Talent

More and more young designers are finding that Hong Kong is a fine place to be discovered. The local heroes listed above have paved the way, and serve as role models and teachers.

Although many of the young designers below are not yet represented in boutiques, they are busy designing private-label goods for large stores. You may never have heard their names, but we think that is just temporary. You just might be buying the next Christian Lacroix.

You can find the latest and wildest designs by these hot young talents in the shops that line Kimberley Road and Austin Avenue. These two streets, in the northern end of Tsimshatsui, have become the SoHo of Hong Kong. The decor of the shops is avant garde; the prices are affordable. Start at the corner of Austin and Nathan roads, walking east. Austin Road turns a corner and becomes Austin Avenue, which will turn again and become Kimberley Road heading back toward Nathan Road. We have listed some of our favorite boutiques under

"Finds" (see page 133). We also have a tour (see page 243) that names even more.

Another great place to search out talented new designers is a store called **HONG KONG DESIGNER'S GALLERY.** The main shop is in the New Territories, at the Hotel Riverside Plaza Arcade, Tai Chung Kiu Road, Sha Tin. A smaller but much more convenient shop is located at Paliburg Plaza, 66 Yee Wo Street, Causeway Bay. Here you will find bits and pieces from many up-and-coming designer lines. At last visit, Designer's Gallery represented Alan Chu, Judy Mann, Jolie by Ada Kuen, Jopej by John Cheng, Batik by Candy Solabarrieta, Eldy Pang, and Mayee Lok.

While shopping, watch for labels from designers whose names we predict will be making headway on the international scene before long. Some names to watch for: Laurence Tang, Paul Cheung, Danny Yu, Jennifer Kwok, Bernard Foong, and Shirley Chan. Some of our favorites include:

IKA BOUTON: Featured in the 1989 Young Designer Show at Fashion Week, Bouton's designs appeal to the career woman looking for both elegance and comfort. Ms. Bouton, who is Indonesian by birth, has studied at both the London College of Fashion and the Far East Dressmaking School in Hong Kong. She has recently opened a boutique attached to her workshop, and is pursuing both the Japanese and European markets.

IKA BOUTON, Humphrey's Building, 11 Humphrey's Avenue, Tsimshatsui, Kowloon

▼

CHUNGYU CHOI: Known as Clara to her friends, Choi lives in Paris, where she designs for the Bell Bonnet label of Orient Forest Ltd., made in Hong Kong. She is well known in Europe due to her work as assistant designer for the House of Chloe and Georges Rech. Her designs are classic and stylish in a French way. Choi hopes to open a Hong Kong boutique in the future, after she conquers Paris.

CHUNGYU CHOI, selected boutiques

▼

SIMON CHOI: Winner of two awards in 1987 at the Hong Kong Trade and Development Council's Young Designer Show, Simon Choi has had a meteoric climb to his own label. Under thirty years old, Choi designs simple and elegant clothing for his Signature label. His own boutique on Kimberley Road features the best of his designs.

SIMON CHOI, Signature Boutique, 61 Kimberley Road, Tsimshatsui, Kowloon

▼

FRANKLIN CHU: The majority of Franklin Chu's work is done for famous overseas clients, who appreciate his breezy coordinates. Designs for Chevalier International are exported to the United States. Designs for Guy Laroche, YSL, and Courrèges are seen in major boutiques around the world. Chu's own line, under the Ron Franco label, can be found in over thirty boutiques.

FRANKLIN CHU, specialty boutiques

▼

RODDY LEUNG: Art and fashion are one, says Roddy Leung when talking about his designs, which are graceful, simple, body-hugging, and meant for the 18 to 30 crowd. Trained at the Hong Kong Polytechnic School, Leung won the Talent Award given by the Hong Kong Fashion Designers' Association for a collection of "motorcycle-racing-inspired sportswear." Trained briefly in the Walter Ma studio, Roddy Leung now designs for the Penguin Cafe boutique.

RODDY LEUNG, Penguin Cafe, 60 Kimberley Road, Tsimshatsui, Kowloon

▼

FLORENCE TSE: Designing under the Florencefreda and J. Juno labels, Florence Tse is very successful. Her look is elegant. We especially like the eveningwear that is bouncy, young, and vibrant. Alas, there is no boutique belonging to Ms. Tse, but her designs are carried in department stores. A third label, Vinca Rose, specializes in contemporary daywear.

FLORENCE TSE, department stores and specialty boutiques

Finds

Some of our favorite stores do not fall into any one particular category. Some we love so much that we have to tell you about them again. The following shops are all favorites of ours for one reason or another:

ASHNELL: One of our all-time favorite resources for dressy handbags in leather, skin, and sequins is Ashnell. The shop is amazingly small, but so are the bags. There is a display case with samples of styles; other colors are stored below. Prices range from $150 to $500, with comparable U.S. prices being double and then some.

ASHNELL, Far East Mansion (1st floor, Shop 114), 5–6 Middle Road, Tsimshatsui, Kowloon

THE COTTON COLLECTION: On a hot, humid day in Hong Kong you will want to thank us for this tip: The Cotton Collection. These floral-print dresses remind us of bolder-looking Laura Ashley styles, and are very pretty. We've seen them all over the United States and France and think they are wonderful in price and design. An average dress is under $100.

THE COTTON COLLECTION
   Hyatt Regency Hotel Arcade, Nathan Road, Tsimshatsui, Kowloon
   D'Aguilar Place, Central, Hong Kong

▼

CROCODILE/CROCO-KIDS: Guess what the logo looks like? Crocodile has gone after the Lacoste look in a big way. They have their own big, bright, shiny stores and their own credit cards. With the Crocodile credit card you get a 10% discount on regularly priced items at Crocodile stores, City Sports stores, and the Palm Restaurant. There is a fee of about $7.00 for the initial card. Children's clothing is fun and colorful. We prefer the men's line to the women's. A polo shirt costs under $20.

CROCODILE/CROCO-KIDS, Hyatt Regency Hotel Arcade (basement), Nathan Road, Tsimshatsui, Kowloon

▼

JOYCE: Ah, Joyce ... our favorite retailer in Hong Kong. Joyce has two of her own boutiques and owns the licenses to big-name designers' shops, including Giorgio Armani, Emporio Armani, Krizia, Genny, Missoni, Sonia Rykiel, Fendi, Maud Frizon, and Issey Miyake. The majority of her shops are in the Landmark, with others in Swire House, the

Peninsula, and New World Tower. Visiting Joyce's shops is a must, especially at sale time.

JOYCE, The Landmark, Des Voeux Road Central, Central, Hong Kong

▼

LEVANTE: Ladies who wear larger sizes will love it here. The shop specializes in washable silks and knits that are flowing and very generously cut. A friend who normally wears a medium and is 5'8" tall took a small. Prices are fair and you can easily put together an outfit for under $100.

LEVANTE, Star House (No. 3), Salisbury Road, Tsimshatsui, Kowloon

▼

M GROUP: M Group is actually a chain of stores under the names Birds, Sports Connection, Circles, Cacharel, Children's Clothing Company, and Attitude. The branch that attracts us the most is Birds. They carry casual, breezy, young fashions. Prices are very moderate as well. Many Birds boutiques will also have a corner devoted to one of the other companies, usually Sports Connection.

M GROUP/BIRDS
The Landmark (ground floor), Des Voeux Road Central, Central, Hong Kong
Harbour City, Ocean Centre (Shops 212, 262, 271), Canton Road, Tsimshatsui, Kowloon

▼

NAG TRADE LIMITED: The British are renowned for their fine saddles, boots, and riding gear. If you are one of the horsey set, you must come to Nag Trade and feel the goods. The shop is located on the 2nd floor of the

Star House Arcade, and is cluttered with bridles, saddles, boots, britches, and other equestrian trimmings. A mother and her daughter run the shop and are extremely anxious to help. You can have custom riding boots made for under $200 that are butter-soft and durable. Riding shirts are also custom-made. The owners are the only agents in Hong Kong for British equestrian supplies, so prices can be kept low. Shipping is no problem. You can also request a catalogue and order from home.

NAG TRADE LIMITED, Star House Arcade (2nd floor), 3 Salisbury Road, Tsimshatsui, Kowloon

▼

LE POMMIER: *Le pommier* in French is the apple tree, and signifies the temptations you will find here. The owner, Prudence Moore, travels to Europe for the designer shows and returns to do her own version of what is in style. There are not many sizes, but if you see something you like and it doesn't fit, usually you can have it made. You have several options in both fabric and design. Many clients are repeaters, and she shops with them in mind. Accessories that are Chanel look-alikes line the walls. We bought a belt that would pass scrutiny (except that it had no CC's) for one third the price of an original. We want to make clear that these are not copies, just similar designs. All accessories come from Europe. Shopping here is like having your own couturier.

LE POMMIER, 39A Wellington Street, Central, Hong Kong

▼

ZHENCHAXUAN/THE BEST TEA HOUSE COMPANY LTD.: Tea is such an important part of Chinese life that it only makes sense that tea utensils are too. We found this very special shop on our Lai Chi Kok outlet day. It is between Splendid and Leighton Stock Sales on Tung Chau West Street. Inside you will find the most wonderful array of teas and Yixing pottery teapots. Some of them are new and some are collector's pieces, signed and documented in a book that the owner keeps to show the artist and his work. The antique and fine-art pots cost $500–$3,000. A small pot is $50–$100. There is another shop in Tsimshatsui, but we prefer the one in Lai Chi Kok.

ZHENCHAXUAN, China Hong Kong City (Room 4, 8th floor, Tower 1), 33 Canton Road, Tsimshatsui, Kowloon

THE BEST TEA HOUSE COMPANY LTD., 1039–1041 Tung Chau West Street (ground floor), Lai Chi Kok, Kowloon

Shopping Centers/Shopping Buildings

Rumor has it that the shopping mall was invented in Hong Kong by a brilliant British tycoon who knew that all tourists want to go shopping and that rain prevents them from doing some of that shopping. Indeed, once you set shoe in any of the plethora of shopping centers and buildings you will not know—or care—if it is day or night, light or dark, winter or summer, rainy or dry outside.

Hong Kong is totally overrun with shopping centers. It's like a contagious disease spreading to all architects, who now feel compelled to equip a hotel or an office building with three floors of retail shops before they get to the actual offices. Somewhere, somehow, they find tenants for all these shops. While stores do come and go in these locations, and there is always some new rumor as to which location is hotter than any other, these shopping centers and buildings do offer all of the riches of the Orient under one roof.

ADMIRALTY
Central, Hong Kong

If you stay in Causeway Bay you will get to know the name Admiralty very well, because you have to change trains at this MTR station to get to Kowloon. There are several layers of shops located between the train tracks and the offices above. Admiralty interconnects (all shopping centers seem to) to United Centre, Queensway Plaza, and The Mall, Pacific Place.

CITYPLAZA II AND III
IIII King's Road, Taikoo Shing, Hong Kong

Cityplaza II and III are rather far from your hotel, but if you are in town for a while you can take the MTR out to Taikoo Shing. This area is developing very rapidly now that the metro makes it more accessible, and many locals say that their best finds are in this area. Cityplaza is famous for its ice-skating rink, roller-skating rink, bowling alley, and assortment of children's toy shops.

Cityplaza is very much a family kind of place. If you happen to be traveling with kids and don't know what to do with them on a rainy day, you can create an excellent family adventure by taking the hoverferry from Central to Taikoo Shing and then catching a bus or taxi to the shopping center. You can shop, use the recreational services, eat, or even take in a movie. Check to see if the movies are in English with Chinese subtitles; most are.

HARBOUR CITY
Canton Road, Tsimshatsui, Kowloon

The shopping complex that occupies most of Tsimshatsui's western shore has been combined under the name Harbour City. It includes Ocean Terminal, Ocean Centre, and Ocean Galleries along with Omni The Hong Kong Hotel, Omni Marco Polo Hotel, and Omni Prince Hotel. There are four levels of shopping from end to end, and if you can successfully negotiate your way from one end to the other, you won't even have to come up for air.

The idea of a shopping complex on the waterfront originated with **OCEAN TERMINAL,** which is the building that juts out into the water beside the Star Ferry Pier. As you come in to dock, you can't help seeing the big Toys "Я" Us sign on the bottom level. Ocean Terminal was so successful that Ocean Centre and then Ocean Galleries were developed. It is hard to tell one from the other unless you look at the distinguishing floor tiles. Ocean Terminal is the least claustrophobic part of the complex because there are windows. Once you get into the bowels of Ocean Centre and Ocean Galleries you need your compass and lots of luck to find your way back out.

Ocean Terminal has chic china shops like **ROYAL COPENHAGEN** and **HUNTER'S;** designer boutiques, including **DIANE FREIS, ALAIN MA-NOUKIAN,** and **BENETTON;** handicrafts shops, including **ARTS OF CHINA** and **MOUNTAIN FOLKCRAFT,** as well as lots of food shops. The entire basement is being turned into a children's specialty floor containing not only one of the biggest **TOYS "Я" US** stores that we have seen, but also furniture, clothing, and other baby-related shopping. As you walk into Ocean Terminal stop at the information desk to pick up a complete listing of all the stores in Harbour City, along with the Harbour City map of Hong Kong. This map contains building locations that will help you get around town more easily.

OCEAN CENTRE is the next shopping complex as you walk away from the Star Ferry, followed by **OCEAN GALLERIES.** Although there are official lobbies, one seems to flow into the next, punctuated with a hotel along the way. The best hotel arcade in Harbour City is at the Omni The Hong Kong Hotel. There is a **JO-SEPH HO** shop on the main level and a mezzanine devoted to antiques shops. We must say that finding your way around Ocean Centre and Ocean Galleries can be confusing. The shops are in blocks and it is easy to get turned around looking for a number. We avoid coming here if there is a branch of the shop we want anywhere else. However, if it is raining, there is a typhoon, or the weather is so hot that you cannot breathe outside, Ocean Galleries and Ocean Centre start to look better. If you successfully make it to the far end, past the Omni Prince Hotel, treat yourself to some *dim sum* at Sun Tung Lok restaurant.

One stop farther up Canton Road is the **CHINA HONG KONG CITY** shopping complex. It is a major mall, with many fine, but ordinary, stores to browse in case you are not exhausted already. We like the dolphin sculpture in the lobby.

THE LANDMARK
Des Voeux Read Central, Central, Hong Kong

The Landmark is one of the best shopping centers in Hong Kong, and is extraordinarily different from all the others. It is totally Western. It is totally elegant. It is made up of two towers, Edinburgh and Gloucester, which are on top of four levels of luxury shops showcasing famous designers and surrounded by fountains and cafés. The basement (the subbasement is a grocery store) is young and hip, with white tile floors and white-fronted stores and even a Pizza Hut. The Landmark has to be seen, but it is closer to Trump Tower than to anything Chinese, British, or Far Eastern. About 80% of the big-name designers have shops in the Landmark, but don't forget to visit the **JOYCE** boutique—which houses even more of your favorites.

NEW WORLD CENTRE
18–24 Salisbury Road, Tsimshatsui, Kowloon

We aren't wild for the New World Centre—to us it seems like more of the same old thing. But people who stay at the Regent Hotel or at the Sheraton love the New World Centre because it's almost out their bedroom door. The New World Centre is yet another massive multilevel, spic-and-span, concrete-and-cold-floor shopping center filled with little shops, one-hour photo stands, and ice cream vendors. It has one of the best air-conditioning systems in Hong Kong, which is important in summer, as well as a cute Japanese department store (called **TOKYU**—open 10 A.M. to 9 P.M.; closed Thursday) on the street level.

THE MALL/PACIFIC PLACE
88 Queensway, Central, Hong Kong

Pacific Place and The Mall are new additions to the shopping center/hotel/office building scene. Located on the eastern side of Central, the buildings sit on a hill overlooking Victoria Harbour. The Marriott Hotel has some of the best views in the region from its lobby windows.

Next to the office towers and hotel is the entry to the shopping mall—Pacific Place. This is the most upscale and chic shopping outside of the Landmark, and is targeting the same audience. Parts I and II join together underground and traverse the entire bottom levels of the hotel and towers. Access to The Mall is via taxi or the Admiralty MTR station, where you walk through the shopping center and then on an overpass to enter The Mall directly.

Major boutiques have opened. There is even a branch of **LANE CRAWFORD.** We think that this shopping mall is a real winner.

PARK LANE SHOPPER'S BOULEVARD
Nathan Road, Tsimshatsui, Kowloon

This addition to Kowloon Park runs the length of Nathan Road from the Mosque at Cameron Road to Austin Road. It is clean and modern and has two stories. The shops either open onto the street or have showroom windows on the 2nd floor. Each store, except for **YUE HWA** (a Chinese department store), is small and oriented toward a youthful clientele. Yue Hwa takes up the whole corner at the Austin Road end and is a great spot to check out Chinese products.

THE PEDDER BUILDING
12 Pedder Street, Central, Hong Kong

The Pedder Building is a yuppie shopping building with a little bit of discount and a lot of interesting offbeat boutiques. At one time it was a secret find for outlet shoppers, but the real estate and rents have forced most of the shops to either up their prices and become what we think of as pseudo-outlets or go out of business altogether. The ones that are left included **SHOPPER'S WORLD SAFARI, SHIRT STOP, TAKPAC** (for the Anne Klein label), and **WINTEX.** The rest of the building is filled with boutiques carrying leather, silk, evening clothing, designer clothing, and talented designers like **DAVID SHEEKWAN.** A bit difficult to find unless you're really looking, it's sandwiched in between the China Building and Marden House, across from the Landmark and Central buildings.

PRINCE'S BUILDING
Ice House Street, Central, Hong Kong

You might think that the Prince's Building is merely a tony office building located across from the Mandarin Oriental and next to Station Square. It is, but, more important, it is home to such big names as **CHANEL, LES MUST DE CARTIER, DAKS, ESPRIT,** and **JEAN-PAUL GAULTIER.** The ground floor is shopping; the upper floors are for business. You will pass by the windows on your way to and from the Star Ferry.

SILVERCORD BUILDING
Canton Road, Tsimshatsui, Kowloon

Located at the upper end of Tsimshatsui, across from Harbour City, the Silvercord Building is devoted more to shopping than to business. If you're interested in computers, fax machines, or other high-tech electronic goodies, head straight to the basement where the **EAST ASIA COMPUTER PLAZA** shops are located. It's a great place to begin your research before buying electronics. There is also a **CHINESE ARTS & CRAFTS** store that is big and fun (four floors), and if you can't find what you're looking for here, you can access the shopping at Ocean Galleries by a footbridge over Canton Road.

STAR HOUSE
Canton Road, Tsimshatsui, Kowloon

Star House is the first building you come to upon exiting the Star Ferry and heading up Canton Road. You will see a large branch of **CHINESE ARTS & CRAFTS.** The interesting shopping actually happens upstairs in the office building, where there are some outlets such as **LEVANTE** (see page 135) and specialty stores like **NAG TRADE LIMITED** (see page 135). Don't let the tacky 1st-floor arcade turn you away.

SWIRE HOUSE
Connaught Road Central and Pedder Street, Central, Hong Kong

Swire House offers some of Central's best shopping under one roof. The Japanese and Chinese designers (**RAGENCE LAM, WALTER MA, JOSEPH HO, KENZO, TOKIO KUMAGAI, MATSUDA,** and **ISSEY MIYAKE**) have opened their shops here. The chic Europeans (**BALLY, BOTTEGA VENETA**) quickly followed. If you really want to be considered "different," this is where you open your shop.

Hotel Arcades

E ver since the 1950s, Holiday Inns of America has hosted little shops in their motel offices where you can buy toothpaste, aspirin, and tampons. Hotels in Hong Kong have taken this basic idea and carried it one step further. They have little shops in their lobbies—or in their arcade areas—that sell everything you might want or need. For life.

There are several reasons for the popularity of hotel arcades in Hong Kong. They're dry in rain; they're cool in summer (like shopping malls); they're handy for the tourist who will spend according to convenience; and, most important, they receive the benefits of trust. Shoppers have come to judge the shops in a hotel to be as reliable as the hotel itself. Thus the fanciest, most deluxe hotels have the most trustworthy shops. Shoppers believe there is a direct correlation between the quality of the store and the quality of the hotel.

Certainly the shops in the Peninsula, the Mandarin Oriental, and the Regent are the most expensive and most exclusive. But that doesn't mean there's anything wrong with the shops in the Holiday Inn. Some hotel arcades offer a handful of shops. Others have three levels of stores and hundreds of choices. Often, a hotel arcade connects to a main shopping center. With the Omni Prince Hotel at the far end of Harbour City, you can walk from the Prince through a shopping arcade to connect to the Omni Marco Polo Hotel, and then go into another shopping center and keep on connecting for a few miles, several hotels, and thousands of stores, and end up at Omni The Hong Kong Hotel.

Japanese Department Stores

Japanese department stores must be considered the eighth wonder of the world. They are so total, so complete, so very staggering in their stock that it's almost overwhelming. Visitors to Japan often go nowhere else but department stores. Visitors to Hong Kong should take some time for a few of these stores just to see what they are like, if not to buy anything.

Basically, Japanese department stores in foreign countries (foreign to Japan) are there to serve Japanese expats. The Japanese department stores in London sell the same things Harrods do; the ones in Hong Kong sell a little of everything. If you expect just Japanese merchandise, you are very, very wrong. Every big-name French and Italian designer is represented in the bigger Japanese department stores. Japanese cosmetics (fabulous) are sold in quantities; and selection of all types of products is maximum. Causeway Bay has several Japanese department stores right near each other, so you may want to check a few of them out while you are there.

Prices in department stores tend to be high, and we don't buy a lot here; we just drool.

One final word to claustrophobics: Don't go during rush hours. Stores are open until 9 or 10 P.M., so relax and enjoy yourself away from the madding crowd.

DAIMARU: Closed on Wednesday in the traditional Japanese habit of closing one day a week, Daimaru is fun and known to us for its clean, well-marked toilets, which we use when in the neighborhood. Asian pop music blares and major designer goods are abundant. Prices are not bargain-basement but are no higher than at other Japanese department stores.

Daimaru is divided into two large department stores, one for fashions and one for housewares and furniture. The stores feel much more Japanese than the other department stores. This is a good "real people" resource if you live in Hong Kong.

Inexpensive Japanese (a fashion style you will grow to appreciate when you see it) is cute and fun—great for teens. There are watches and pearls here, but the selection and quality are not as snazzy as at Mitsukoshi. Daimaru is more middle-class than some of the other stores; the real buys here are in Japanese fashions. Hours are 10:30 A.M. to 9:30 P.M.

DAIMARU, Fashion Square, Paterson Street, Causeway Bay, Hong Kong

▼

ISETAN: Isetan is more young at heart than the other Japanese department stores. It's a great place for fun clothes, although there is a good selection of international designers. This store also has several basement levels, but is not attached to an MTR station. Fun for teens; convenient enough to your basic Kowloon shopping spree that you can pop in for a few minutes. Hours: Daily, 10 A.M.–9 P.M.

ISETAN, Sheraton Hotel Arcade, 20 Nathan Road, Tsimshatsui, Kowloon

▼

MATSUZAKAYA: This department store closes on Thursday, but otherwise it's open from 10:30 A.M. to 9:30 P.M. It feels a lot like Sears but has pockets of designer clothes here and there. If you crave Godiva chocolates, you can buy them here. The ground floor has cosmetics, perfumes, handbags, and accessories; the 1st floor is ladies' and children's ready-to-wear; the 2nd floor is men's and sports; and the 3rd floor is housewares, stationery, and toys.

The overall quality is everyday Hong Kong, which probably is not your look back in the United States. Display of fashion is not good, and we aren't wild for the store—except for its good cosmetics department and those marvelous Godiva chocolates.

MATSUZAKAYA
Paterson Street, Causeway Bay, Hong Kong
Queensway Plaza, Central, Hong Kong

▼

MITSUKOSHI: This is our favorite Japanese department store—in Hong Kong, anyway. It's built a bit like a bomb shelter and seems to have no relationship to the real world. It just goes on forever, and there are no windows. In fact, a good bit of it is underground. Floors are numbered with substreet numbers—for example, B3 means it's the third floor down, not up. This bothers some, but not us.

Mitsukoshi can be appreciated even before you set foot in the actual store. Occupying most of the ground floor of the marbled

Hennessy Centre, it is one of the largest and fanciest of the Japanese department stores in Causeway Bay. Just looking at it is exciting. Fine watches, pearls, leather handbags, and some designer labels dot the ground-floor display cases. Compared to other Japanese department stores, Mitsukoshi is one of the most lovely and elegant—especially on the main floor. Prices here are Japanese standard, which means there are no bargains.

As you descend into the guts of the store, each floor gets less and less American. The lower-level fashions downstairs are geared more for Hong Kong taste and budget. As you go down, the lights get brighter and the music seems louder. Don't go if you have a headache.

Mitsukoshi has designer clothes and accessories—Gucci, Lanvin, Christian Dior, Guy Laroche, Chloé, Mila Schön, etc. The housewares department is great fun; there is also a grocery store on B3. Hours are Sunday through Friday, 10 A.M.–9 P.M., and Saturday till 9:30 P.M. (closed Tuesday).

MITSUKOSHI, Hennessy Centre, 500 Hennessy Road, Causeway Bay, Hong Kong

▼

SOGO: Sogo is right over the Causeway Bay MTR station, which makes it very convenient. (Or, if you are driving, there is free parking for two hours at Windsor House.) Sogo is open daily from 10:30 A.M. to 10 P.M., so you can get in some nighttime shopping with pleasure. All the big designers are represented here. Prices are good on Japanese designers such as Hiroko Koshino, whom we have been buying in Milan or at Alma in New York.

Sogo plays recognizable Muzak as you zip up and down escalators—designers on the ground floor; ladies' fashions, cosmetics, and shoes on B1; food on B2. There is more ladies' fashion on floors 1 and 2; don't miss the cos-

metic bar on the 1st floor; men's fashions are
on 3; 4 is sports and hi-fi equipment; 5 is
household goods and furniture; 6 has babies'
and maternity items; and 7 offers stationery.
On the 1st floor there's an adorable "Cafe
City" decorated with pink-and-black Art Deco
and ready to convince you that you aren't in
Hong Kong. Sogo claims to be the world's
largest department store.

SOGO, Lockhart Road, Causeway Bay, Hong
Kong

British Department Stores

I t seems perfectly normal for there to be
British department stores in a British crown
colony—especially one that was set up for
the sole purpose of trade—but we are sorely
disappointed that Harrods doesn't have an outlet in Hong Kong.

DODWELL: Dodwell is a bargain basement
of the British variety. It is not Chinese but
British in nature, even though the Chinese like
the store as much as everyone else.

Dodwell is not the place to pick up souvenirs, but if you need inexpensive clothing,
Western-style, there are bargains galore. Little
girls' dresses cost $10–$15; cotton T-shirts are
$3.50; socks are $2.

There are several Dodwell stores; the one in
the Landmark is the snazziest.

DODWELL
  Excelsior Hotel, Causeway Bay, Hong Kong
  Cityplaza, Taikoo Shing Road, Hong Kong
  Elizabeth House, Causeway Bay, Hong Kong
  The Landmark, Central, Hong Kong
  Harbour City, Kowloon

LANE CRAWFORD: Lane Crawford is the most prestigious Western-style department store in Hong Kong, and a jewel to those who work and live here but who crave the elegance of Old World charm in a retail setting. Lane Crawford is not huge by American standards, but it's large enough to give comfort and to offer the leading brands of merchandise. It is not really there for tourists, but it does offer the guarantee that you are not getting fakes, seconds, or inferior merchandise. Snobs often like to buy their jewelry here.

Lane Crawford was created as a full-service English department store for the people who live here. It doesn't have the food halls of Harrods or the young-working-girl selection of Selfridge's, but it does offer cradle-to-grave services along with the merchandise. Yes, you can take your Maine Chance Day at the Elizabeth Arden here.

We have never seen anything in Lane Crawford we didn't see anywhere else, and find the store worthwhile only if you seek to escape the realities of Hong Kong (and many do ... if only for an hour), or want to see a lot of merchandise in a manner you can deal with—as opposed to the wretched excesses elsewhere in Hong Kong.

LANE CRAWFORD
Lane Crawford House, Queen's Road Central, Central, Hong Kong
74 Nathan Road, Tsimshatsui, Kowloon

▼

MARKS & SPENCER: Marks & Spencer has three stores now open in Kowloon. The more accessible one, located in the Harbour City complex, has 10,800 square meters of shopping on two levels. It is small, but packed with delicious specialty items. Level 1 has the St. Michael brand underwear that everyone loves, along with nightwear and other lingerie, some in sizes up to a 16. Level 2 is complete with a cosmetics counter, menswear, ladies' wear, and a specialty food shop. The St. Michael brand cosmetics and natural skin products are fun and fresh. You can buy cleansers and toners made with oatmeal and rosemary, rosewater and glycerine, or apricot, almond, and avocado. The second Marks & Spencer, located in Cityplaza, has 20,000 square meters of space. The third is in Mong Kok.

MARKS & SPENCER
Harbour City, Canton Road, Tsimshatsui, Kowloon
Cityplaza, 1111 King's Road, Taikoo Shing, Hong Kong

Chinese Department Stores

There are several Chinese department stores in Hong Kong, but the most glamorous of them is run by the Communist Chinese government. They have nothing to do with the other Chinese department stores, which are owned and operated by locals.

CHINESE ARTS & CRAFTS STORE: This store is shocking to most Americans because it is so downright elegant. (There are several branches, the biggest one being in Wanchai, but all are very nice.) Stores are open every day of the week, including Sunday.

There are several shops and each is slightly different, but most of the merchandise is the same. *One warning:* The shops are meant to bring cash into the Communist Chinese government, as we've already said. To make the most, the most is asked. These stores happen to be very expensive, for what they are selling. By American standards, the prices are good. By local standards, they are outrageously high.

Eddie Lau has his own boutique in each store; the jewelry departments are glorious. You may find merchandise here that you can get cheaper in the United States.

The silk fabric (yardgoods) department is fun, although the prices are cheaper in Jardine's or the Lanes. We love the porcelain, baskets, and tablecloths. We've been told by those who know that this is a reputable place to buy jade. There's no imitation passed off as real here. Be warned, however, real jade is quite pricey. The store will ship for you; sales help have been very pleasant to us. We like it here, but we seldom buy much only because we find prices are *cher*. Hours in all stores are basically Monday to Saturday, 10 A.M. to 6:30 P.M.; some stores may be open on Sunday.

CHINESE ARTS & CRAFTS STORES (H.K.) LTD.

Shell House, Queen's Road, Central, Hong Kong

Silvercord Building, 30 Canton Road., Tsimshatsui, Kowloon

China Resources Building, 26 Harbour Road, Wanchai, Hong Kong

▼

WING ON: Wing On has Western-style merchandise at about one quarter the U.S. price. Many prices are less expensive than at Stanley Market. We're not talking Calvin Klein, but you can find some inexpensive work clothes here. Large-size Americans need not apply. This store was really a shocker in that it offered so much. Needless to say, there are not a lot of tourists here.

WING ON

361 Nathan Road, Yaumatei, Kowloon
26 Des Voeux Road, Central, Hong Kong

YUE HWA: If you can't make it all the way to China, stop by here for a taste of the real thing. If you need acupuncture needles, stop by the counter on the 1st floor. (Promise her anything, but give her acupuncture needles. . . .)

Besides the medicines and herbs and spices, inexpensive menswear is on the 1st floor. The 2nd floor has rows and rows of Chinese working clothes. This is not what you came to Hong Kong for. There is a fur corner on 2—the furs are of questionable origin and bring immediately to mind the question of U.S. Customs. You will need a country-of-origin form to bring the fur into the United States. If the thought of a fur appeals to you, call your district Customs office to ask about GSP breaks on fur and which animal fur cannot be brought into the United States.

The 3rd floor has lots of fun gift items, jade flowers, little wallets, cloisonné bracelets, children's Chinese pajamas, beaded evening bags, and Suzy Wong gowns. They mail to the United States—a 10-kilo package (25 pounds) costs $30 to ship. Not bad at all. Hours are daily from 9:30 or 10 A.M. to 8 or 9 P.M.

YUE HWA

Main store, 301–9 Nathan Road, Yaumatei, Kowloon

Park Lane Shopper's Boulevard, 151 Nathan Road, Kowloon

Factory Outlets

The words "factory outlet" are music to the ear of any true shopper. Once the ultimate fantasy of the tourist visiting Hong Kong, factory outlets have now become an integral part of the shopping scene. There are, in fact, hundreds of factory outlets in Hong Kong. It is a trend in Hong Kong's manufacturing business to have your own. They are located in nice neighborhoods, out-of-the-way neighborhoods, scary neighborhoods, and chic neighborhoods. Finding them all is easy; getting to all of them in a short amount of time (three days) is impossible. But don't panic; many of them are not worth finding.

Each year more and more factory owners have gotten wise to the fact that the tourist wants a bargain, wants to buy at a factory, and is disappointed when she cannot do so. Some of them advertise in the *South China Morning Post* and in the tourist handouts that are provided at the airport by the HKTA. Many of them actually belong to the Hong Kong Tourist Association and have received their approval and sticker. The outlets in Kaiser Estates have made shopping easy by banding together and forming an association. The result of all this activity has been to generate mass "factory-mania" in the industry. Some of the most commercial outlets have let their merchandise become shoddy and second-rate. The real bargains have disappeared and been replaced by manufactured bargains. Factories that are new to the game are competing hard for the business. Many have opened beautiful, clean "outlets" staffed with English-speaking sales help. The merchandise is as good as you would get in a boutique—definitely not seconds. We don't complain too much as long as the bargain is still there and the price is right. In many cases this is not true. High rents mean higher prices. Don't expect to find a great deal in a factory-outlet shop that has a tony address.

The famous designer labels that you might hope to find in the outlets have put restrictions on their factories because of the serious problem of rip-offs that has plagued them in the last few years. Current merchandise has been known to "disappear" from the factory and reappear under a different label at a factory outlet. Sometimes the style is slightly modified; sometimes it is not even changed. Many factories that you would hope to visit are closed and guarded.

Having learned and relearned it all the hard way (hours on the MTR in search of a bargain and winding up with junk; being frightened to death in the back hallways of Kaiser Estates; wearing through many pairs of shoes walking the back alleys of Kowloon and the New Territories), we are here to keep you from making the same mistakes we first made. We have revisited, edited, added, and listed only those outlets that we think are worth visiting. If we have left some out, it is either because they are too inaccessible or because the quality of the merchandise was not up to our standards. If you have only three to five days in Hong Kong, you don't have time to waste. Be sure that you are not planning your factory-outlet visits on a public holiday, and especially not during the Chinese New Year, when everything will be closed up tight. Remember that factories and their outlets close during lunch, usually from 1 P.M. to 2 P.M. One of our readers, visiting Hong Kong on a cruise, ended up being there over Chinese New Year. It was colorful and fun, but there was no shopping. She was miserable. We list our select outlets by area and in our tour section (pages 249–251). If you are pressed for time, we suggest you just pick a tour and follow it.

Ambience in the outlets varies widely. Some good outlets are in the factories themselves, and are exciting to visit. Other outlets are funky but have good-quality merchandise mixed in with seconds. More and more of our favorite outlets are quite elegant, have large, modern showrooms, and accept credit cards; nevertheless, they offer quality merchandise at discount prices. One thing to remember about shopping in an outlet is that there are no returns or credits. Once you leave the store, the merchandise is yours, even if you find a huge hole in the sleeve when you return to your hotel room. Always check the merchandise for dye lots and damages before you buy it. Always try on an item; verify sizes. Most outlets will have some place for you to try on items. Sizes are not always marked correctly. As with the rest of Hong Kong shopping, the motto is "Buyer Beware."

One note of warning: In Hong Kong, stores seem to move about faster than the prevailing winds. Despite our best efforts to keep this book current, a few stores will, no doubt, fall between the publication of one edition and the next. If a store is no longer at the address we have listed, we apologize. We no longer list the specific designer names carried by the outlets, unless they themselves advertise it, for the exact same reason. Designers jump from one manufacturer to the next at a moment's notice, leaving the once great outlet high and dry. If the outlet is particularly out of your way, you might want to double-check that it is still there. Remember, this is Hong Kong ... expect anything.

Central

Central is the main retail shopping, banking, and business hub of Hong Kong. The rents are very high. Get the message? Because more and more tourists are looking for factory outlets that are convenient, more and more manufacturers are complying by opening branches in Central. However, you cannot expect to get a fabulous bargain in a shop where the overhead is outrageous. We recommend shopping the Central outlets for fun and convenience. It sure beats an hour on the MTR and getting lost in Kwun Tong. But you will pay the price for this convenience. For many, time is money. Unless we have specifically noted, these outlets all accept some form of credit card, usually MasterCard, Visa, and/or American Express.

BETU: Betu is located in the tony Pedder Building, which used to be a rehab waiting to be finished, and now looks too chic for discounts. Nevertheless, Betu carries private-label merchandise that is better priced than what you find in the department stores. There are no fabulous designer-label "deals," but the shop is clean and convenient, and the merchandise is well organized. The bigger, better Betu is in Kwun Tong, but that is a trip you wouldn't want to take just for this. The entrance to the Pedder Building is just after the Escada shop, across from the Landmark. Hours are Monday–Saturday, 9:30 A.M. to 6:30 P.M.

BETU, Pedder Building (Room 106B), 12 Pedder Street, Central, Hong Kong

▼

CAMBERLEY: This is the easiest Camberley location to find, although there are two others, one in Kowloon and one in Hung Hom. Camberley has pared down its outlet business since it no longer carries the Anne Klein II label. However, we still have luck here. They manufacture for other top designers, and we have seen clothing from two big-name designers hanging on the racks. Camberley's quality surpasses that at most factory-outlet shops. We like their silk blouses under $100 and their suits in gabardine or silk/linen blends for under $200. A famous-name designer's silk dresses were selling for $100. The shop is located upstairs in Swire House. Hours are Monday to Saturday, 9 A.M. to 6 P.M.

CAMBERLEY, Swire House (Room 813), Connaught Road Central, Central, Hong Kong

▼

ÇA VA: One of the "office building" outlets in Central, Ça Va carries export merchandise, not seconds. They do not claim to be a true factory outlet, and are straightforward about the fact that they sell the Marisa Christina and Ciao Sports lines in the shop. During the January–February and June–July–August sale periods, they dispose of all the factory samples through their three outlets. This is the time to come and save money. Ça Va manufactures a full line of clothing, mostly in silks and gabardines. Prices are midrange, with a suit costing $250 and silk blouses $100. To find the shop, enter the Central Building (next to the Landmark) to the left of the Polo/Ralph Lauren shop. The elevators are in the back of the building. Ça Va is open Monday–Friday from 10:30 A.M. to 6 P.M., and Saturday from 10:30 A.M. to 5 P.M.

ÇA VA, Central Building (Room 1522), Pedder Street, Central, Hong Kong

▼

LESLIE FAY: We discovered Leslie Fay one day as we were heading out of the Hilton Hotel. One block east of the hotel is Duddell, a dead-end street between Ice House and Wyndham. We spotted a very well-dressed lady heading into this little building and decided to follow. Much to our surprise and happiness she led us directly to the Leslie Fay outlet. Major design lines are carried here, with an emphasis on sports and business clothing. Prices are extremely good on major brands. There are many items suitable for "larger" (size 10) Americans, which are hard to come by in many Hong Kong stores. Other Leslie Fay outlets are located in Kowloon in the Wing On Plaza (Room 207), and in the Sun Plaza at 28 Canton Road. Hours for the

Central shop are Monday–Saturday, 10 A.M. to 7 P.M.

LESLIE FAY, Baskerville House (Shop M1), 13 Duddell Street, Central, Hong Kong

▼

JENNIE: Across the street from a very tony interior-design showroom is a little black hole-in-the-wall building that houses the tiny but impressive Jennie outlet. The merchandise includes sweaters, silk blouses, pleated silk skirts, gabardine blazers, and cotton knits of all varieties. The average price of anything is $50. The outlet is crowded with Hong Kong locals. There are no labels that we recognize, and the merchandise looks like upscale private-label to us. If you really like the look, try the Quarry Bay shop (Cornwall House, 19th floor, Taikoo Trading Estate, 28 Tong Ching Street), which usually has more selection. Central is often shopped out. Hours in Central are Monday–Saturday, 10 A.M. to 5 P.M. No credit cards.

JENNIE, Cheong Sun Building (Room 503), 52–54 Wellington Street, Central, Hong Kong

▼

SHIRT STOP: This outlet has become so popular that it has multiplied and spawned many others around town. We still come to the original shop because it looks more cluttered and outlety than the others. Shirt Stop specializes in men's shirts, most especially from a major French designer with three initials. They are very upfront about displaying the merchandise, labels intact and all. Other designer goods have labels cut, but it is still possible to read them. Shirt Stop is a good place to stock up on everyday shirts at good prices. A button-down cotton runs $20 or less. There are also sweaters in wool and cashmere for sale. The heavy knits are less expensive and a better value than the cashmeres. Other outlets are located in Causeway Bay at 518 Lockhart Road, in the Excelsior Hotel at 281 Gloucester Road, and at 19–312 Yee Wo Street (Shop 3). In Tsimshatsui you will find Shirt Stops at the Hyatt Hotel, on Nathan Road, and at 2A Prat Avenue. Hours at the Pedder Building are Monday–Saturday, 10 A.M. to 7 P.M. Credit cards on charges over $100.

SHIRT STOP, Pedder Building (Room 506–507), 12 Pedder Street, Central, Hong Kong

▼

SHOPPER'S WORLD SAFARI: This is what a factory outlet should look like. It was one of the first, and may be one of the last. It is dingy, crowded, and packed with people and merchandise. You have to be Inspector Clouseau to find the designer goods here, but they are here. Much of the merchandise looks like it has been around since the store opened. We don't think it has been; it is just factory rejects, seconds, or damages. Over the years we have found major big-name designer goods in the racks. You will either luck out or be sorry you bothered. The seasons make a big difference. Other shops are located in Kowloon, at the Sands Building (Room 708), 17 Hankow Road, and at Jade Mansion, 40 Waterloo Road. Hours at the Pedder Building are Monday–Sunday, 9:30 A.M. to 6:30 P.M.

SHOPPER'S WORLD SAFARI, Pedder Building (Room 104), 12 Pedder Street, Central, Hong Kong

▼

TAKPAC: A new, smart, modern outlet has been opened in the Pedder Building, and we say "Yawn." There are lots of choices to make in lots of colors. We don't know where the merchandise is sold retail, however, because it is not typical U.S. goods. A lot of the clothing is sample size. A lot of the clothing looks old. Prices are no better than a good sale would be in the United States. Look in and see if you find anything. Chantal Thomas clothing is also sold. The location certainly is convenient. Hours are Monday–Saturday, 9:30 A.M. to 6:30 P.M. A retail/wholesale shop is open in Tsimshatsui at 67 Chatham Road, 2nd floor.

TAKPAC, Pedder Building (Room 301), 12 Pedder Street, Central, Hong Kong

▼

WINTEX: One of the tonier outlets in Central, Wintex carries the Lisa Ferranti and Vanessa Van Cleef labels. (They have them on their card.) All the clothing is spanking clean; much of it is still in plastic. Prices average around $100–$200 for a blouse, which we don't consider to be much of a bargain for these lines. They advertise "wholesale prices," but we don't think these goods would retail for double what you will pay here. You can put together a complete outfit and not worry about holes, however. Hours are Monday–Friday, 9 A.M.–6 P.M., and Saturday till 5 P.M.

WINTEX, Pedder Building (Room 401), 12 Pedder Street, Central, Hong Kong

Some outlets listed elsewhere have secondary shops in Central. You might also want to look in on these:

FASHIONS OF SEVENTH AVENUE, Sing Pao Centre (Room 12A), 8 Queen's Road Central, Central, Hong Kong (see page 172)

FOUR SEASONS GARMENTS, South China Building (10th floor), 1–3 Wyndham Street, Central, Hong Kong (see page 171)

GAT DESIGN LTD., Cosmos Building, 8–11 Lan Kwai Fong, Central, Hong Kong (see page 165)

TOP KNITTERS, Tak Yan Commercial Building (12th floor), 30–32 D'Aguilar Street, Central, Hong Kong (see page 163)

VICA MODA, Bank of East Asia Building (Shop 1-B), 10 Des Voeux Road Central, Central, Hong Kong (see page 170)

Tsimshatsui

Tsimshatsui and Tsimshatsui East are the focal areas where Kowloon Peninsula's "retail" outlet shops have located. These outlets, usually found in commercial buildings, cater to the tourist trade, while still trying to pass on a bargain or two. We must warn you that looking for an address is frustrating, however. Many buildings are old, and their numbers have been worn away or buried under shop signs. In our listings, we give building names for this reason. The name of any building seems to be more clearly marked than the street address is. Travel with the HKTA map book put out by A-O-A Publications. You can match up buildings by name and location in the block to find the right doorway. We give as specific directions as possible, but even we still get lost. Credit cards are accepted at these shops unless so noted.

THE SANDS BUILDING
17 Hankow Road, Tsimshatsui, Kowloon

The Sands Building is not a factory-outlet building, although you might think so from all the listings. It is an office building, located right in the heart of the action, next door to the Chung Kiu Department Store. The entrance to the

Sands Building is to the right of the store. Go to the back to find the elevators to the shops:

ORIENTAL PACIFIC, Room 602. O.P. is an old hand at the outlet business, and we are glad they still have good prices. We could ramble on for hours about the bargains we have found here, the sweaters we are still wearing, the single- and double-ply cashmeres that are unbeatable for design and price. O.P. is a real find. The shop is quite large, with sweater bins and racks lining three of the four walls. Displays are arranged by quality. Summer cottons are in one area, children's clothing in another, cashmeres on the wall nearest to the cash register. Sizes all tend to be marked large, but there is stock in the back; just ask. If a salesperson tells you that is all they have, ask the manager. Trust us, the back room has boxes upon boxes of sweaters.

Some of the sweaters may appear worn or old at first glance. Examine them carefully and you'll probably see that it's a combination of the lighting, the wool, and the colors. We stock up on kids' wool sweaters because they are so cheap ($15–$20). They are not, we repeat not, designer sweaters. If you expect glamorous styles here you will be disappointed. These are basics. These are bargains. Oriental Pacific has recently opened in Star House (6th floor, 3 Salisbury Road), and that is a prettier, fresher, and newer store. The stock is all the same. Expect to pay $150–$200 for a cashmere pullover. We think the best buys are the men's heavy woolen sweaters. Hours in both stores are Monday–Saturday, 9 A.M. to 6 P.M.

TOP KNITTERS, 10th floor. This is the one outlet where we lose our cool. Top Knitters produce knitwear for some of the major, major, major European designers. If you are up on sweater designs, you will recognize them. The best buys are in men's woolen sweaters. A heavy Italian designer sweater runs $200. The comparable U.S. price would be $450. Cotton-and-linen-blend sweaters are under $200, cashmeres the same. Styles come and go from this shop. Mirrors by Krizia merchandise is always carried, but only a small selection. Don't expect cheap at this outlet. Hours are Monday–Friday, 9 A.M. to 6 P.M., Saturday till 5 P.M.

MISS O, Room 801. The silk dresses in Miss O bear the Miss O for Oscar de la Renta label, and the outlet makes no bones about letting you know that. We know and love Oscar's clothing and don't see much resemblance between his regular label and the Miss O for Oscar de la Renta one. The dresses are very nice, don't get us wrong, and the price is right, under $150. But these are simple dresses, not high-fashion styles at all. Most of the clothing is a sample size 8 or 10, so bring your credit cards if you are, too. The shop also carries a washable silk line that is casual and fun. Hours are Monday–Saturday, 9:30 A.M. to 5:30 P.M.

Nathan Road

Nathan Road runs the length of Kowloon Peninsula, from Salisbury Road near the water to the never-never lands of Sham Shui Po. There is no other street quite like it in the world. It makes 42nd Street in New York City look like a country lane. Shop after shop after shop is filled with clothing, electronics, watches, jewelry, and bargains. Some of them are even factory outlets. However, there is only one that we really love.

DORFIT: After the Peninsula Hotel, and before you reach the Hyatt Hotel, is Shui Hing House and Dorfit. Enter the building beside the grocery store and walk downstairs and to the back to find the elevators. Dorfit is just off the elevators to the left, on the 11th floor. Be aware that some of the elevators do not go to all the floors.

Dorfit is a small version of Oriental Pacific. There are sweaters piled all over the room. Some are a little seedy, but if you ignore these and concentrate on the cashmeres and cottons, you will love it here, too. A good two-ply cashmere man's or woman's pullover should run no more than $200. Dorfit also carries a fun and inexpensive line of children's sweaters. There is another outlet in the Tsimshatsui Centre at 66 Mody Road, and one in the Ocean Centre, on Canton Road. The shop on Nathan Road is open every day from 9 A.M. to 7 P.M.

DORFIT, Shui Hing House (Room 1107–8), 23–25 Nathan Road, Tsimshatsui, Kowloon

Granville Road

Granville is the perhaps Hong Kong's most controversial shopping street. Once a busy, unobtrusive avenue, Granville is now a pseudo–bargain-hunter's paradise. Every shop says "Factory Outlet" or "Wholesale." Unlike Kaiser Estates, where there really are factories, Granville is mostly business. Don't believe the signs; don't fall for the sales pitch. You still might find something fun and worthwhile, but *be aware.* We guide you to and through this area with care. If you have only a few days in Hong Kong, we would even suggest skipping it altogether.

To find Granville Road, follow Nathan Road away from the waterfront and to the park. You will see the Park Lane Shopper's Boulevard on your left. Granville Road will be on your right.

GAT DESIGN LTD.: Previously called Geis and Tijan, GAT is located in the Taurus Build-

ing. Enter the building (next to McDonald's)
and walk up the stairs to find the elevator.
Take it to the small showroom on the 12th
floor. Most of the stock is factory overruns, so
you can never be sure what to expect. The
quality and styling are midrange casual, the
kind of thing you might expect to find in the
sportswear department of a large department
store. Prices for silk shirts are in the $50 range,
while matching pants are $40. This is a real
factory outlet—don't expect glamour. Hours
are Monday–Friday, 9:30 A.M. to 6 P.M. The
shop is closed from 1 to 2 P.M. for lunch.
There is another outlet in Central in the Cosmos Building, 8–11 Lan Kwai Fong Street.

GAT DESIGN LTD., Taurus Building, Room
21A-B Granville Road, Tsimshatsui, Kowloon

▼

A-WIN GARMENTS MANUFACTORY:
A-Win is what all outlets used to look like. It
is hard to find, and then once you have found
it, you are not sure why you bothered. If you
are not used to outlet shopping, and think that
camping is tough, skip this one. However, if
you are into adventure as we are, give it a try.
We have had great luck here and we have had
no luck here. Don't blame us.

Our airline friends first introduced us to
A-Win. To get there from the Taurus Building, or McDonald's, walk along Granville Road
until you see the Fung Lum Restaurant. There
is a minisign above it pointing to A-Win. Enter through the tiny and tacky notions store,
and go up the rickety steps to the 1st floor.
You will think that for sure we are crazy at
this point. However, once you get inside and
take a look around you may love us forever.
The merchandise here is mid- to lower-end
goods. Nothing is expensive. There are a lot of
jeans, casual pants, ski jackets, knit shirts,
sweatshirts, and sweatpants. Hours are Monday–

Saturday, 11 A.M. to 8:30 P.M., and Sunday, 11 A.M. to 7:30 P.M. (double-check this if going on Sunday; phone 3-697070). No credit cards accepted.

A-WIN GARMENTS MANUFACTORY, 23 Granville Road, Tsimshatsui, Kowloon.

Secondary Tsimshatsui outlets to check include:

BETU, 16 Observatory Road, Tsimshatsui, Kowloon

ÇA VA, Star House, 1726 Salisbury Road, Tsimshatsui, Kowloon

DORFIT, Ocean Centre (Shop 518), Canton Road, Tsimshatsui, Kowloon; and Tsimshatsui Centre (Room 106), 66 Mody Road, Tsimshatsui, Kowloon

LESLIE FAY, Wing On Plaza (Room 207), Tsimshatsui East, Kowloon; and Sun Plaza (Shop 11), 28 Canton Road, Tsimshatsui, Kowloon

ORIENTAL PACIFIC, Star House (6th floor), 3 Salisbury Road, Tsimshatsui, Kowloon

SHIRT STOP, Hyatt Hotel (basement), Nathan Road, Tsimshatsui, Kowloon; and 2A Prat Avenue, Tsimshatsui, Kowloon

SHOPPER'S WORLD SAFARI, Sands Building (Room 708), 17 Hankow Road, Tsimshatsui, Kowloon

TAKPAC, Oriental Centre (2nd floor), 67 Chatham Road, Tsimshatsui, Kowloon

WINTEX, Star House (5th floor), 3 Salisbury Road, Tsimshatsui, Kowloon

Hung Hom

Once you are out of Tsimshatsui, you have entered the world of true factory outlets. Hung Hom is the neighborhood closest to Tsimshatsui, and was the first to make factory-outlet shopping an event. Kaiser Estates Phase I, II, and III are the mainstays of Hung Hom, although there are three other buildings where outlets have popped up as well.

Getting to Hung Hom is best done in a taxi. We hate to give in to convenience, but if you have never been there before, it really is the smart way to go. The taxi ride costs $35 (H.K.). Ask to be let out in front of Kaiser Estate Phase I, as the majority of the shops are located either in Kaiser Estates or in the Winner Building across the street. If you are compelled to come by bus, routes 5C, 8, and 25 leave from the Kowloon Star Ferry Terminal. Get off at Ma Tau Wei Road, just after Station Lane. Walk to Man Yue Street for Kaiser Estates. To return, backtrack and catch the bus on the other side of Ma Tau Wei Road marked "'Star Ferry." Taxis come and go on a regular basis in front of Kaiser Estate Phase I.

We will tell you upfront that we are not fans of Kaiser Estates. We think it is a waste of valuable time. However, since every tour in the world comes here, and every tourist in the world has heard of it (like the Sphinx), we feel compelled to at least lead you in the right direction. If you are stuck on a tour, listen and look, then come back on your own. Most tours concentrate on the jewelry and fur factory showrooms because the tour director can make the most "commission" here. If you want to buy something, ask for the "commission" as a discount. It usually is 10%. Most of the outlets are geared for tourist business and now accept plastic. It is smart to bring more than one card, in case they don't take them all. If an outlet does not take credit cards we have noted it in their listing.

Before attacking Kaiser Estates, be prepared for dark hallways and dirty toilets. The shops that have opened for tourist business are nice enough; the rest of the estates are not. Don't go looking for your own bargains. Trust us, if they want your business you will know. New outlets, or factories getting rid of merchandise, post signs on the street, employ people to pass out flyers in front of their building, or advertise in the *South China Morning Post*. Otherwise, we find these outlets most worthwhile:

MORELLE: Across the street from Phase I is a strip of fancy shops. Morelle is in the Winner Building, but has a ground-floor entrance. The windows remind you of a Rodeo Drive boutique. They are plate glass and go on for miles. Inside, there are racks upon racks upon racks of dresses, blouses, washable silks, and the like. Most styles are nice, but none will make you jump up and down and be glad that you came. Prices for a silk shell average $40. You can put together an outfit for $100. There are lots of size 8 and 10. Look for the sale racks for bargain-basement goods. Hours are daily, 10 A.M. to 6 P.M.

MORELLE, 40A Man Yue Street (ground floor), Hung Hom, Kowloon

▼

ÇA VA: We don't want you to miss this branch of Ça Va, if you didn't visit it in Central. Ça Va is well known for silks. You can buy shirts, still in the plastic wrap, for under $50. The styles are not exciting, but we are happy wearing them under suits. Marisa Christina sweaters are also featured. If you come at the right time of year, there is a good selection. Sample sale times are January–February, June, and July–August. You will get your best buys then. Hours are Monday–Friday, 10:30 A.M. to 6 P.M., Saturday to 5 P.M.

ÇA VA, 34 Man Yue Street (ground floor), Hung Hom, Kowloon

▼

VICA MODA: Vica Moda actually has two locations in Hung Hom. One is across the street from Phase I, and the other is in Phase II. We shop both, but prefer the one on Man Yue Street for convenience. Vica Moda is known for its casual coordinates. We fell in love with a silk-and-cashmere sweater here that was $200 worth of scrumptious. There were also washable silk pants for $40, and silk shells for $20–$40. Hours are Monday–Saturday, 9:30 A.M. to 6:30 P.M.

VICA MODA
> Winner Building, 32 Man Yue Street, Hung Hom, Kowloon
> Kaiser Estate Phase II, 51 Man Yue Street, Hung Hom, Kowloon

▼

JOSEPH HO: If you've checked out Joseph Ho's line in any of the retail boutiques (see page 125) and like it, then this outlet is worth the trip. Enter the building and go to the 1st floor (remember that the 1st floor is the floor above the main floor, or the 2nd floor, to those from the United States), turn left, then left again. The shop is clearly marked. Inside you will find racks and tables full of damages, seconds, and last year's goods. Sizes are plentiful, especially in sweaters, and are marked with European, United Kingdom, and U.S. equivalent sizes. Be aware that the merchandise is often flawed. Look carefully for damages before you pay. The shop is open Monday–Saturday, 9:30 A.M.–5 P.M. Call to confirm, as store hours were in flux when we visited. Telephone 3-620401.

JOSEPH HO, Winner Building, (Flat 2C, 1st floor), 36 Man Yue Street, Hung Hom, Kowloon

▼

CAMBERLEY: No longer the huge showroom on Man Yue Street, Camberley has regrouped in a smaller, nicer space around the corner. There are still some designer labels, and very good clothing, but no more Anne Klein II. This is a very reputable house. The new showroom is in the Eldex Building, on Ma Tau Wai Road. Take a left on Ma Tau Wai after leaving the Winner Building shops, and look for the building name. It is in the first block. The elevator panel has no numbers; push the top right button for the 12th floor. Enter the main offices and the shop is to the left. We prefer the outlet in Star House, but if you are in Hung Hom anyway, it is worth a visit. Hours are Monday–Friday, 9:30 A.M.–5: P.M.

CAMBERLEY, Eldex Industrial Building (12th floor), 21 Ma Tau Wai Road, Hung Hom, Kowloon

▼

FOUR SEASONS GARMENTS: We would say "Don't waste your time," but you won't listen, so go and look. Four Seasons was one of the first factory outlets to open its doors to the public. There is a factory. However, success has gone to their heads and now the outlet is run purely for profit from the tourist. We do like the items made just for gifts, such as the Chinese silk happy coats for $50, or the packaged and labeled silk shells for $8. Regular silk blouses are now $50 and up. That's the price of glory. The shop is located in Phase II, at the top of the escalators to the left. Hours are Monday–Saturday, 10 A.M.–6 P.M.

FOUR SEASONS GARMENTS, Kaiser Estate Phase II (1st floor, Room G1), 51 Man Yue Street, Hung Hom, Kowloon

▼

LIM YING YING: Lim Ying Ying used to have an outlet in Central, but now this is it. We have followed this line from small crowded shop to small crowded shop. All of our favorite lingerie designers are hanging on the racks. Granted there's not a big selection of all designs in every size, as you would find in Neiman Marcus. But if you luck out, you really luck out. We found a big-name designer robe for under $50 on our last visit. It would have retailed for triple that at Neiman's. There are a lot of Joseph Ho look-alikes and midrange cotton sweaters as well. The air conditioning is great, and there is even a couch to sit down on. We had to force ourselves to leave. Don't forget to check the silk lingerie for damages. Remember, that's how it got to be so cheap! The Hang Fung Industrial Building is across the street from Kaiser Estate Phase III. Enter on Hok Yuen Street, which intersects Man Yue Street after it turns the corner. Lim Ying Ying is on the 1st floor. Hours are Monday–Saturday, 9:30 A.M.–5 P.M.

LIM YING YING, Hang Fung Industrial Building (1st floor), 2G Hok Yuen Street, Hung Hom, Kowloon

▼

FASHIONS OF SEVENTH AVENUE: If you like a certain well-known U.S. designer whose claim to fame is the bodysuit-knit look, you should check out Fashions of Seventh Avenue. We think the similar designs you'll see at home are of much higher quality. However, this is a hot source for locals. The racks are cleaned out as quickly as the merchandise comes in. Fashions of Seventh Avenue is located in the most out-of-the-way part of Kaiser Estates, in Phase III. You must brave the hallways and the elevators to get there, so be aware. As you exit the elevator on the 9th floor, look for an office marked "M." The outlet is inside. The boutique is simple and spare. There are lots of good-quality silk body-suits and knits hanging along the perimeter. Sizes are strange and prices are high. There are no labels. There is also an outlet in Central (8 Queen's Road). There was no crossover in merchandise between these two stores when we visited. Hours are Monday–Saturday, 9 A.M.–6 P.M.

FASHIONS OF SEVENTH AVENUE, Kaiser Estate Phase III (9th floor, Unit M), Hok Yuen Street, Hung Hom

▼

LILY CHAO: The clothing in this outlet is about as upscale as you will find anywhere in Hong Kong. Some of it we loved; some of it was just too much. Stop in at the retail boutique in the Landmark to check out the styles before coming. The designs are dramatic in a glitzy way. The outlet is bigger than most stores, and well supplied with beaded and sequined sweaters, dresses, and separates. The prices in the outlet are not cheap, but they are cheaper than those in the Landmark by a hair. It's unlikely you will find anything for under $50. Hours are Monday–Friday, 10 A.M.–6 P.M., and Saturday till 1 P.M. It's located in the Focal Industrial Centre, across the street from Phase III. The building is white and clearly marked. Be sure to find the entrance for Block A. Some of the elevators only go down. Look around the corner for the ones that go up and down.

LILY CHAO, Focal Industrial Centre (9th floor, Room 06–07), 21 Man Lok Street, Hung Hom, Kowloon

▼

KOLZANO LIMITED: Now, *this* is what we call a factory outlet. As a matter of fact, we think it really is a selling office that has decided to offer samples to those of us who are crazy enough to stop by. We did, and found fabulous sweaters. High-style cashmeres are the specialty here. Prices are high ($250 for a cardigan), but the styles are so much better than anything we saw elsewhere we still thought it was a good price. There are basic pullovers as well, for far less money ($125). The outlet is in the office, so don't look for showroom windows. Remember lunch-hour closings. Hours are Monday–Friday, 9 A.M.–6 P.M. (closed for lunch 1–2 P.M.), and Saturday, 9 A.M.–noon.

KOLZANO LIMITED, Focal Industrial Centre (12th floor, Room 1213), 21 Man Lok Street, Hung Hom, Kowloon

Lai Chi Kok

Now we are talking factory town. Lai Chi Kok is midway on a factory tour between Kowloon and Kwun Tong. It is safe, the MTR access is great, and all of these outlets are within walking distance. You are in a real factory town, even though it's one of the nicest, so expect to get lost and become frustrated, confused, and anxious as you search for that elusive bargain. But trust us, the bargains are out there waiting. Get out your courage and forge ahead.

Getting to Lai Chi Kok is the easy part. From Central or Tsimshatsui station, get on the train marked "Tsuen Wan." Stay toward the front of the train to be near the right exit, which is at Lai Chi Kok station. Follow the signs for Leighton Textile Building and Tung Chau West Street. When you reach the street, walk ahead and cross Tung Chau West to locate Splendid. *Note:* When crossing back and forth on Cheung Sha Wan Road and Tung Chau Road, don't be too brave, or foolish. The traffic is terrible. Use the lights to cross.

SPLENDID: Once you find the 916 address, walk back to the garage and then to the rear, where you will find the elevators, marked "lifts." Splendid is located on the 7th floor, behind gray doors, in a large showroom attached to the factory. It looks too modern and clean to have good bargains, but don't let the nice appearance stop you. Splendid manufactures upscale leather clothing for European stores. Many lines are made specifically for Germany and Italy. The styling is top-of-the-line. Men's jackets come in every size and many styles. We especially like the bomber jackets, which sell for $200–$300. A comparable jacket in New York would be $750. Women's leather suits are a tad more expensive at $375–$500; but again, a suit of comparable quality would cost double in the United States. Stock up on leather pants in various colors ($150). The factory is to the right as you walk in, if you care to watch the work in progress. Hours are Monday–Saturday, 9:30 A.M.–5 P.M.

SPLENDID, Sun Ping Industrial Building (7th floor, Unit A), 916–922 Cheung Sha Wan Road, Lai Chi Kok, Kowloon

▼

LEIGHTON STOCK SALES: Just down the street from Splendid you will see a big sign and an arrow pointing to the Stock Sales outlet. This is an especially fine resource for men. The whole back of the large showroom space is devoted to suits, pants, sweaters, and blazers. Styles are not way-out or European chic, but we saw some definite winners. A pair of nice wool pants was selling for $20. A great wool car coat was $50. There are even less expensive selections piled in the bins. Some pants were as low as $10. Leighton also sells women's and children's clothing, but we didn't get too excited about either. Hours are Monday–Saturday, 9 A.M.–5 P.M.

LEIGHTON STOCK SALES, 868 Cheung Sha Wan Road, Lai Chi Kok, Kowloon

▼

AH CHOW PORCELAIN: Backtrack on Cheung Sha Wan Road until you see the alley between buildings 489 and 491. The entrance to Ah Chow is down this alley, which is really a driveway, in the building to your left. Be sure that you are in Block B before going to the 7th floor. Room numbers B1 & B2 will lead you to porcelain heaven. The showroom is crammed with huge jardinieres, waiting to go to a mansion or hotel, and lamps and vases of every size imaginable. Directly ahead from the entry is a room full of sample dishes. If you were a buyer for one of the major department stores, you would go in here and pick one from column A and one from column B. Many of the pieces on the floor have "Sold" signs (in Chinese, of course) on them. We asked; that's how we knew. If you look at the fine Chinese-style ashtrays, lamps, and ceramic goods in American department stores, you will recognize Ah Chow's merchandise. While they will make any pattern you want, or copy anything you want, it is easier to just pick from the overrun stock sitting around the shop. We shipped a set of ginger jars, and they arrived in perfect condition—wrapped better than a mummy. The shipping cost more than the jars, but who wants to handcarry china for fifteen hours on a plane? If you buy a lamp, be sure to discuss the electrical current and type of plug you need. It may take a long time for your order to arrive, so be patient. We find this store to be quite honest in their business dealings.

The place is a little bit dusty, but this only adds to the charm. Breakables are piled high—

don't bring the children! No credit cards are accepted, but traveler's checks are OK. Hours are Monday–Saturday, 10 A.M.–7 P.M.

AH CHOW PORCELAIN, Hong Kong Industrial Centre, 489–491 Castle Peak Road, Block B (7th floor, Room B1-2), Lai Chi Kok, Kowloon

▼

SANG WOO: Cross Cheung Sha Wan Road to get to Sang Woo. The building is located opposite the Leighton Textile Building, at number 883. Take the elevators to the 6th floor and turn right for Room 604. This is another great leather source with big (and we mean BIG) name designers represented ... especially American. The outlet is air-conditioned (important in summer), and neatly arranged so you don't have to rummage. The biggest selections are in leather jackets for men. A bomber jacket sells for about $300. Soft leather pants were $200, and a chamois sweatshirt $100. This is upscale styling and prices. Try your luck and hope that a shipment has just arrived. Hours are Monday–Saturday, 9:30 A.M.–5:30 P.M.

SANG WOO, Elite Building (Room 604), 883 Cheung Sha Wan Road, Lai Chi Kok, Kowloon

▼

LA TESSILE/LE BARON: This factory outlet is known by both names. To find the Yeung Yiu Chung Industrial Building, walk away from the main street, Cheung Sha Wan, on Cheung Lai Street. At the corner, one block away, turn right. No. 19 will be toward the beginning of the block. Enter through the garage and look on the wall for a sign that says "Yeung Yiu Chung (No. 6) Industrial Building." Take the elevators in the rear to the 7th floor to find the La Tessile factory. This is an honest factory. You will think for sure that we have sent you to the wrong place. However, point to the book and look lost. Someone in the office will come to rescue you. The factory shop is in the middle of the factory. You will be surrounded by knitting machines and boxes of finished cashmere sweaters. La Tessile manufactures the basic, warm variety of cashmere. A crewneck style costs under $100, with the most expensive one running $200. No credit cards or traveler's checks. Bring cash. Hours are Monday–Friday, 9 A.M.–5:30 P.M.; Saturday till noon.

LA TESSILE/LE BARON, Yeung Yiu Chung (No. 6) Industrial Building (7th floor, Flat B), 19 Cheung Shun Street, Lai Chi Kok, Kowloon

▼

TEAM-LEE FASHION KNITTERS: Located in the same building but on the 9th floor, Team-Lee is a factory shop within the offices. You enter a very nice reception area, and the outlet is to the right, through glass doors. The knitwear here will make you wish you had a bigger suitcase. There are boxes and boxes of sweaters in colors and styles that are chic. You can find wool and cotton designs that are geometric or appliquéd. The styles change according to the season. We are sure these are private-label goods for great stores. Prices are fair, with the most expensive design costing under $300. No credit cards are accepted; cash only. Hours are Monday–Saturday, 9 A.M.–5:30 P.M. Everything closes for lunch from 12:30 P.M.–2 P.M.

TEAM-LEE FASHION KNITTERS, Yeung Yiu Chung (No. 6) Industrial Building (9th floor), 19 Cheung Shun Street, Lai Chi Kok, Kowloon

▼

BROADWAY SPORTSWEAR: Broadway Sportswear is located on the other side of Cheung Sha Wan Road. To get there, cross over to the MTR station and take a left to Tung Chau West Street. Take a right here and walk two blocks to Wing Hong Street, where you take another left to reach No. 7. Easier still, simply take a taxi. The building has a huge sign on top that says "Broadway," so once you are close you can't miss it. You will be more than pleased that you came. Broadway Sportswear is the single best source for designer raincoats in Hong Kong and Kowloon. The labels read like a *Who's Who* of European and American design.

The inside of Broadway is massive and confusing. Don't make this your last stop when you are already tired, or you will turn around and walk out. To the left of the entrance are racks of coats and jackets. Some of them are regular sports coats (for a major U.S. label); some are sports jackets and skiwear. A men's khaki sports coat in cotton was selling for $20 and a wool tweed blazer was $50. The tweedy country look is very prominent since the fashions are those of one particular designer label. Along the side and back walls are the raincoats, heavier coats, and still more jackets. A major-designer–label raincoat, which we saw in Bloomingdale's the season before, was ⅓ the price here. It was a sample size. A wool-and-fur designer overcoat was $500. We happen to know this designer's coats never sell for under $1,000. There are coats with major department store labels and coats with major designer labels. We love this outlet. Hours are Monday–Saturday, 9:30 A.M.–5:30 P.M. Closed for lunch 1 P.M.–2 P.M.

BROADWAY SPORTSWEAR, 7 Wing Hong Street (ground floor), Lai Chi Kok, Kowloon

Kwun Tong

If you liked Lai Chi Kok, wait till you see Kwun Tong. Lai Chi Kok is glamorous by comparison. However, the farther you go from the big city, the better the bargains get. There aren't many in Kwun Tong, but those that are here are quite spectacular. Getting to Kwun Tong is only slightly more complicated than getting to Lai Chi Kok. It is about an hour's ride on the MTR from Tsimshatsui or from Admiralty station in Central. Get on the train for Tsuen Wan and change at Mong Kok station for the Kwun Tong line. When you leave the train, follow directions for the outlet you have chosen. There is a map in the main station that will make things clearer if you feel lost. Many of the signs are in Chinese, but don't let that deter you.

With the opening of the Cross-Harbour Tunnel Kwun Tong is now linked to Quarry Bay. If you are coming from Central, consider this route as an option.

LEATHER CONCEPTS: When Leather Concepts opened its shop in the Pedder Building we were concerned about the factory outlet. We thought that perhaps they had decided to go the way of so many factories and turn "retail" while still trying to pretend that they were wholesale or discount. Not so. The shop in the Pedder Building is very nice, very clean, and very retail. If you want bargains, however, the outlet is the place to go.

To get to Leather Concepts from the MTR, take the Hoi Yuen Road exit and go down the stairs to the left as you face the exit. Once on Hoi Yuen walk straight ahead until you come to Hing Yip Street (look for the Security Pacific Asian Bank Ltd. on the corner) and then take a left. Almost at the end of the block you will see the building number "20" above a garage door on the right side of the street. Enter the garage and look for the elevators on the left. Do not go up the stairs to the second bank of elevators. The ones through the brown door have an elevator operator and are nicer. Once you reach the 11th floor, walk straight ahead into the shop and the factory outlet will be to your left.

You will be pleasantly surprised at the selection and prices at Leather Concepts. Hannah Ping is the designer who creates styles for many major European and American designers. Some clothing has labels, but most does not. We saw plastic sheets on outfits being shipped out that had designer names all over them. Since Leather Concepts is a jobber, designer goods change on a seasonal basis. The prices have gone up, but a good pair of leather pants will still cost under $150. We saw a beautiful quilted leather coat for $300, and a stamped leather jacket for $700. The expensive jacket was still a good buy if you would have considered buying it retail for $1,200. Leather Concepts now takes MasterCard and Visa. We don't know if that is the good or the bad news. Hours are Monday–Saturday, 9 A.M.–5 P.M. (closed 12:30 P.M.–1:30 P.M. for lunch).

LEATHER CONCEPTS, Union Hing Yip Factory Building (11th floor), 20 Hing Yip Street, Kwun Tong, Kowloon

▼

TRINITY TEXTILES: Trinity Textiles is around the corner from Leather Concepts, so if you are looking for menswear you should stop here next. Go back to Hoi Yuen Road and turn toward the MTR station. Turn right at the next street you come to, which is Shing Yip Street. Trinity Textiles is on the right on either side of a driveway. The two showrooms carry two very different types of merchandise, so be sure to look in both. The casualwear shop may not be open every day, although they tell us they are. One of our readers went and they were closed.

The line, both business and casual, is well-styled in a European way. The production quality is excellent, as are the prices. We found summer cotton jackets for $75 that would have been $150 in the United States. A good-quality casual T-shirt was selling for $20. Across the driveway, the showroom specializing in suits and formalwear had suits for $100 and up. The quality is similar to that of a good department store. In the summer they have linen/polyester blends; in the winter, wool. The showrooms are on the ground level, air-conditioned and very pleasant. Hours are Monday–Saturday, 9:30 A.M.–5:30 P.M. (closed for lunch).

TRINITY TEXTILES, 10 Shing Yip Street, Kwun Tong, Kowloon

▼

DIANE FREIS: All right, ladies, this is what you bought the book for, right? Let's be honest. Diane Freis dresses travel better than anything you have ever worn. You never look wrinkled or tired in them because they have a life of their own. Do you mind last season's model? If not, run to the Diane Freis outlet.

Getting here is easiest if done via the MTR stop. Pretend you have just gotten off the train again. The exit is marked "Tsun Yip Lane" and "Sime Darby Industrial Centre." (Look in the main part of the station to find a locator map.) Go down the stairs by the exit and turn left. You should be on the right side of Kwun Tong Road. Walk in the direction of McDonald's (across the street) until you find the Chung Nam Centre at 414 Kwun Tong Road. Take the elevator to the 7th floor and enter the Diane Freis offices. Be prepared to be over-

whelmed with a sea of colors. The outer office
has been turned into a factory outlet. Dresses
line both sides of a very long, narrow room.
There are long and short styles, dressy and day
styles. Some have sequins, some are knits. Prices
are 20% to 30% below retail. The average
range of prices in the outlet is $100–$300.
Much of the merchandise is returned goods
from shops in the United States that have no
sales. With a Diane Freis dress, last season is
just as wonderful as this season. Hours are
Monday–Friday, 9:30 A.M.–5 P.M. (closed for
lunch 1 P.M.–2 P.M.), Saturday, 9:30 A.M.–12:30
P.M.

DIANE FREIS, Chung Nam Centre (7th floor),
414 Kwun Tong Road, Kwun Tong, Kowloon

Made-to-Measure

Any gentleman who comes to Hong Kong
and doesn't indulge in at least one be-
spoke shirt or suit has missed one of the
island's pleasures. It is the British way,
and the Hong Kong way. It can be an inexpensive or an expensive way, depending upon
your desire and pocket cash.

There are more tailors in Hong Kong than
anywhere else in the world. Many of the better
tailors learn their trade as they are growing up.
It is a family tradition. Others just see a good
thing for what it is and jump in. The important thing for you to do is to distinguish between
these two types of tailors. Cheap prices usually
mean inferior work. But there are exceptions:
One of the favored tailors in Hong Kong has
so many "under tailors" working for him that
he can afford to turn out his garments for a
very good price. Smaller tailor shops, where

time and energy are spent producing a garment, are more expensive.

Our best advice comes from a friend who lives in Hong Kong. He feels that although many tailors have the ability to construct a good suit, there are only a handful who understand Western tailoring and the Caucasian male or female body. The well-known tailors are well known for a reason: A bargain is not a bargain if it doesn't fit.

The tailors we have listed are well versed in the styles popular in Europe. However, it is always best to bring a photograph of the suit you want copied, to attach to your work order. This is particularly true of women's garments, where the diversity of detailing is enormous. The tailors will do exactly what you ask them to do, so it is important to be specific about the minutest details. If the photo you show him does not have pleated pants but you want them, put it in writing.

After you leave, the tailor will remember only the work order and what is written down. Make sure you have a copy of the invoice with all the details, and a fabric sample, before you leave Hong Kong. If you receive an order with no pleated pants after you had requested them in writing, you have some recourse. If you have no confirmation of the request, well . . . we hope you're satisfied in the first place.

We've comparison-shopped the tailors extensively and have had several suits fitted on our husbands and friends' husbands, and we offer these tips:

▼ Start your search for a tailor the minute you arrive. Leave yourself time for three fittings while in Hong Kong. The first will be for measurements and choice of fabrics; the second fitting will be a loose fabric or muslin fitting; the third will be to detail the finished garment. Shirts sometimes take only two fittings, and then you receive the finished goods after arriving home. When ordering a suit, keep in mind your life-style at home and when you plan to wear it.

▼ Most tailors carry a full line of imported fabrics from Italy, England, and France. Ask whether the thread they use is imported also. If it is not, ask to see the quality, and test it for durability. Remember all those horror stories you have heard about suits falling apart? It wasn't the fabric; it was the thread.

▼ Check the quality of the lining. The better tailors have beautiful choices in lining fabrics, some imported and some not, but all in good taste. Be sure to specify a fully lined jacket.

▼ Check the inner-lining material to make sure it is stiff enough to hold the shape of the suit.

▼ Check the quality of the shoulder pads and the buttons. A tailor could save a lot of money by using inferior goods.

▼ Well-made suits from a Hong Kong tailor are no longer as inexpensive as they used to be. Imported fabrics run about $10–$40 per yard, and an average-sized suit will take 3½ yards. The silk/wool blends and cashmeres cost more. The finished price for a suit will run in the area of $200–$800. You could do better in some cases with an off-the-rack suit in the United States, but the quality would not be the same. Ask for tailoring prices with and without the material. In some cases you might wish to supply your own. At the very least, you will know what the tailor is charging for labor versus cost.

▼ The shop will want a 50% deposit to start the work. If less is demanded, the suit will probably be turned out by a manufacturing house. Finished shirts will run $25–$75 depending upon your choice of material and style. French cuffs cost more than plain ones. White collars cost an extra $9–$12.

▼ If you are having the tailor ship the suits to you, remember to figure in the Customs charges and shipping. On average, it costs $20 per suit to air-freight them to you. Shirts can be shipped for $30 per dozen. Once you have established an account with a tailor or a shirtmaker and he has your measurements on file, you can simply get the fabric swatches sent to you for the new season and do your shopping through the mail—or in a local hotel.

▼ Check to see if the tailor you have chosen makes trips to the United States to visit customers. Chances are, if you live in a major city (New York, Washington, Los Angeles, or Chicago), he will. Most of the tailors we recommend either come in person once a year or send a representative with fabric books and order forms. At that time, new measurements can be taken in case you have lost or gained weight. However, we recommend only making minor changes. Any major change should be done in Hong Kong, where a new muslin can be cut.

▼ The tailors we recommend have been tried and tested by one of us, our husbands, relatives, or friends. There are many other tailors in Hong Kong. There is at least one in every hotel shopping arcade. There are even tailors who set up booths at the various night markets. Unless you have a personal recommendation, we say "Beware." Your suit might be cheap, but will it be good?

ART'S: Art's was the personal recommendation of a friend of ours who has lived in Hong Kong for many years. It is on the mezzanine floor of Swire House. There are two tailors on the premises to fit you, although the tailoring is done elsewhere. The atmosphere is not especially low-key, but the sales staff is informative and friendly. Only two fittings are required, unless you have time for three, which is always better. It will take ten days from the time you place your order to get a finished product. Suits run about $500, depending upon the material.

ART'S, Swire House (Shop 112), Chater Road, Central, Hong Kong

▼

H. BAROMAN LTD.: Tycoon alert: This is a No. 8 warning. If you wonder where the real financial heavyweights have their clothing made, wonder no more. H. Baroman has been in the business for forty years, serving the elite. His reputation is so above the rest of the world that we are surprised his shop hasn't been moved to Savile Row. When you go to choose suit fabric from H. Baroman, you receive a little booklet containing a photo of the shop, a brief description of the H. Baroman philosophy, a page where you can paste your sample cutting, a memo page for notes, a dollar conversion chart, and a very nice map to help you find your way back.

A made-to-order suit takes at least seven days. The average suit price is over $750. Shirts average $100. H. Baroman does not send representatives to the United States.

H. BAROMAN LTD., Swire House, Chater Road, Central, Hong Kong

▼

W. W. CHAN & SONS TAILOR LTD.: W. W. Chan is one of our favorite tailors in Hong Kong. We find ourselves returning time and again to their shop on the 2nd floor of the Burlington Arcade building on Nathan Road. After you enter the building there are stairs to the left or an elevator around the corner.

W. W. Chan has a spacious fitting and sample room with a great view of the Park Lane Shopper's Boulevard. This is the perfect spot for the businessman who prefers quiet and privacy while ordering his suits. Most of the British and American businessmen we know shop here. W. W. Chan offers incredible tailoring and personal attention to detailing. Mr. Chan has been in the business for over forty years. His son, Peter, who now runs the shop, has been tailoring for twenty years. This is one of the old-fashioned family businesses that we admire. The tailoring is not farmed out but done on the premises. Henry is Peter Chan's associate and right-hand man. If Peter misses a detail, Henry picks it up.

The shop has an extensive selection of materials from Italy and England; they need three fittings to complete a suit but can do it with two if there is little time. Producing the suit takes a little longer due to Peter's attention to detail. We suggest having it shipped, and not rushing the process. Peter travels to the United States once a year to show his clients new fabric swatches and to take orders. Suits begin at $450, shirts at $65.

W. W. Chan recently opened a ladies' department next door that is equally pleasant. One of us had a cashmere coat tailored on our last visit and was thrilled with the outcome. We gave them a jacket that had the right "look," and they translated it into a full-length style with no problem.

W. W. CHAN & SONS TAILOR LTD., Burlington Arcade (Shop 2F), 92–94 Nathan Road, Tsimshatsui, Kowloon

▼

ASCOT CHANG CO. LTD.: This well-known shirtmaker has three branches in Hong Kong and Kowloon. Our favorite is in the Peninsula Hotel. Like all the other bespoke-shirt shops, this one is tiny but filled with wonderful fabrics imported from Switzerland and France. Prices are competitive with David's, and they offer mail-order once your measurements have been taken. Shirts run between $40 and $125 depending upon the fabric and style.

ASCOT CHANG CO. LTD.

The Peninsula Hotel (MW6), Salisbury Road, Tsimshatsui, Kowloon

Regent Hotel (R107), Salisbury Road, Tsimshatsui, Kowloon

Prince's Building, Chater Road, Central, Hong Kong

▼

JIMMY CHEN & CO. LTD.: Jimmy Chen is another Hong Kong favorite for many travelers. Jimmy Chen is a good resource in Tsimshatsui. He is one of the few good tailors who will cut men's summer suits in cotton. He has a shop in the Peninsula Hotel, where he holds court and helps anxious buyers decide what wonderful fabric to pick for a suit. A lightweight suit will average $350–$400. Three fittings are requested. There are nine Jimmy Chen shops in all.

JIMMY CHEN & CO. LTD., The Peninsula Hotel (MW4), Salisbury Road, Tsimshatsui, Kowloon

▼

A-MAN HING CHEONG CO. LTD.: Fondly referred to as "Ah-men," this tailor shop in the Mandarin Oriental Hotel turns out quite a few garments for the rich-tourist-and-businessman trade, and therefore has become very adept at relating to the European-cut suit. They don't even blink twice when you ask for an extra pair of trousers. They just smile and ask for an extra $120. The prices here are on the higher side, with a jacket and one pair of pants costing $500 and requiring over a week to make. However, the quality is excellent, and that is what you are paying for. Anyone can buy off the rack. This is a Savile Row–quality suit.

A-Man will also do custom shirts for approximately $50. If you wish to cable them, their cable name is "Luckylucky." You will feel lucky lucky when you get home and enjoy your new bespoke clothing.

A-MAN HING CHEONG CO. LTD., Mandarin Oriental Hotel (M4), Connaught Road Central, Central, Hong Kong

▼

DAVID'S SHIRTS: David's is one of the most popular and famous custom-shirt shops in Hong Kong. They are so popular, in fact, that they have opened a branch in New York City. The main shop in Hong Kong is in Kowloon near the hot young designers on Kimberley Road. We don't think it is the most convenient, however, and usually shop in the Mandarin Oriental Hotel branch. The shop is tiny and crowded with fabrics standing side by side, like soldiers in a British regiment. The fabric colors are muted, and may at first glance seem rather ordinary. However, as each bolt is brought out and unraveled, the quality of the fabrics and subtleties of design become apparent. If you didn't know better you would swear you were in London.

To order custom shirts, two fittings are necessary—one for the measurements and then one with the garment. David's will copy any favorite shirt you may have. Just bring it with you and plan to leave it. They also have a framed illustration of collar and cuff styles that you can choose from. Mail-order is not only possible but common with repeat customers. If you cannot get to Hong Kong, ask for a current swatch and price list. Return a shirt that fits you perfectly and a check, along with fabric and collar/cuff choices. Approximately four to six weeks later a box of new shirts will arrive. If you want to contact their New York store call (212) 757-1083.

DAVID'S SHIRTS

> Mandarin Oriental Hotel (M-7), Connaught Road Central, Central, Hong Kong
>
> Wing Lee Building (ground floor), 33 Kimberley Road, Tsimshatsui, Kowloon (main store)

▼

ROBERT TAILOR: While Robert Tailor makes men's sport jackets and suits, we have also used him for women's clothes, and find him to be excellent. Gentlemen's suits take under a week to do and require three fittings; prepare to be there every day. Suit prices start at $350. Shirts cost $45 and up.

> ROBERT TAILOR, Mandarin Oriental Hotel (M-12), Connaught Road Central, Central, Hong Kong

▼

SAM'S TAILOR: Sam is the most famous tailor in Hong Kong, and he has no qualms about letting you know that. Sam is, in fact, three people, a father and two sons, all Sam. We have met all three on various visits, and they are all quite charming. Sam's is well known for good prices (suits average $200–$300) and service. They have a large staff cutting and sewing in their workroom. A suit can usually be finished in three days. If the showroom in the Burlington Arcade is not overflowing with customers, you can chat about fabrics, styles, and prices with one of the owners. Most people who come in order a suit or shirts or both. Don't forget to look at the photographs of Sam's famous clientele; they boast of princes and dignitaries from all over the world. Sam's is fun. If you are coming to Hong Kong on a cruise ship, you will probably meet Sam. He or a group of his staff fly to the port of origin, take orders, do fittings, and then return to make the garments. By the time the ship arrives in Hong Kong, everyone has a suit or two—or three—waiting for them. Pretty good business.

SAM'S TAILOR, Burlington Arcade (Shop K), 92–94 Nathan Road, Tsimshatsui, Kowloon

▼

YING TAI LTD.: Coming to Ying Tai is like coming to a party where you are the guest of honor. The shop in the Hilton Hotel is enormous, has big showroom windows opening onto the 1st-floor arcade, and is full of tailors and sales staff so that you don't ever have to wait. Like the shop, the selection of fabrics for suits and shirts is enormous. The work done is excellent, and the staff is used to working with the Western figure. There is another shop in the Peninsula Hotel. Suit prices start at $300.

YING TAI LTD., Hong Kong Hilton Hotel, 2 Queens's Road Central, Central, Hong Kong

Shoes and Leathergoods

I f you are a shoe fanatic, read carefully, because there's no business like shoe business in Hong Kong.

First things first: In Hong Kong, shoes are usually sized in the European manner. There are few, if any, women's shoes above a size 40 (U.S. size 9½). American and European women with large feet spend a lot of their time in Hong Kong complaining about the difficulties in finding shoes. If you wear a large size, and are in an emergency situation, the good news is that the Marks & Spencer department stores carry large-size shoes (up to size 10 or 10½). These are private-label, not designer, styles but they are good, "sensible" English shoes, and are reasonably priced at around $35 a pair. You can also have shoes made, of course, but it does take a few days.

We remain disappointed in the shoes available on Leighton Road in Happy Valley. Locals keep recommending this area, but to us these shoes, with their "Made in Italy" labels, are one more of Hong Kong's scams. The shoes are manufactured in Hong Kong and then printed with Italian labels. Expect that they will not last that long. However, at these prices you might not care how long they last. For the most part, these are inexpensive shoes that are copies of fashion styles. They sell for about $40–$60 a pair. We vote a "pass" on Leighton Road.

There are many European shoe boutiques in Hong Kong, and many of them have quality goods at prices about 20% less than in the United States. Charles Jourdan has an extensive stock at savings against U.S. prices. Gucci we find more expensive; Bally is about similar. Finely crafted leathergoods are equally available at the designer boutiques. They just aren't at bargain prices.

You may find shoes and handbags in Stanley Market; many more handbags are sold in the Lanes. Running shoes happen to be an excellent Hong Kong value, and major name brands are available at Stanley Market, among other places.

As for leather clothing, if you were a true devotee, you would not be reading this book; you would be out shopping at Leather Concepts (see page 180). There is a large market in leathergoods in Hong Kong, but a good percentage of it is poorly made. This is a matter of taste and opinion.

We investigated having shoes made and came

up with both satisfied and not-so-satisfied customers. However, in our opinion this is more what you came to Hong Kong to find. Custom-shoe shops usually look like holes in the wall, junked up with dusty shoes. Even the fanciest ones in the fanciest hotels don't look like John Lobb in London. If you really want shoes made, ignore the surroundings and walk in. The shoes you see displayed are samples of what can be made. Some people come to Hong Kong with shoes and ask to have them copied. Others decide once they are there, and have no idea what they want. All of the custom shops have similar policies:

▼ Once you have decided on a style, a canvas will be made of your foot. This will then be turned into a mold from which the shoe will be made. If the shoemaker you have chosen simply takes measurements, leave. This is not what you are paying for. You won't be happy with the results.

▼ Unless you specifically ask to pick out your skins the shoemaker will do it for you. We suggest you pick your own and mark the backs so that no one else will use them. In the case of leather, ask to see the hides and examine the quality. Be able to verify that your skins were indeed used.

▼ Many kinds of leather or skin are used in making exotic shoes and boots. The following cannot legally be shipped into the United States: kangaroo, elephant, shark, antelope, gnu, sea lion, lizard, sea turtle, or alligator.

▼ The shoemaker usually has a base price list from which he works. A basic pair of men's cordovans cost $87, say. Then you add the extras. This is especially true of boots, where you might decide to have fur lining ($20), zipper sides ($5), or double leather soles ($4). If a man's foot is bigger than 12½, a special quote will be made.

▼ If you are having shoes shipped to you, allow for shipping charges. Surface mail postage for shoes or a handbag should cost $15. Airmail for the same will be $20–$30.

▼ The shoemaker will want a deposit (at least one third, possibly one half) or full payment before he starts to make the shoes. This is negotiable depending upon the store.

▼ If at all possible, pick up your shoes yourself. If they are uncomfortable, it is easier to remedy the problem while you are there.

▼ Prices vary from $20 to $100 from shop to shop. Some sample prices that we were quoted are: men's calfskin laceups, $75–$175; ostrich-skin shoes for ladies or men, $250–$350; calf-skin ladies' boots, basic style, $100–$200. Golf shoes cost the basic shoe cost plus extra for cleats and flaps. Alligator handbags run anywhere from $350 to $1,200 depending upon size and skin quality.

If you have the time, shop a few stores before settling on one. Each shop we tried was different. The ones we felt comfortable with and had either friends or relatives recommend were **LEE KEE BOOT AND SHOE MAKER LTD.,** 19–21B Hanyee Building, Hankow Road, Tsim-shatsui, Kowloon; **LILY SHOES,** Peninsula Hotel (M13), Salisbury Road, Tsimshatsui, Kowloon; **LOTUS CO.,** Hotel Miramar (AR325, 2nd floor), Nathan Road, Tsimshatsui, Kowloon; **MAYER SHOE CO.,** Mandarin Hotel Arcade (M23), Connaught Road, Central, Hong Kong; **SHOE-MAN LAU,** Hyatt Regency Hotel Arcade, Nathan Road, Tsimshatsui, Kowloon; and **VIP SHOES AND GIFTS,** Regent Hotel Arcade, Salisbury Road, Tsimshatsui, Kowloon.

If you are looking only for handbags, try the above-mentioned sources as well. If you are looking for great-looking evening bags, or for dressy day bags that look like a famous designer's bags, try **ASHNELL,** Far East Mansion (Shop

114, 1st floor) 5–6 Middle Road, Tsimshatsui, Kowloon. The Far East Mansion is a tacky old building located opposite the Sheraton Hotel, and it is hard to find your way to the 1st floor.

Furs

When you begin saving money for your Hong Kong trip, remember to put a little (well, a lot actually) away for a new fur coat. You will be saving by spending, if you know what we mean. The cost of labor in Hong Kong is far less than in the United States, and this is where the savings comes in; pelts cost the same on the world market. This can be good and bad news. Yes, you want to save money, but no, you don't want to cut costs and have the coat fall apart. Pick a reputable store, preferably a member of the HKTA, and enjoy.

If you are having a coat specially made for you, the process will take longer. We discuss this in Chapter 5 (see page 87). For the best design and workmanship try **SIBERIAN FUR STORE.** Their big showroom is at the corner of Chatham and Mody roads, No. 21 Chatham Road. Here you will be assured of getting the finest quality in every way. If you are really gung ho, you can stop at their factory in Kwun Tong. It is located at 6 Shing Yip Street. Make arrangements ahead of time, as this is a real factory neighborhood and you don't want to make the trek and be disappointed that they are closed, or out to lunch, or that the one person who speaks English is on vacation.

Two major mass-market furriers operate out of Hong Kong as well. **JINDO FUR SALONS** has shops in the Kowloon Hotel, Middle Road, Tsimshatsui, Kowloon, and at the Prince Hotel Shopping Arcade (3rd floor), Canton Road,

Tsimshatsui, Kowloon. You will be bowled over by the selection the first time you walk into their shop. Prices run the range from inexpensive to expensive. It is possible to get that mink coat of your dreams for an affordable price (under $5,000). However, you must inspect each coat very carefully for flaws, bad skins, or poor workmanship and fit. These coats are mass produced for Jindo shops worldwide.

The other major furrier in town is **DESPINA FURS.** There are two shops and the factory, where you can also shop. In Kowloon, showrooms are located in the China Ferry Terminal (Shop 21/22), Tsimshatsui, and at Sun Plaza (Shop 40), 28 Canton Road, Tsimshatsui. The factory and factory shop are located in the Merit Industrial Centre (3rd floor, Shop B10), 94 Tokwawan Road, Kowloon. (Call 3-339235 for directions on how to get there.) This is real off-the-rack fur. However, since manufacturing is done in Hong Kong (as well as in New York, Greece, and China), you can have alterations done on the spot. Bargain for a better price. You should receive a 10% reduction at least. Despina has a branch in New York City, at 305 Seventh Avenue, if you have problems upon your return to the United States.

If you are interested in shopping the higher end of price and quality try Mody Road in Tsimshatsui, Kowloon. Aside from Siberian Fur Store, there are many others you can browse through. Start at Siberian, then just work your way down the street.

Jewelry and Gemstones

H ong Kong trades every variety and quality of gemstone. It is the fifth-largest diamond-cutting center in the world. The money changing hands in this industry totals billions of dollars per year.

The good news about buying gemstones in Hong Kong is that you can bring them (unset) back to the United States for a negligible duty (or for no duty at all). The bad news is that finding good stones requires a Ph.D. in gemology. You'll also require Sherlock Holmes at your side, and a jeweler's loupe. Actually, what you need is someone like our friend Elizabeth Li, who has family in the business and explained it all to us.

The jewelry and gemstone businesses are separate, and converge into one business only at the wholesale level, where you will never be admitted without a bona fide dealer. If you are serious about buying stones, you should be introduced to the wholesale dealers. This requires personal contact from a dealer here, or from a friend who is Chinese and living in Hong Kong. It is a very tight business. Don't expect to just walk into a shop off the street and see the best stones or get the best prices.

We have many jewelers we actually trust in Hong Kong. However, our trust has been earned through experience. Friends who live there have their favorite people and have been kind enough to share sources with us. Other friends have been buying from one family or firm for fifty years and have shared sources with us. There is risk in every purchase, but if you are dealing with a reputable jeweler that risk is minimized. Reputation is everything. If you are looking for good pearls, diamonds, opals, jade, or ivory, educate yourself first. Take the time to learn before you leap.

Jewelry

Jewelry is the word we use to describe decorative baubles made of gold and either precious or semiprecious stones. There are almost as many jewelry shops in Hong Kong as there are tailors. As you walk down almost any street in Hong Kong, your eyes are constantly drawn to windows full of magnificent pins, rings, and earrings. Much of the Hong Kong jewelry is made with 18K gold, which is popular in Asia. This is a yellower gold than the 14K gold Americans usually prefer. Jewelers used to dealing with overseas clients keep pieces on hand for both markets. Decide which you prefer before you begin serious negotiations on a piece. 14K is less expensive than 18K. Gold will be marked with either a K label or an alternate that reads "375" (9K), "585" (14K), or "750" (18K).

One of the best buys in the jewelry field is in custom-made pieces. If you have a favorite Tiffany, Harry Winston, or Van Cleef & Arpels catalogue, take it with you. A good jeweler can translate any basic design into something just for you—at half the cost. To make certain that you get value for your money we suggest the following:

▼ Look at many things in the shop, both expensive and inexpensive. We discovered a tremendous buy on lapis beads by just being curious. You never know what the jeweler uses as a promotion piece in order to get you going as a client. These beads were selling in Lane Crawford for $250, and we bought them for $60.

▼ Ask questions. If the jeweler is not willing to spend time with you, leave.

▼ Negotiate prices on a few items before you get down to business on the one that you really want. If the jeweler knows that you are looking for a good price at the beginning, the process will happen faster.

▼ Ask if you can get an outside appraisal of the piece of jewelry that you are considering. If the jeweler hesitates, question why.

▼ Remember that you will pay duty on set versus unset stones coming into the United States. Use this as a negotiating tool.

▼ Always get a written certification of the gold content of your piece of jewelry. This is important for insurance and Customs.

▼ Also get a receipt from the store quoting the exact price that you paid. Don't leave it up to U.S. Customs to evaluate your goods.

▼ If you choose to have the jewelry sent to you, confirm that it will be insured, and for how much.

▼ If you are buying a piece of jewelry with large stones, have a separate appraisal done on them. It should include a photograph and a detailed description of each stone.

The jewelers we recommend are of the larger variety, and reputable. We like them all for different reasons. Many of them carry jade, pearls, and other collector's pieces along with fine jewelry. We have not bought personally from each and every one, but each and every one has been strongly recommended by someone who has. Interview a few of them before settling on one.

GEMSLAND, Mandarin Hotel (mezzanine), Chater Road, Central, Hong Kong, is a great source for custom work, pearls, and set pieces at fair prices. Ask for Richard Chen or his mother, Mrs. Chen. There is another branch in the Hilton Hotel.

CHARISMA, 1509 Melbourne Plaza, 33 Queen's Road, Central, Hong Kong, is good for large custom pieces and unset stones. Derrick Mace is a wholesaler full-time, and has his showroom for custom work within the office. Only serious buyers should go here.

HENRY JEWELLERY LTD., 29 Nathan Road, Tsimshatsui, Kowloon, is where the Beverly Hills ladies like to shop. Set pieces are very elegantly glitzy.

KEVIN, Holiday Inn Golden Mile, 50 Nathan Road, Tsimshatsui, Kowloon, has some very unusual and creative pieces of jewelry. Not the usual stuff you see in the hotel arcade shops.

JIMMY LAW GEMS CENTRE, 6 Carnarvon Road, Tsimshatsui, Kowloon, is the place to go for cubic zirconias set in gold. Be sure to bargain hard.

LARRY JEWELRY, the Landmark, Central, Hong Kong, specializes in glitzy and large pieces. This is a very popular place with the ladies who lunch.

KAI YIN LO, the Mandarin Hotel (mezzanine), Central, Hong Kong. We consider this jewelry with an ethnic flavor to be both serious and fun. Her designs using gold and semiprecious gemstones are unique in Hong Kong.

KING FOOK GOLD & JEWELRY CO. LTD., 30–32 Des Voeux Road Central, Central, Hong Kong, is popular with Asian shoppers. Much of their work is done in 18K gold.

CHINA HANDICRAFTS & GEM HOUSE, 55 Haiphong Road, Tsimshatsui, Kowloon, is known for good prices on set and unset stones. One of our readers bought a diamond here and had it appraised for considerably more in the United States.

Pearls

If you are searching for pearls and pearls alone, you will have many options. Every jewelry store has them in the window. The question is, Who do you trust? When we were doing our research for *Born to Shop: Tokyo*, we were told that all the pearls that make it to Hong Kong are the rejects from Tokyo. It is true that pearl prices in Tokyo are higher than in Hong Kong, but we don't believe that all the pearls are inferior. The story does, however, point out that some jewelers might be selling inferior quality.

The bigger jewelry shops are a safe bet for buying quality pearls. The price tag will be higher than on the street, but you have some assurance that, should you have a problem with your second appraisal back home, they will make amends. The following are all considered reputable shops for pearls:

TRIO PEARL, Peninsula Hotel, Salisbury Road, Tsimshatsui, Kowloon. Lily and her friends all agree that one of the best places to go to in Hong Kong is Trio, whose reputation for high prices and higher quality is well known.

GEMSLAND, Mandarin Hotel (Shop 20/mezzanine), Central, Hong Kong, is where we bought our pearls. Gemsland looks like a fancy shop, but Richard Chen or his mother are happy to spend hours rolling pearls to find the best ones. We even know people who mail-ordered pearls through Richard and were happy with the quality.

OM-INTERNATIONAL LTD., 6 Carnarvon Road (1st floor, Suite A3), Tsimshatsui, Kowloon. Om-International is a favorite of many of our friends. They are pearl wholesalers who have a semiofficial shop in their offices. If you are a serious shopper you can match sets, or they have a few made up. Prices are good if you know your quality and will bargain.

MA'S JEWELRY, Sands Building, 12 Peking Road, Tsimshatsui, Kowloon. A favorite of the Bulgari set, Ma's has good pearl prices and sixteen years of experience dealing with Americans.

MIKIMOTO PEARL SHOP, Matsuzakaya Department Store. If you want a guarantee that you are buying the very best in pearls, Mikimoto is where you should come. They are Japanese, guaranteed top-quality, and quite expensive.

Opals

We have only one suggestion when it comes to buying opals: Buyer beware. Opals are mined in Australia, among other places, and brought to Hong Kong to be cut, polished, and shipped out again. Considering this, it is surprising that there are not more opal stores. You will see opals in fine jewelry stores, but you will not see many. One company in particular, **OPAL CREATIONS,** has cornered the tourist opal trade. They have set up one shop in Burlington Arcade, Tsimshatsui, that is a re-creation of an opal mine, with illustrations and samples of what to look for and what not to look for. It is informative and fun, especially if you are with children. The mine opens up into the (surprise!) retail store with opal choices galore. There are big stones and little stones, set stones and unset stones. All the opals are guaranteed to be authentic and not tampered with in any way. Prices are high, and the sales pitch is strong, but for small pieces, there are many choices. Comparison-shop elsewhere before coming, and then bargain once you are there. Opal Creations is on the ground floor of the Burlington Arcade, 92 Nathan Road, Tsimshatsui, Kowloon. Otherwise, simply shop in good jewelry stores. It is easy to be duped with opals.

Diamonds

Diamonds come into Hong Kong duty-free from around the world. It is one of the world's largest diamond-trading areas. If you wish to buy diamonds, check with the Hong Kong Tourist Association, which publishes a list of some 200 jewelers they recommend. Also contact the **DIAMOND IMPORTERS ASSOCIATION, H.K. LTD.,** Diamond Exchange Building (Room 401), 8–10 Duddell Street, Hong Kong, for their list of authorized agents. The Diamond Importers Association also publishes a variety of educational leaflets that you can send for ahead of your trip. Or call 5-235497 when you are in Hong Kong.

When looking for diamonds, judge their value by the four C's—Cut, Clarity, Color, and Carat. The cut of the diamond is determined by your personal choice. No one cut is more valuable than others, although the round cut is the most classic and salable because it allows for the most brilliance and fire. Clarity in a diamond is judged by absence of inclusions, then number, size, and position of existing inclusions. A "flawless" diamond is unusual.

Color is an important factor in the value of the stone. A perfect blue-white stone is the most valuable. The more intense the color, the higher the price. Colorless diamonds are rare.

Carat is the weight of the stone. One carat equals ½₀ gram. Price goes up as carat weight increases. There are 100 points per carat. A 4.02 carat stone would weigh 4 carats 2 points. A flawless stone larger than 1 carat is considered of investment quality because of its rarity.

Before you buy any stone get an independent appraisal done by the **GEMOLOGICAL LAB OF HONG KONG,** Luk Hoi Tong Building, 31

Queen's Road Central. Phone 5-262422 for an appointment and directions. It usually takes five working days to certify a diamond. It's worth the time to make sure that you don't get caught buying a cubic zirconia thinking it is a diamond.

Watches

Any type of watch you ever hoped to find is in Hong Kong. The trick is finding the right watch at the right price. You can pay anything from $50 to $10,000. If you are in the market for an international brand of watch, you are wisest to go to one of the authorized dealers for that brand. They are all listed in the phone book as well as through the Hong Kong Tourist Association. All of the companies expect to lower their prices by 10%. You might expect to get an even better discount if you pay in cash.

If you are looking to buy a fun, or interesting, watch, but don't care if it's a name brand, there are some things to be aware of before you buy:

▼ Check the movement to see that the whole watch and not just the movement was made by the manufacturer. A common practice in Hong Kong is to sell a Swiss watch face and movement with a Hong Kong–made bracelet. The bracelet is probably silver with a gold plating. This can work to your advantage if you do not want to spend $5,000 for a solid-gold watch but want the look. A reputable dealer will tell you that this is what you are buying, and price the watch accordingly. These watches can cost anywhere from $150 to $400. We have found that you have the greatest bargaining power in this area, because the profit for the watchmaker is so high. On the other hand, dealers of name-brand watches have a limited play in their prices.

▼ Check the serial number on the inside movement with the serial number of your guarantee. If you do not receive a worldwide guarantee, don't buy the watch.

▼ If you are buying from a name-brand dealer, do the same careful checking as if you were buying from a small no-name shop on the street. We know of someone who bought a name-brand watch from a reputable dealer, got the watch home, and had problems. When she went to the U.S. dealer for that name, they told her that yes, indeed, she had bought one of their name watches, but the movement was five years old. She had bought a current body with a used movement!

▼ As to imitation name-brand watches: We can only tell you that they are cheaper on the streets of New York City than they are in Hong Kong or Kowloon. If you are determined to buy one, browse through the **CHUNG KING ARCADE,** 36–44 Nathan Road, Kowloon. This is an arcade of ordinary watch dealers, and you won't see any fakes in sight. However, if you go into one of the stores (we can't say which one) and sit on the couch and they believe you are not going to have them arrested, you can look through a sample book of "real" name-brand watches and pick. Of course, they may all have picked up and moved by the time you read this book. These operations are not exactly legitimate. Try standing on the street near the Sands Building. Two or three boys will sidle up to you and say "Wanna buy a watch, lady?" They don't mean any old watch, you can be sure. We find the subject of these imitation watches a tricky one. It is illegal to sell them, and illegal to bring them into the United States. Someone must be willing to risk it, however, since these streetcorner salesmen are quite firm about their high asking prices. Frankly, we don't think it's worth the risk.

The list below will give you a starting point for finding a reputable store. In the case of companies like Rolex, the main service center will supply you with a current list of dealers, and a suggestion of who might carry the model you want. If you are buying a name brand, we suggest buying through an authorized dealer, in order to protect your repair rights at home. Don't forget to get a worldwide guarantee containing the dealer's stamp, serial number of your watch, and date of purchase:

TIME WATCH COMPANY, 54 Nathan Road, Tsimshatsui, Kowloon

BASEL WATCH COMPANY, 33 Queen's Road, Central, Hong Kong

LES MUST DE CARTIER, Prince's Building, Central, Hong Kong

CHOPARD, the Landmark, Central, Hong Kong

DICKSON WATCH & JEWELLERY COMPANY, the Landmark, Central, Hong Kong

GIRARD-PERREGAUX SERVICE CENTRE, the Landmark, Central, Hong Kong

LONGINES HONG KONG LTD., 1120 Ocean Centre, Canton Road, Tsimshatsui, Kowloon

PIAGET, the Landmark, Edinburgh Tower, Central, Hong Kong (information and showroom)

ROLEX LTD., Jardine House, 1 Connaught Place, Central, Hong Kong (service and information)

SEIKO, the Landmark, Gloucester Tower, Central, Hong Kong

If it's not necessary that you find a name-brand watch, and you are simply looking for something unusual and fun, try the following:

CITY CHAIN: There is a particularly good branch of this popular chain at 16 Mody Road, Tsimshatsui, Kowloon. City Chain carries Seiko, Bulova, and Zenith among their name brands.

They also carry fashion watches like Smash (a takeoff of Swatch).

SWATCH SHOP, 6 Great George Street, Causeway Bay, Hong Kong. Swatch is a big seller in Hong Kong. Prices are no cheaper than in the United States, but you might see some different styles.

Cameras

B uying a camera in Hong Kong is confusing unless you are quite knowledgeable about the equipment and comparable prices. Every year there are new top-of-the-line models available in every brand, and they're all for sale in Hong Kong. Most shopkeepers will tout what they have in stock, and not necessarily what you need. Begin your search armed with the exact details of what it is you want. There is a Canon showroom in the Silvercord Building Arcade where you can test various models. You must supply your own film. Once you are quite sure of what you want, price-shop. Try several different stores and bargain as if you were going to buy. Don't buy, however, no matter how good the price seems. Wait and go back. If you got a good price the first time you will probably get it again. If you are buying a lot of equipment, ask for a larger discount. Take a copy of a recent ad from 47th Street Photo (these double-page ads run every Sunday in the *New York Times* and will give you an excellent reference point for U.S. prices on cameras and other small electronic goods).

After you have decided where you are going to buy, insist on the following:

▼ Each piece of equipment needs its own warranty (worldwide). The serial number of the piece must be clearly marked on the card, along with the agent's stamp and a complete address of where you purchased the item.

▼ Make sure you are not being charged for extras that should have been included in the original purchase. For example, camera cases usually come with the camera. You should not pay extra for the case.

▼ Watch your purchase being packed, and check each item as it goes into its box. Don't trust the store owner to pack and deliver your purchase to the hotel. When you get back you might discover that a few small items somehow got lost.

▼ Keep your receipts separate. Customs most likely will not want to open and go through all of your equipment if your receipts are clear and in order.

▼ For the name of an authorized importing agent for a name-brand camera, call the Consumer Council at 5-277662.

Our strongest recommendation for buying a camera comes from our friend Libby, who lived in Hong Kong and is a professional filmmaker. She depended on Mark's Photo Supplies. There are a few other shops we liked as well:

MARK'S PHOTO SUPPLIES, 20 Des Voeux Road, Central, Hong Kong. Steven Mark is the managing director of this shop, which has been in business for over seventeen years. It is not flashy or showy—as a matter of fact, it is not even very easy to find. Although the address is on Des Voeux Road, the entrance is actually on Theatre Lane.

FRANCISCO CAMERA COMPANY, 53 Nathan Road (Hyatt Hotel Arcade), Tsimshatsui, Kowloon. If you're a camera buff your eye will immediately gravitate to the front window full of Leicas and Rolliflex models. This is right in the middle of the tourist path; items are priced accordingly.

ASIA PHOTO, 5 Queen Victoria Street, Central, Hong Kong, and **CROWN PHOTO SUPPLIES LTD.,** 14 Queen Victoria Street, Central, Hong Kong, are both large, well-stocked, convenient shops that cater to the tourist trade.

If you really know your stuff, the inside secret is that all of the local professionals shop at the many smaller camera stores located on Stanley Street and Hing Lung Street. Hing Lung Street is a bit difficult to find. Walk toward Central Market on either Queen's Road Central or Des Voeux Road. Hing Lung Street intersects both just after Jubilee Street, walking west. They'll be able to spot an amateur in these shops, and you'll pay accordingly.

Computers and Small Electronic Devices

We have one important thing to say about buying computers: **ASIA COMPUTER PLAZA,** in the basement of the Silvercord Building, 30 Canton Road, Tsimshatsui, Kowloon, is the place to go to, to be safe. There are authorized dealers here for most of the big names in the computer world. There are bookstores (try **LEED & WOOD,** Shop 21) that sell programs and have information galore. You can get fax machines, laptops, and typewriters with memories. Prices are very good (but there are some great deals in the United States if you are connected to the right source). As with all electronic equipment, you can get computers in Hong Kong.

The question is whether you want to or not. The big names like Apple, IBM, and NEC are sold at authorized stores in the East Asia Computer Plaza. You can haggle and bargain . . . probably even make a good deal. Make sure, however, that the machine you buy is wired to work on the voltage where you will be using it. The Hong Kong voltage is 220, while standard voltage in the United States is 110. Don't let a salesperson convince you that a converter will do. Computers are much too sensitive, and you don't want to risk losing your program because of a power failure. Also make sure that the equipment you buy will work with the monitor you have at home.

If you are a little more adventurous, take the MTR to Sham Shui Po to visit the **GOLDEN ARCADE SHOPPING CENTER,** 44B Fuk Wah Street, Sham Shui Po. This area of town is very much a "real people" neighborhood, filled with street stalls selling blue jeans for $2, T-shirts, bed linens, ducks, and roosters. The street odor is strong. People are jammed into every nook and cranny of the area. In the midst of this craziness is the Golden Arcade Shopping Center, a supermarket filled with computer hardware, software, and educational material. As you get out of the MTR you will be right there. . . . Just look up to see the arcade marquee. There is a directory listing all 120 of the shops, but it really doesn't matter. The only way to shop here is to wander and compare. Each shop has a different type of computer, and many if not most of them are clones. You have to know your equipment to shop successfully here. In the basement are software companies selling unofficial programs.

Important note: Take the time to open the package and run the program. One of our readers found that half the program would not boot. They ran a new copy for him on the spot. This is definitely a bargain-hard shopping environment.

Optical

I f we weren't nearsighted, we'd be perfect. Lucky for us, we wear glasses and consider them a fashion accessory, not a liability. When we are in Hong Kong we're likely to buy a few new pairs. If you're used to paying $150 to $200 for prescription eyewear in the United States, you'll be pleased to know that you can get three or four pairs for that price in Hong Kong.

Many Americans—snobs and opticians—will question whether you are being properly fitted with prescription lenses in Hong Kong. We are not guaranteeing that you will be properly fitted in Hong Kong, or anywhere. So we offer several suggestions:

▼ Have your eyes examined at home and carry your doctor's prescription with you to Hong Kong.

▼ Have your Hong Kong glasses checked out once you return home.

▼ Buy only the frame, and have the prescription lenses inserted once you're back home, especially if your prescription is in any way tricky or out of the ordinary.

▼ Do not buy glasses if you wear contact lenses.

▼ Use reputable sources in Hong Kong, and negotiate adjustments and/or refunds before you order.

THE MANDARIN OPTICAL CO., 51 Queen's Road, Central, Hong Kong, is our choice of optician. They offer a good selection of frames to choose from and professional service. **PIONEER OPTICAL SUPERMARKET CO. LTD.,** 568 Nathan Road, Kowloon (as well as several other branches), is truly a supermarket of styles, and is by far the least expensive place we've seen. A good bet if you're just planning to buy the frames.

THE OPTICAL SHOP, LTD., with about twenty-five shops throughout Kowloon and Central, must be doing something right.

PRINCETON PROFESSIONAL, Wing On Plaza, Mody Road, Tsimshatsui East, Kowloon. We found fashion frames here for about $35 that would have cost more than twice that at home, as well as a good selection of designer sunglasses, including Ray-Ban, Porsche, and Christian Dior.

A few words about contact lenses:

1. If you wear contact lenses most of the time, remove them twenty-four hours prior to an eye examination so that your eyeballs may return to their natural shape.

2. Many people buy extra sets of contact lenses (all types) in Hong Kong. We didn't do this, but we saw many taking advantage of brand names and low prices. One British woman walked into Mandarin Optical while we were there and said crisply, "Do you have a [some style, size and number] Bausch & Lomb lens?" They did, and she bought them. The entire transaction was like buying wallpaper. We don't know enough about contact lenses to guide you; you probably want to discuss this with your regular eye doctor. Disposable lenses were not available in Hong Kong at the time this book went to press.

Fabrics and Notions

As one of the ready-to-wear manufacturing capitals of the world, Hong Kong has more fabrics and notions than just about any other city we've seen. Prices for even the most luscious Chinese or Japanese silks are reasonable—although Chinese silk is much less expensive than Japanese. (Japanese silks are much more intricately printed; the Chinese rarely run multiple screens on their silks.)

There are two basic fabrics and notions neighborhoods: Jardine's Bazaar and the Lanes. When you go to Jardine's Bazaar weave in and around all the little streets behind the market itself; you'll find numerous fabrics, notions, and yarn shops with incredibly low prices.

Wool yarn is very inexpensive in Hong Kong. You'll find some excellent knitting shops in the Lanes, and there are several in Causeway Bay. We bought Jaegar alpaca, in the 50-gram size, for $4. There were many 100-gram packages of 100% wool selling for about 50¢ each. Try **PICK 'N' PAY HOUSE OF FANCY WOOL,** 16 A3 Kai Chiu Road, Causeway Bay, Hong Kong, or 42A Yun Ping Road, Causeway Bay, Hong Kong. For yarn and sweater patterns try **PATRICIA ROBERTS,** 3244 Ocean Galleries, Canton Road, Tsimshatsui, Kowloon. If you are shopping the Lanes, try **MUI TONG CO.,** 11 Li Yuen Street West. They have another branch at 28 Bonham Strand East, Central, Hong Kong.

Raw and finished silk are incredible buys. See Chapter 5 for details on silk. You can buy fabrics from most tailors; there's a large selection of Chinese silks in all Chinese Arts & Crafts Stores. A nice jacquard or raw silk runs about $15 per meter. Bespoke tailors always have a large selection of fabrics for men's suits and shirts, but you cannot buy these goods off the bolt. The oldest and perhaps most well known store for fabrics, especially silks, is **THE OLD PEKING SILK CO. LTD.,** 219 Nathan Road, Tsimshatsui, Kowloon. It is just up the road from the Park Lane Shopper's Boulevard. The selections here range from French couture brocades to classic Chinese silks.

One of our best resources for colored thread in fashion colors is **TAI HING CO.,** Lee Fat Building (1st floor), 30–38 Jardine's Crescent, Causeway Bay, Hong Kong. For the best in sequins, diamond trims, and doodads, **MUI KEE CO.,** 40 Stanley Street, Central, Hong Kong, is another good resource. And of course **WING ON STREET** is not called Cloth Alley because it sells cameras! Wing On Street is near Western Market in Central.

Embroidery and Whitework

The Chinese are famous for their embroidery. One variety that we particularly like is done on linen or cotton, by machine and hand, and we refer to it as "whitework," which is actually a Victorian name describing the white-on-white variety. Antique embroidered goods are quite valuable. Tablecloths, napkins, place mats, sweaters, jackets, and fabric purses are all sold with embroidery. The best drawn embroidery is supposed to come from Swatow in China.

Since more and more of our friends are becoming collectors of whitework we get requests to bring it back from all over the world. We shopped in Spain and Portugal for embroidered goods and were surprised to find a lot of Chinese imports there. Be careful to learn the look of hand embroidery versus machine embroidery. Most of the shop goods are machine-made. Hand embroidery is very expensive. If you want finely crafted pieces try:

HANDART EMBROIDERIES, Hing Wai Building (Shop 106), 36 Queen's Road Central, Central, Hong Kong. This shop offers a particularly good selection of bed linens, place mats, and doilies.

SWATOW DRAWN WORK CO., World Wide Plaza (C2), 19 Des Voeux Road Central, Central, Hong Kong. The finest embroidery in China, drawnwork from the Swatow region is known for quality.

THE CHINESE BAZAAR, Prince's Building, Chater Road, Central, Hong Kong, or 10A–B Carnarvon Road, Tsimshatsui, Kowloon. This store offers a huge selection in table linens, napkins, duvets, coasters, and children's clothing. They have been in business since 1905.

HAND EMB'D COMPANY, 41-E Mody Road, Tsimshatsui, Kowloon. There is a very wide range of quality and styles here, from Irish linen fabric embroidered by hand to sheets, place mats, and the like.

LACE LANE, Silvercord Building (Shop 204), 30 Canton Road, Tsimshatsui, Kowloon and Wing On Plaza (UG5), 62 Mody Road, Tsimshatsui East, Kowloon. These two shops are our favorites for pricing, selection, and service. The hand-smocked dresses for little girls are especially wonderful.

WAH SING LACE COMPANY, 7 On Lan Street, Central, Hong Kong. On Lan Street is a short block full of wholesalers and manufacturers. Not all may offer retail, but this is a good lane for finding bargains. Wah Sing manufactures and does export, in case you want to buy lots.

With all of the above shops, bargaining is acceptable. The smaller the establishment, the harder you should bargain. We found that they all had comparable starting prices for the same goods. You can expect to pay $50 for a set of twelve napkins, $30 for a hand-embroidered little girl's dress, $300 for a queen-size duvet cover, and $10 for a dozen coasters.

Cosmetics and Fragrances

Cosmetics and fragrances are not as inexpensive in Hong Kong as in Paris, but may be less than in the United States. Expect to save about 10% to 20%. The best thing is that scents that have been introduced in Europe, but not in the United States, are available in Hong Kong. So if you want to sniff out the latest, Hong Kong offers you that opportunity.

We have comparison-shopped all the big department stores—British, Japanese, Chinese, you name it—and we find that they all have pretty much the same prices. We buy our cosmetics at a duty-free because we can sometimes wrangle a big discount. Most of the markets sell cosmetics, although they are not usually American or French brands, or even names that you recognize.

Take note: Major big-name cosmetics companies manufacture for the Far East in and around Hong Kong; often they will have a product with the same name as the product you use at home, but it will be slightly different. They may also have a product, or shade, that you will have never heard of and will never find again anywhere else in the world.

KIN CHUEN COSMETICS CO. LTD., 67–69 Wing Lok Road, Western, Hong Kong, is an importer of European cosmetics and fragrances. Our secret brand of French cosmetics, not available in the United States, is called Bourjois, and we stock up in Hong Kong, where eyeshadow costs about $6.

FANDA PERFUME COMPANY, 21 Lock Road, Tsimshatsui, Kowloon, or World Wide Plaza, Pedder Street, Central, Hong Kong. Lily and her friends all buy their perfumes and cosmetics at this convenient shop where prices are discounted on many items, including Badedas.

THE BODY SHOP, the Landmark (B28), Gloucester Tower, Central, Hong Kong, or The Mall/Pacific Place (Shop 110), 88 Queensway, Central, Hong Kong. We love this English natural cosmetics line that has taken the United States and Hong Kong by storm. All the products come in biodegradable containers and are made from natural ingredients. There is a complete line of cosmetics as well as soaps with scents like sandalwood and jasmine. Treat yourself to a bottle of Peppermint Foot Massage Creme after a hard day of bargain hunting.

SHU UEMURA, the Landmark (B25), Central, Hong Kong, and Ocean Centre (Shop 204), Canton Road, Tsimshatsui, Kowloon. We first discovered this line of cosmetics and skin-care products in Tokyo, then in Paris. L.A., New York, and now Hong Kong. Nobody does better colors in eyeshadow.

China and Crystal

Y ou may not think of Hong Kong as the place to stock up on your Wedgwood. However, think again. Because of British rule, Hong Kong is an excellent source for many British products. Prices are exactly the same as in retail stores in England and considerably less than in the United States.

The largest china and crystal stores are in or near the major hotels and shopping centers. They all ship and take orders from overseas. The only problem arises when the store is out of stock. You can have many dinner parties before your missing pieces arrive. Check on availability before you place your order. European lines stocked locally include Royal Crown Derby, Royal Albert Spode, Royal Brierley, Royal Worcester, Hammersley, Edinburgh, Robbs and Berking, Royal Minton, Royal Doulton, Lladró, Limoges, Herend, Ginori, Saint Louis, Boehm, Rosenthal, Baccarat, Lalique, and Wedgwood.

To find your favorite European big name try any of the following shops. Most have catalogues; many will ship:

BACCARAT, the Landmark, Central, Hong Kong

CRAIG'S, St. George's Building, 2 Ice House Street, Central, Hong Kong (next to the Mandarin Oriental Hotel); Ocean Centre (Shop 341), Canton Road, Tsimshatsui, Kowloon

GRENLEY'S, Swire House (Shop 25C), Pedder Street, Central, Hong Kong

HUNTER'S, Peninsula Hotel (BE14), Salisbury Road, Tsimshatsui, Kowloon; Ocean Terminal (Shop 2122), Tsimshatsui, Kowloon

EILEEN KERSHAW, Peninsula Hotel, Salisbury Road, Tsimshatsui, Kowloon; The Landmark (G44), Central, Hong Kong

LLADRÓ, Peninsula Hotel (BL5), Salisbury Road, Tsimshatsui, Kowloon; Alexandra House, Des Voeux Road Central, Central, Hong Kong

ROSENTHAL, Prince's Building, Ice House Street, Central, Hong Kong

ROYAL COPENHAGEN, Prince's Building (Shop 122), Chater Road, Central, Hong Kong

WATERFORD SHOP, Peninsula Hotel, Salisbury Road, Tsimshatsui, Kowloon

WEDGWOOD, the Landmark (G7A), Central, Hong Kong

Chinese China also is available, and there are many outlets. One of the easiest sources for vases and tea sets is the Chinese department stores. We like **CHINESE ARTS & CRAFTS**, in either of their stores: Star House or Silvercord Building, Tsimshatsui, Kowloon. Also in Kowloon, try **CHUNG KIU CHINESE PRODUCTS EMPORIUM LTD.**, 17 Hankow Road, Tsimshatsui, or **YUE HWA**, 301 Nathan Road, Tsimshatsui.

Chinese factories are a popular shopper's attraction—you can see some of the goods in production if you catch a good day. The factories are not easy or convenient to get to, so we suggest that you plan your day around the visit, leave plenty of time, and remember that factories close for lunch, usually between 1 P.M. and 2 P.M. Also remember public holidays when factories close (see page 27). One of our favorite factory outlets for Chinese porcelains is **AH CHOW FACTORY**, Hong Kong Industrial Centre, 489 Castle Peak Road, Lai Chi Kok, Kowloon. We also like **WAH TUNG CHINA COMPANY**, Grand Marine Industrial Building, 3 Yue Fung Street, Tin Wan, Aberdeen, Hong Kong.

Chops (and We Don't Mean Lamb)

Of course we know what a chop is. It's served for dinner and comes in the pork, veal, or lamb category. Or so we thought.

It turns out that in China, a chop is a form of signature stamp (not made of rubber) on which a symbol for a person's name is carved. The chop is dipped in dry dye (instead of an ink pad) and then placed on paper to create a signature stamp—much like a rubber stamp.

The main difference between rubber stamps and chops is that rubber stamps were invented after the Bessemer process and became trendy only in the early 1980s, whereas chops were invented about 2,200 years ago.

Since chops go so far back, you can choose from an antique or a newly created version. Antiques are quite pricey, depending on age, importance of the carving, materials used, and maybe even the autograph that is engraved. New chops have little historic importance but make great gifts.

Although chops vary in size, they are traditionally the size of a chessman, with a square or round base. Up to four Chinese characters or three Western initials can be inscribed on the base.

The quality of a chop varies greatly, based on the ability of the person who does the carving. We have done enough chop shopping to know that the very best place to get a chop is in Man Wa Lane. But every hotel has at least one gift shop that will have your chop engraved. (You must allow at least twenty-four hours.) While prices vary on chops, obviously, we paid $20 for a fabulous one—midsize but brilliantly carved. This is a little high, but we didn't bargain on the price. Our craftsman was chosen by the lines in his face and the twinkle in his eye. He does not speak English. . . . **HON JAI,** Man Wa Lane, Hong Kong. Possibly any other engraver in Man Wa Lane is as good. None of the chops we had made at various hotel gift shops was nearly as fine.

You can buy little pots of the proper dye in any gift shop ($1) or use a regular old ink pad. Red is the color for your true love's chop ink.

Arts, Crafts, and Antiques

Hunting down bargains in arts, crafts, and antiques is one of our favorite shopping adventures in Hong Kong. Our definition of arts and crafts is broad enough to include handwork of any kind, from hand-carved teaware to cloisonné that has been done within the last 100 years. We include pottery that is original or copies of originals, ivory carvings, jade carvings, handmade dolls, and papercuts. The how and why of some of these subjects we tackle in Chapter 5. The where to get them is not so precise a topic. Antiques are often arts and crafts that are over 100 years old. Some of our sources carry antiques and arts and crafts. Some just carry fun crafts. Some just carry antiques.

A good way to get a fix on the arts, crafts, and antiques of China is to begin with a visit to some of Hong Kong's museums:

HONG KONG MUSEUM OF ART, High Block, City Hall (10th and 11th floors), Central, Hong Kong, has a collection of 2,800 antiquities, including ceramics, bronzes, cloisonné, snuff bottles, papercuts, and embroidery. Paintings and calligraphy dating from the 17th to the 20th centuries are represented as well. Educational material is available, and there is a gift shop with replicas and postcards. This museum is closed on Thursday. Other days it is open 10 A.M.–6 P.M., and on Sunday, 1 P.M.–6 P.M.

FLAGSTAFF HOUSE MUSEUM OF TEA WARE, Victoria Barracks (enter from Cotton Tree Drive), Hong Kong, is a branch of the Hong Kong Museum of Art. It is housed in the oldest Western-style building left in Hong Kong. There are 560 pieces of teaware, mainly

Chinese, with a good selection of Yixing teapots. The museum is closed Wednesday and open 10 A.M.–5 P.M. every other day.

We feel that arts and crafts and antiques are wonderful buys. It is hard to comparison-shop for them, because you never see two things of the same kind. If you do, you shouldn't be buying them anyway.

The Hong Kong Tourist Association publishes a list of factories that produce brassware, carpets, carved furniture, Chinese lanterns, pewter, and china and are open to the public.

For the ultimate thrill in antique collecting, frequent the auction galleries. Auctions are advertised in the *South China Morning Post*. Large auctions of priceless porcelains make front-page news. If you wish advance notice or catalogues before you visit, write to:

ASSOCIATED FINE ARTS AUCTIONEERS, LTD., Entertainment Building (13th floor) 30 Queen's Road Central, Central, Hong Kong (telephone: 5-222088)

CHRISTIE MANSON & WOODS LTD., Alexandra House, Des Voeux Road Central, Central, Hong Kong (telephone: 5-215396)

LAMMERT BROTHERS, 10 Stanley Street (9th floor), Central, Hong Kong (telephone: 5-223208)

SOTHEBY'S H.K. LTD., Lane Crawford House, Queen's Road Central, Central, Hong Kong (telephone: 5-248121)

Arts and Crafts

EILEEN KERSHAW: This shop, in the Peninsula Hotel, is on the upper end of fine arts and crafts stores. Their business card is a three-way foldout with the Chinese dynasties listed along the entire back half. The front has a list of birthstones, in case you want to buy a present for a friend, as well as a place for notes on what you have seen.

The shop is extremely large, but seems less so because there are pieces of stonework, display cases, packing crates, and porcelain jars everywhere you look. The sales help is very understanding and pleasant. Prices are average. The antique vases are displayed on the highest shelves, so that curious travelers cannot touch. Antique paintings, china, carpets, and wall hangings are a large part of the store's business, but do not involve the usual walk-in tourist. If you are interested in a special type of item, ask. The store will do mail-order as well.

EILEEN KERSHAW, The Peninsula Hotel, Salisbury Road, Tsimshatsui, Kowloon

▼

AMAZING GRACE ELEPHANT COMPANY: Amazing Grace carries handcrafted items from all over Asia. In particular we like the Taiwanese temple carvings. You can also buy silk pillow covers, brass carts, bowls, and candlesticks, incense burners, jewelry, Korean chests, paper carvings, fans, dolls, bird cages, mirror frames, tea sets, and more. This shop has a broad appeal and can be a good source for small, inexpensive gift items.

The warehouse/outlet, in the New Territories, is open to the public. If you are doing serious shopping it might be worth the drive. You cannot get there any other way but by car, so take that into consideration. We suggest you stop in the Ocean Centre shop and get directions. This is a warehouse situation, so be prepared. Wholesale prices are predicated on how much you buy, or on the cost of the goods. You can save a small fortune—and spend one too.

AMAZING GRACE ELEPHANT COMPANY, Harbour City, Ocean Centre (Shop 349), Canton Road, Tsimshatsui, Kowloon
AMAZING GRACE OUTLET, Yeu Shing Industrial Building, 4 Kin Fung Street, Tuen Mun, New Territories

STONE HOUSE: If you are looking for an easy and fun gift, try a carved chop or figurine from Stone House. The shop, located in the Omni The Hong Kong Hotel Arcade, specializes in snuff bottles, stone carvings, chops made out of ivory, jade, agate, and stone, and printing. If you need a business card, you can get a chop and card at the same time.

STONE HOUSE, Omni The Hong Kong Hotel Arcade (3rd floor), Canton Road, Tsimshatsui, Kowloon

▼

YUE KEE CURIO COMPANY: Yue Kee has many options in fine art curios, including carvings, wall pieces, floor pieces, screens, and statues. There are also Chinese vases in every size. The shop is very crowded, and we don't suggest that you bring children or large shopping bags. It will take some time to make your mind up here. Yue Kee also has antiques.

YUE KEE CURIO COMPANY, Omni The Hong Kong Hotel Arcade (Shop 3032A), Canton Road, Tsimshatsui, Kowloon

▼

MOUNTAIN FOLKCRAFT: One of our favorite shops for handcrafted items, Mountain Folkcraft has a tendency to move around. If it is not at this address call their head office (5-232817) to get a new one. Mountain Folkcraft carries a little bit of everything in a small amount of space. When you go into the shop, shed your coat and bags at the door, because you are going to need room to stoop, bend, and sift through the items that are displayed, in order to see the ones below. We love their dolls, papercuts, woodblock prints, antique fabric pieces, batik fabric, boxes, chests, puppets, baskets, toys, and pottery.

The Central shop is located on a tiny street that cuts off D'Aguilar Street, just after Wellington and before Wyndham. The Ocean Terminal shop is easier to find.

MOUNTAIN FOLKCRAFT
Harbour City, Ocean Terminal (Shop 239B), Lantao Gallery, Canton Road, Tsimshatsui, Kowloon
12 Wo On Lane, Central, Hong Kong

▼

BANYAN TREE LTD.: Banyan Tree is a mass-market kind of handicrafts shop that sells rattan furniture, fabrics, figurines, lamps, porcelains, rugs, screens, and hundreds of other items for the home on both a retail and whole-sale basis. They have a large exporting business, and can deliver anything you buy to your hometown. We would trust Banyan Tree to pack and ship anything.

BANYAN TREE LTD.
Harbour City, Ocean Galleries (Shops 238, 304, 311), Canton Road, Tsimshatsui, Kowloon
Prince's Building (Shop 214–217), Chater Road, Central, Hong Kong

▼

REASON COMPANY: This odd little shop in the Princess Shopping Plaza is a good resource for *netsuke*. We realize that *netsuke* is Japanese in origin, but the new hot collector's item is *netsuke* carved in Hong Kong. The figures bear no relationship to antique custom. The elders would be turning over in their graves. These *netsuke* are of men and women in erotic poses . . . movable. Need we say more? Prices are high, considering that they are all new. However, we did not see many shops selling them, either. Reason Company has quite a few pieces, as well as regular jade, lapis, and stone carvings. Prices for the *netsuke* run $200–$300.

REASON COMPANY
Princess Shopping Plaza (2nd floor, Shop 330), Miramar Hotel, 118 Nathan Road, Tsimshatsui, Kowloon

Furama Hotel (Shop E), Connaught Road Central, Central, Hong Kong

▼

CHUNG KIU CHINESE PRODUCTS EMPORIUM: This smallish department store inside the Sands Building in Tsimshatsui has four floors, three of which are devoted to handicrafts products. On the main floor look for jade, cloisonné, ivory, and semiprecious stone carvings. The 1st floor has jewelry, embroidery, silk, and tailoring. For Chinese carpets go to the 4th floor.

CHUNG KIU CHINESE PRODUCTS EMPORIUM,
17 Hankow Road, Tsimshatsui, Kowloon

▼

ORIENTAL ARTS & JEWELLERY COMPANY: Oriental Arts & Jewellery is an importing company located on the 3rd floor of a Nathan Road office building near the Park Lane Shopper's Boulevard.

Go around the corner to find the entrance, take a rickety elevator, step over straw in the hall, and look for the red door that says "A." Come prepared to stay, because this is arts and crafts nirvana. As you walk into the room you see warehouse-type display racks in front of you. On them are a variety of vases, cloisonné items, porcelain, and stone carvings in jade and lapis. Behind and to the side are crates and more crates. Some have their tops opened; some have not yet been touched. The shipments are, for the most part, from mainland Chinese factories. On our tour through mainland China a few years before, we visited factories where cloisonné work was done. The factories all had shops. The prices here were cheaper for the same size vase, two years later. (A 6″ vase was $20.) The imports are mostly new copies of old pieces. However, there are also some old pieces that are offered for sale. One Chinese couple who were there when we came in sat for the entire hour we were there negotiating the price of a 3′ lavender jade carving. This shop is magnificent and one of our best Hong Kong finds. George Chan is the owner.

ORIENTAL ARTS & JEWELLERY COMPANY, 80 Nathan Road (3rd floor, Shop A), Tsim-shatsui, Kowloon

▼

WAH TUNG CHINA COMPANY: One of the largest antiques reproduction facilities for china in Hong Kong is located in Aberdeen. Wah Tung produces plain white porcelain in various shapes and sizes, including large jardinieres and small vases. Their craftspeople then handpaint each piece in the tradition of a period or style. The factory and the showroom are enormous. They take special orders from individuals, decorators, or stores. Custom dinnerware is also available. Wah Tung is a favorite of big-name decorators.

WAH TUNG CHINA COMPANY, Grand Marine Industrial Building, 3 Yue Fung Street, Tin Wan, Aberdeen, Hong Kong

▼

TAI PING CARPETS: One of the major crafts industries in China is carpet-making. These are still made by hand, and many take years to complete. Tai Ping is one of the leading manufacturers and importers. You can visit their retail shop and order a custom carpet (takes 6–12 weeks), or check out the factory shop on Mondays and Thursdays from 2 P.M. to 4 P.M. Call 0-6565161, ext. 211, to arrange the visit.

TAI PING CARPETS
    Hutchison House, 10 Harcourt Road, Central, Hong Kong
    Wing On Plaza, Mody Road, Tsimshatsui East, Kowloon
FACTORY SHOP
    Tai Ping Industrial Park, Ting Kok Road, Lot No. 1687, Tai Po Market, New Territories

Antiques

MARTIN FUNG ANTIQUES AND FUR- NITURE COMPANY: At the far end of Hollywood Road are the Cat Street Galleries and Martin Fung's showroom. Most of the stock in this two-level shop is lacquer furniture. However, the variety is enormous. You can get antique lacquer chests or boxes, or new ones. There are complete living room, dining room, and bedroom sets. Martin Fung deals mainly with decorators and store buyers, but will sell and ship to anyone. If you are placing a large order, talk wholesale.

MARTIN FUNG ANTIQUES AND FURNITURE COMPANY, Cat Street Galleries (1st floor), 38 Lok Ku Road, Central, Hong Kong

▼

P. C. LU & SONS LTD.: A fine antiques dealer with showrooms in the major hotels,

P. C. Lu's family has been in the business for four generations and runs one of the finest resources for antique ivory and jade, porcelain, and decorative work. The three sons, who now run the business, work closely together. Stop in at any of the galleries and browse.

P. C. LU & SONS LTD.
The Peninsula Hotel (ML7 and W-10), Salisbury Road, Tsimshatsui, Kowloon
Mandarin Oriental Hotel (M9–11), Connaught Road Central, Central, Hong Kong

▼

CHARLOTTE HORSTMANN & GERALD GODFREY LTD.: One of the most popular and well-respected antiques shops in Hong Kong, Charlotte Horstmann and Gerald Godfrey offer a wide range in museum-class Asian antiques. There are pieces from Korea, Burma, China, Japan, Indonesia, and India. Choices include *Noh* masks, Chinese scrolls, Ming tapestries, T'ang horses, and period furniture made of sandalwood, rosewood, and blackwood. It has been rumored that the shop may move from Ocean Terminal. If so, call 3-677167 to get their new address.

CHARLOTTE HORSTMANN & GERALD GODFREY LTD., Harbour City, Ocean Terminal (2104 & 2100D), Canton Road, Tsimshatsui, Kowloon

▼

JADE HOUSE: Small but impressive, Jade House has been run by members of the C. K. Liang family for five generations. Mr. Liang's personal collection of early jade is magnificent. The shop specializes in antique jadeite and nephrite, as well as snuff bottles. Telephone:

3-680491. There is another branch in the Kowloon Hotel.

JADE HOUSE, 1-D Mody Road, Tsimshatsui, Kowloon

C. K. LIANG & SONS, Kowloon Hotel (B-203), Middle Road, Tsimshatsui, Kowloon

▼

HONEYCHURCH ANTIQUES: Located on Hollywood Road, Honeychurch deserves to be singled out for its quality and honesty. Glenn and Lucille Vessa are the owners, and they are extremely knowledgeable in the ways of antiques. Their store carries a wide variety of merchandise and they are always willing to give advice on where to go if you have a special need.

HONEYCHURCH ANTIQUES, 29 Hollywood Road, Central, Hong Kong

HOLLYWOOD ROAD

The single best way to shop for antiques without overexerting yourself is to wander Hollywood Road, from Pottinger Street to Cat Street. There is shop after shop filled with Asian finds. Some of them are good, some of them are fake, and some of them are worth bargaining for. Whatever you do, bargain, bargain, bargain. If you are a dealer or plan to purchase in quantity, deal only with the owner. The shops that have been recommended to us as reliable ones by dealers and Hong Kong residents alike include **IAN MCLEAN ANTIQUES,** 73 Wyndham Street (around the corner before Pottinger Street), for fine furniture, paintings, and works of art. On Hollywood Road try **ATFIELD FINE ARTS GALLERIES** (Nos. 1 and 42A) for quality antiques and works of art. (They may be moving due to building renovation at No. 1.) **C. P. CHING FINE ORIENTAL ART** (No. 21) specializes in Asian textiles and one-of-a-kind antiques. **KUNG WAH LEE CHINA-WARE COMPANY** (No. 25) are porcelain wholesalers and exporters. **YAU SANG CHEONG** (No. 39) are brushmakers and stationers. **HANART** (No. 40) is a source for Chinese paintings both ancient and contemporary. **EASTERN DREAMS** (No. 47A) sells porcelains, screens, and furniture. **TAI SING COMPANY** (No. 122) has early Chinese ceramics and porcelain. **MASTERPIECES OF NETSUKE ART,** 3 Upper Lascar Row, offers a good selection of carved ivory, including the erotic figurines.

One note: Hollywood Road is undergoing extensive renovation, and some shops may be moving. If you arrive to see a construction site, go to one of the other shops and ask to use the phone directory. Another of our other favorite dealers has gone wholesale only. If you are a serious buyer looking for fine antiques, contact Helen Bennett at 5-444988 for an appointment, or write before you begin your trip to 27 Hollywood Road (2nd floor), Central, Hong Kong.

8▾TOURS

Hong Kong on a Schedule

We have put more tours in this book than in any of our other books because we think you need the help—but forget this section if you aren't interested. There are no listings here that have not been mentioned elsewhere, but the details or directions might be more explicit in this chapter. If you don't know your way around Hong Kong and do not have a car and driver, we think you should try one or two of our tours. With the average stay in Hong Kong a mere three days, you need to see (and shop) as much as possible. Our tours cram it all in.

Tour 1: Hong Kong—Central and Sane

Your first day in Hong Kong should be easy and fun. The Hong Kong side, especially Central District, is the most understandable place to start. This is the area where all of the large shopping centers, as well as the majority of office buildings, are located.

1. If you are staying in Kowloon, come across the harbor on the Star Ferry. This is the best way to view Central for the first time, as the skyline is spectacular. Crossing under Connaught Road Central will bring you up between Statue Square and the Mandarin Oriental Hotel. If you are staying on the Hong Kong side, taxi to the Hilton. Start your tour here. Then walk to the Mandarin after you've shopped the Hilton arcade.

2. The Mandarin Oriental Hotel is home to two of the most popular tailor shops in town. On the mezzanine level you will find David's (shirts) and A-Man (suits). Also on the mezzanine don't miss the jewelry shop, Gemsland.

3. As you leave the hotel, take a left and then left again on Ice House Street. Craig's is one of our favorite shops for loading up on English bone china and crystal, and is right on the corner of Ice House Street and Connaught Road Central.

4. After leaving Craig's, turn left again on Connaught Road Central, and walk to Swire House (in the middle of the block and before you get to Pedder Street). Swire House is a perfect example of an office building/shopping center. Within the Swire House arcade, you will find Issey Miyake (No. 108), Bruno Magli (No. 19), Fendi (No. 20), Ragence (No. 21), Matsuda (No. 10), and a variety of lesser-known designer boutiques.

5. Leave Swire House via the Chater Road exit, take a right, and then an immediate left onto Des Voeux Road Central, where you will be in front of the Landmark. Enter the Landmark after visiting Hermès (entrance on the street) and Dickson Watch & Jewellery Co. Ltd. (also on the street). One entrance into the building is beside Gucci. Walk past Gucci, down a somewhat claustrophobic hallway, toward the throngs of people and center atrium. Once in the atrium, spend some time gawking like the rest of the tourists. We gawk every time we visit the Landmark. The biggest names in design are here. If you are looking for discount shopping only, don't waste your time. . . . Move on, or grab a bite to eat. However, if you are not going to Europe soon and want to purchase expensive fashions from the top designer houses, start

shopping. In the Landmark you will find Celine, Lanvin, Cacharel, Krizia, Ellesse, Jaeger, Versace, Ferré, Vuitton, Gucci, Courrèges, Ungaro, Montana, etc., and a score of other fun shops. The Landmark could be an all-day adventure in itself. We suggest, however, that you make your major designer purchases here and wait to buy gifts until you visit some of our discount sources.

6. One discount source we like is in the Bank of East Asia Building, which connects to the Landmark via a ramp on the top mezzanine. The shop is called Vica Moda and has a good selection of silk blouses at reasonable prices. You will find the same merchandise slightly less expensive in some other outlets, but if your time in Hong Kong is limited, this is a good place to buy.

7. After visiting Vica Moda, go back into the Landmark and break for lunch. The rest of our tour is going to be fun but not so elegant. Choose your restaurant from the many (including a Pizza Hut in the basement) that are available, and work out your budget for the rest of the day. If you need more cash, there is an American Express bank in Swire House.

8. Exit the Landmark via the Pedder Street door, cross at the corner of Queen's Road Central, turn right down Pedder Street, and look for the Pedder Building (No. 12: small entryway right next to the China Building). If you get to the Mandarin House, you have gone too far. The building is a renovated warehouse/factory. The spaces now occupied by chic designer boutiques were once, not so long ago, workrooms. Start at the 5th floor and work your way down. Don't miss Shirt Stop on the 5th floor and Wintex (4th floor) for factory prices on Lisa Ferranti. On the 3rd floor is Takpac,

carrying Anne Klein II and Chantal Thomas. On the 2nd floor you will find David Sheekwan. The 1st floor has Shopper's World Safari (Room 104) and Betu (Room 106B).

9. If you still have the energy at this point to go on, exit the Pedder Building, take a right, and then another right onto Queen's Road Central. Stay on the harbor side of the street and walk in the direction of Pottinger Street. If you are interested in buying sunglasses or prescription glasses, stop at the Optical Shop (ground floor of the China Building) or Mandarin Optical (No. 51). Both shops offer incredible value for the dollar, and both are honest and reliable.

10. Your last stop of the day should be the Lane Crawford Department Store, across the street from Mandarin Optical and farther toward Pottinger Street. Here you can find a sampling of anything you want, from truly fine art to portrait photography, from china and crystal to Mikimoto pearls. You can even get a pedicure for your very tired feet at Elizabeth Arden.

11. Taxi back to your hotel with all of your packages. If you like night markets and still haven't had enough adventure (you're our kind of person), make reservations for an early dinner and plan to be at the Macao Ferry Pier at about 8 P.M. This is a very simple night market compared to the ones in Kowloon. The merchandise is cheap/fun junk. There are also scores of food stalls selling every kind of Chinese specialty.

Tour 2: Antiques Adventures

It is possible to be in Hong Kong and not experience the flavor of this exciting, energetic city. If you visit only the Landmark, the Hilton Hotel, and Swire House, your view would be that Hong Kong is a very civilized, clean, modern, disciplined city. However, the real Hong Kong is more than just shopping centers, luxury hotels, and large office compounds. The street life is what makes the city vibrate. This adventure is for the person who enjoys the sensuous aspects of a city—and we don't mean the red-light district!

Put on your walking shoes and bring your umbrella (useful as both a parasol and a walking stick). Get ready to experience Hong Kong.

1. Begin your day at the foot of Pottinger Street, next to the China Products Store on Queen's Road Central. Pottinger is a very steep-stepped street with scads of stalls and an equal number of steps. The stalls have very diverse merchandise, including handbags, clothing, and food.

   If you are truly an adventurous soul and like all kinds of markets, before you climb Pottinger Street go farther along Queen's Road Central (away from Lane Crawford), to the large Central Market. This is the source of much of the produce purchased by restaurants and hotels. Here you will see an amazing range of Chinese fruits, vegetables, and, of course, fresh meat . . . very fresh!

2. When you make it to the top of Pottinger Street you will be at the crossroads of Chinese antiques and curios heaven—better known as Hollywood Road. Hollywood Road became popular in the early 1950s, after the Revolution in China. At that time many Chinese had fled the People's Republic with possessions in hand. In order to raise cash, they pawned them on Hollywood Road. The tradition remained, and Hollywood Road is still the center of merchandise coming out of China. Most of what you see in the shops today is not antique but antique repro. The

true finds are in the back rooms and are saved for dealers. However, if you are an antiques collector, let the shop owner know immediately upon entering the store that you are in the market for fine pieces and are willing to deal. Often it is better to have an introduction to a dealer in town who can shop and negotiate with you. For the majority of shoppers who want a curio to take home, rummaging through dusty shelves for the "perfect" piece is a lot of fun! Just remember that there are no Ming vases on the shelves. Ask lots of questions, and bargain. Try to pay cash, as credit cards often add 4% to your bill. Make sure you get a receipt stating the age of your purchase. If you are buying a true antique you are entitled to a certificate of authenticity. Customs will want to see these papers. In the more established shops, shipping is no problem and the goods arrive safely. If you are planning to buy in quantity for any reason, ask for the dealer price. Bring along your business card and negotiate on a quantity basis. Many of the shops are used to dealing with interior designers who buy for their clients.

Hollywood Road is actually an extension of Wyndham Street. Except for Ian McLean of 73 Wyndham Street, however, the chicest shops begin at Pottinger Street and continue toward the Man Mo Temple. The closer you get to Ladder Street, the tackier the shops become. After the temple the shops become a mix of Chinese herbalists, furniture makers, and curio stores. Be sure to go into a Chinese medicine shop and look at all the wonderful, exotic substances in glass jars. The wizened old men concocting remedies for any ailment you might have probably are the only true antiques left on Hollywood Road.

3. At this point you will have passed the Man Mo Temple. If you didn't go into this shrine,

do so. There is nothing to buy, except a Coca-Cola from a stand at the corner, but the experience is important for an understanding of Chinese life. The burning incense, filtered light, larger-than-life statues, smoke-filled rooms, and candles all contribute to a visual sense of the Chinese life-style.

4. Exit the temple and go to the corner of Hollywood Road and Ladder Street. Ladder Street is another of those wonderful stepped streets that looks like it has been there for centuries. Most of the street actually runs uphill, but you will be thrilled to know that you will be going downhill. Pass by the street hawkers selling jade (you can make a better deal at the Jade Market), go to Cat Street (also known as Upper Lascar Road), and turn left. This is a really fun street to walk and shop for junk. Vendors have not set up stalls. All the merchandise is displayed on blankets laid on the ground. Each vendor specializes in a different variety of "junk." Farther along the street you will see workshops making furniture and forging metals. Dealers who sell mostly to the design trade have their showrooms in the Cat Street Galleries, which is in the middle of the block on the harbor side of the street. The actual address for the gallery is on the next street down the hill, so if you miss the building on Cat Street, walk to the end of Cat Street, turn right, duck under the hanging laundry, and turn right again on Lok Ku Road. Showrooms are at No. 38.

5. If you have the energy to walk, go down the steps of Ladder Street to Man Wah Lane. If you can't walk, you can almost roll. Man Wah Lane is the only place to buy a chop and is also the best place to have your business cards made up in Chinese (a great gift for the person who has everything).

6. If you have strength for one more adventure, walk the few extra blocks to Wing Lok, which runs parallel to Bonham Strand East. At Nos. 61–69 is our favorite cosmetics and perfume importer, Kin Chuen Cosmetics Co. Ltd. Chances are you need to flag a taxi and limp to your hotel.

Tour 3: Half-Day Adventures—Yet More Bargains (Includes Stanley Market)

These two tours are at opposite ends of the Hong Kong world, so divide them in half by lunch, or separate them into two different days if you have time. We suggest lunch in or near your hotel, because you'll want to make a pit stop to drop off your packages.

1. MTR Lai Chi Kok. This is a lot closer to downtown Kowloon, and while the outlets we suggest do not offer the exotic treasures you'll find at Leather Concepts, we were quite pleased with ourselves on the day we bought the raincoat for $10. See page 180 for directions and actual listings for this part of town. We suggest this as a morning tour.

2. Stanley Market. Take the bus or a taxi to Stanley Market in the afternoon. We go by taxi because we are anxious to get to the bargains and return by bus. Yes, it's rush hour by then, but the traffic is going the other way. The bus will be empty when you get on it at Stanley Market and will fill as you approach town, but you will get a seat. Look out the windows to get a bird's-eye view of the real Hong Kong. See page 97 for directions to and suggestions for Stanley Market.

Tour 4: Central Street Markets

This tour is for the person who wants to spend some more time in the Central District before heading on to a meeting or to Stanley Market in the afternoon. These stops should not occupy more than three hours of your time, unless you hit gold at one of them.

1. Start your spree in the Pedder Building across from the Landmark (see Tour 1 for a description of what the Pedder Building has to offer and how to get there).

2. Turn left for Mark's Camera. This is the shop where all the professional photogs shop for their equipment. Steven Mark is very knowledgeable and more than willing to give you his professional advice on equipment. The camera shop (20 Des Voeux Road) is farther down Theatre Lane, toward Queen's Road, Central.

3. Turn right on Queen's Road, Central, and walk three blocks to Li Yuen East, where you will turn right, walk to Des Voeux Road, turn left, and then walk up Li Yuen West. Li Yuen East and Li Yuen West are the most famous market streets in the Central District. The street vendors sell absolutely everything except counterfeit. Li Yuen East and West used to be where you could find all those brand-name goods for bargain prices, but Hong Kong has had a major housecleaning and now the streets are squeaky clean. You will find briefcases that look amazingly like Gucci but without the GG, watches that look just like Chanel but have no logo, and purses that should carry an LV but instead say LL. These two streets do have a wonderful selection of sweaters, purses, underwear, and odd merchandise you will not see elsewhere.

4. After finishing Li Yuen West, turn right on Queen's Road and proceed to Pottinger Street. If you have not climbed the steps and peered into the stall boutiques, you might want to do it now. Otherwise take a right and proceed until you see or smell the Central Market. Depending upon your sensibilities, peer in or tour it.

5. After you leave the Central Market, take a long breath of fresh air and then keep walking on Queen's Road, Central, until you reach Wing On Street. This is a market street that specializes in fabrics. Its nickname is Cloth Alley. If you don't look hard you will walk right by. Cloth Alley is a good place to pick up Chinese silk.

6. Walk to the end of Wing On Street and turn left onto Wing Lok Street. Walk two blocks then cut up Man Wa Lane (on your left) to Bonham Strand East (to the right). Man Wa Lane is where you will see the chop makers. If you want stationary, or your name engraved on a chop, this is the place.

7. Bonham Strand East is the place to pick up a snake for dinner. Even if that doesn't appeal to you, it is interesting to see all the snake shops doing business. Snake soup is considered a delicacy in Hong Kong. Along the street you will also see great and authentic rattan shops. These shops cater mostly to the local crowd who know good quality. A rattan weaver must apprentice for three years before being allowed to handle weaving on his own.

8. Bonham Strand East turns into Bonham Strand West past the Macao Ferry Pier. This area of town is known for its medicines and ginseng. Shop after shop is filled with barrels and jugs of herbs and roots. Men and women stand in line to talk to the herb doctor, who prescribes combinations to cure their ills.

9. Bonham Strand West dead-ends into Des Voeux Road West, where you should take a left for one block before taking a right on Sutherland Street and then a left onto Queen's Road West. Look here for wedding shops, embroidery shops, and paper shops. The wedding shops and embroidery shops sell all varieties of magnificent fabrics in different weights and colors. The paper shops specialize in paper to be burned as offerings. You can buy houses, cars, and boats, all meant to be burned at the funeral of a loved one. The images are supposed to accompany the departing spirit and make life more comfortable in the afterworld.

10. If you keep walking straight you will enter the back end of Hollywood Road near the coffin and provision shops. The other choice is to stay on Queen's Road West until it turns into Queen's Road Central, and take the bus or hail a cab home. If you stay on Hollywood Road, do our Hollywood Road tour backwards (see page 236). If you stay on Queen's Road, notice the tea shops and art-supply shops.

Tour 5: Kowloon—All-Day Bargain/Treasure Hunting: Outlets, Markets, Hot Young Designer Boutiques, and All That Stuff

Kowloon has many different shopping areas, each of which should be a day's adventure. In our one-day tour we will cover only our favorites; there are many more in our listings. And you will have no trouble finding adventures of your own, no matter where you wander. Begin your day early. The shops all open by 9:30 A.M., and you should be at our first shop at that time. Our second stop is a market that opens at 10 A.M. and closes around noon, so judge your time accordingly.

1. If you are staying in Kowloon, walk to the Ocean Terminal, just to the right of the Star Ferry Pier. If arriving via the Star Ferry from Hong Kong, turn left as you exit and look for the Omni The Hong Kong Hotel and the entrance into Ocean Terminal just beside it. Ocean Terminal is one of the few massive shopping complexes we recommend you even peek at. There are another three miles of Harbour City shops that connect Ocean Terminal, the Omni The Hong Kong Hotel, Ocean Centre, Ocean Galleries, and the Omni Marco Polo and Omni Prince hotels. Wandering for miles and miles of shopping becomes a surrealistic experience after the first half hour.

   In Ocean Terminal, stop first at the information desk and pick up the *A-O-A Map Directory* to Hong Kong. We found these maps to be invaluable resources because both the streets and building names are drawn and listed. Very often an address is impossible to see, but every building has its name prominently displayed. After leaving the information desk, go upstairs and start hoofing. There are hundreds of shops.

2. Next stop is the Jade Market, which opens at 10 A.M. and closes just after lunchtime. If you choose to take a taxi, ask the driver for the corner of Reclamation and Kansu streets, across from the Yaumatei Market (produce market building that is across the street). If taking the MTR, exit at the Nathan and Jordan roads terminal, walk past the Yue Hwa Department Store, past the Wing On Bank and Department Store, past the Hotel Fortuna, and take a left on Kansu Street. You will then see ahead of you blocks of stalls with umbrellas. These are produce vendors. The Jade Market is an enclosed area just after you pass Shanghai Street. Walk through the chicken-wire enclosure and pass around the market (approximately a hun-

dred stalls crammed together under umbrellas). Especially take note of where the Chinese people seem to be buying. We have had our best luck following Chinese shoppers, watching how they negotiated for their jade, and then counting the money as the sale was being finalized. It sounds a little silly, but unless you are a jade expert, how else can you know the fair market value for a piece of stone? We found that the prices vary enormously for stones that look similar to an untrained eye. Once you, too, have spent a day staring at green rocks they will look enormously different, but to the first-time buyer it is very confusing. Look also for the vendors selling jade pieces for practically nothing (50¢ to $5). Sometimes you can pick up some attractive pieces of jade to combine with a larger good piece for a necklace. No matter what it is you want to buy, remember that this is the time to act like you don't care, and to bargain.

3. By now you will be starving. At least we always are after visiting the Jade Market. Not only will it be after noon, but also you should be so highly stimulated by the deals you were able to make, that your body will need to be refueled. If not, continue on. In either case we recommend grabbing a taxi and going to the Peninsula Hotel. There are plenty of restaurants in the area, and our next shopping stop is the hotel itself. In the Peninsula you will find the best selection of big-name designer boutiques in Kowloon. The shopping arcade is to the right and left of the center court restaurant as you are standing facing the front doors to the hotel. There are three floors of shops. Famous names you will not want to miss are Cartier, Leonard, Mila Schön, Bally, Chanel, Trussardi, Ascot Chang Co. (custom-made shirts), and Charles Jourdan. All of these shops carry a small amount of stock but are repu-

table dealers. If you want to buy a Cartier watch, you can feel comfortable that the watch will indeed be Cartier inside and out.

4. The next stop is at our two favorite sweater outlets. Both are in the Sands Building, 17 Hankow Road. Exit the Peninsula Hotel on the Hankow Road side, turn right, cross Middle Road, and continue until Peking Road. Cross Peking Road, make an immediate left, and cross Hankow Road. You will be at the corner of the Sands Building. Entrance is on Hankow Road. First go to Top Knitters on the 10th floor. Here you will find Mirrors by Krizia, and many other famous knit lines. Labels often are cut out, so you have to know your designer look to appreciate what you are buying, which is quality. Our other favorite resource is Oriental Pacific in Room 601. O.P. carries private-label knit goods at incredible prices. In the summer, their cotton sweaters cost from $10 to $50. The same merchandise at a chic boutique in the United States would be three times as expensive. We know—we have made the mistake of buying it! They also carry gorgeous single- or double-ply cashmeres for men and women. These two resources are a must if you have birthday or holiday shopping to do.

5. If you bought too much at Top Knitters and O.P., you might have to return to your hotel to stash your goods. Possibly you can leave your bags at O.P. and retrieve them after you explore Nathan Road, our next stop. As you exit the Sands Building, turn right and then left on Peking Road. Walk three blocks to Nathan Road and turn left. Nathan Road is bargain central. We get dizzy trying to count the number of watch and camera shops along this strip. Next stop is at the Burlington Arcade (92–94 Nathan Road). Sam's Tailor is on the main floor as you enter, and is an experience you don't

want to miss. We are not sure how Sam does business in this tiny shop, but his clients swear by his quality and promptness. Most of his business is, in fact, local businessmen and repeat customers. (Rumor has it that his suits are sent to Canton by train and brought back the next day after they are completed.) Our best choice in tailors is one floor up, in Room 2F. W. W. Chan & Sons has a spacious and quiet shop where the more private client can pick out beautiful English wools for his suits and fine English cottons for his shirts. Prices are a touch more than Sam's, but you pay for the quiet!

6. Just off Nathan Road is Granville Road, which seems to be becoming discount heaven. As you leave the Burlington Arcade, turn right and continue up Nathan Road past Cameron Road. The next right is Granville Road. You will see many shops listing "discount." Some are, most are not. On this street, the factory outlets are upstairs, where the rent is cheaper . . . and the factories are located. Some of these shops are bargain-basement, some are better. We always check in at GAT Design Ltd., in the Taurus Building (21A-B Granville Road), and A-Win Garments Manufactory (23 Granville Road).

7. Now backtrack on Granville Road and take a right on Carnarvon Road until you reach Kimberley Road. Here take a right and follow Kimberley in a U as it becomes Austin Road, then Austin Avenue and returns to cross Nathan Road. This is the young designer section of Kowloon. Kimberley Road and Austin Avenue are lined with trendy boutiques selling the latest in Hong Kong–and Japanese-designed fashions. A few of our favorites include: Pink House (19–23 Austin Avenue), for young slinky fashions; Onitsuka (15 C-B2 Austin Avenue), for way-out fabulous Japanese warrior decor and experimental designs; Legend (22A Kimberley

Road), for Laurence Tang designs that are verging on couture; Nunsex Monkrock (68 Kimberley Road), clothing by Eldy Pang that is New York chic with a Japanese flair; Vee, Gee and Front First (31, 56, and 49 Kimberley Road), three shops showcasing Walter Ma's younger looks (you can shop in all three and coordinate your payments in one); Signature (61A Kimberley Road), for Simon Choi and Joseph Ho designs; and Seduction (54A Kimberley Road), for wild and weird Christian Lacroix type looks that are also fun and fanciful.

8. Either return to Nathan Road and grab a cab to go back to your hotel or continue to our one last stop for the day, which is on Bristol Avenue, between Carnarvon and Mody roads. If you turn left on Carnarvon, turn right on Bristol, and just before you come to Mody you will see Young's Fashions. From the front this doesn't look like the kind of place we would send you to. However, ignore the ready-made jackets and talk to David Young about custom. Bring out that picture of the Gucci leather dress that you have been carrying in your wallet; Mr. Young will create it for you from his skins (which you select) for a lot less. You must have three days for fittings.

9. Make your dinner plans so you can be available to go to the best night market (called the Ladies' Market) in Kowloon, at about 9:30 P.M. Whole families stroll the Ladies' Market area shopping for whatever the vendors have brought in for the night. You can take the MTR to Mong Kok and exit the subway on Argyle. Mong Kok is the stop after Yaumatei. The market is mostly on Argyle. At the market you can find Fila shirts, Japanese toys, underwear, watches, electronic goods, and knits. Just about everything manufactured can be found in some vendor's pushcart. The streets have an energy similar

to that of a carnival. Even the regular stores stay open late to accommodate the crowds.

Tour 6: Kowloon Out-of-the-Way Factory Outlets

If you did not get your fill of factory bargains in Tours 3 and 5, this could be your choice for a third day, or half day if you are fast. These outlets are not easy to find and often are in areas you won't believe—areas that make the New York garment district look like Fifth Avenue. However, go with a friend, and have a ball.

Don't expect to be able to find a taxi in many of these locations, so arm yourself with a good MTR map and a new tourist pass. Pack some fruit and cheese in case you get hungry and don't want to try a street market. The majority of factory outlets in the out-of-the-way areas do not take credit cards or checks, so bring enough cash to get by. Remember when scheduling your time that this is a working area and therefore the majority of shops close for lunch (1–2 P.M.). However, the outlets are open during regular business hours on Saturday.

1. Go to the MTR stop Kwun Tong. Kwun Tong is the last stop on the MTR Kowloon East line and therefore is the name of the line (makes it easy). Coming from Admiralty or Tsimshatsui, you will change trains at the Mong Kok station for the Kwun Tong line. Expect the trip to take forty-five minutes from Central or thirty minutes from Tsimshatsui. The train goes above ground about halfway to Kwun Tong, which makes the trip quite interesting. Most of the people will have gotten off the train before the last stop, but you might find a few factory work-

ers or other avid bargain shoppers to keep you company.

2. Exit the train and take the escalator down to the main floor. Take the stairs across and over Hoi Yuen Road if you want to go to Leather Concepts and Trinity Textiles.

3. Walk straight ahead on Hoi Yuen Road (traffic now will be on your right) until you reach Hing Yip Street. The Security Pacific Asian Bank is on the corner in case you can't see any street signs. Take a left and walk until you are almost at the end of the block. The number "20" is displayed over a very large garage door. This is what you have been searching for: Leather Concepts Ltd. Enter the garage and look for the elevators on the left. There are actually two elevators. The one through the brown doors has an operator, the one up the stairs does not. Go to the 11th floor and ask the security guard at the desk for someone to help you in the showroom. He won't understand a word you say but will know what you want just by looking at your guidebook and seeing your desperate expression. All of your walking, riding, searching, and schlepping will be rewarded here in leather heaven.

4. Trinity Textiles Limited, 10 Shing Yip Street. Upon leaving Leather Concepts, turn right onto Hing Yip Street, then left onto King Yip Street and take another left onto Shing Yip Street. (Who was Mr. Yip, anyway?) The neighborhood is less than wonderful, but keep in mind that this is the real world, not the Landmark! The reality of the neighborhood makes the Trinity Textiles showrooms (two) seem like stage sets from *The Twilight Zone.* We keep thinking that Rod Serling should come out of a dressing room modeling one of the men's suits that Trinity manufactures. Both showrooms are modern and look like any nice showroom in one of

the Harbour City underground shopping arcades. The best part, in case you have dragged your husband or a male friend with you, is that these two shops sell *only* menswear. The one to the left of the garage has suits and formalwear, the one to the right of the garage sells the casual line. They even take American Express and Diner's Club!

5. To get to Diane Freis we suggest that you return to the MTR station. To do this, take a left upon leaving Trinity Textiles, and then a right back onto Hoi Yuen Road. Now turn to page 182 for directions to Diane Freis.

6. Retrace your steps to get home and enjoy the cool clothing (Diane Freis) and hot pants (Leather Concepts) that you bought. We like tea at the Peninsula after a day like this, just because it is such a contrast.

Size Conversion Chart

WOMEN'S DRESSES, COATS, AND SKIRTS

American	3	5	7	9	11	12	13	14	15	16	18
Continental	36	38	38	40	40	42	42	44	44	46	48
British	8	10	11	12	13	14	15	16	17	18	20

WOMEN'S BLOUSES AND SWEATERS

American	10	12	14	16	18	20
Continental	38	40	42	44	46	48
British	32	34	36	38	40	42

WOMEN'S SHOES

American	5	6	7	8	9	10
Continental	36	37	38	39	40	41
British	3½	4½	5½	6½	7½	8½

CHILDREN'S CLOTHING

American	3	4	5	6	6X
Continental	98	104	110	116	122
British	18	20	22	24	26

CHILDREN'S SHOES

American	8	9	10	11	12	13	1	2	3
Continental	24	25	27	28	29	30	32	33	34
British	7	8	9	10	11	12	13	1	2

MEN'S SUITS

American	34	36	38	40	42	44	46	48
Continental	44	46	48	50	52	54	56	58
British	34	36	38	40	42	44	46	48

MEN'S SHIRTS

American	14½	15	15½	16	16½	17	17½	18
Continental	37	38	39	41	42	43	44	45
British	14½	15	15½	16	16½	17	17½	18

MEN'S SHOES

American	7	8	9	10	11	12	13
Continental	39½	41	42	43	44½	46	47
British	6	7	8	9	10	11	12

INDEX OF STORES BY NEIGHBORHOOD

Hong Kong

Central, Hong Kong

CONNAUGHT ROAD

MANDARIN ORIENTAL HOTEL
Fashion: Eddie Lau, p. 126
Jewelry: Gemsland, pp. 200–201, 202; Kai Yin Lo, pp. 127–128; 201
Tailors: A-Man Hing Cheong Company Ltd., pp. 189–190; David's Shirts, pp. 190–191; Robert Tailor, p. 191

P.C. LU & SONS, LTD., *Antiques/Home Furnishings,* pp. 229–230
REASON COMPANY, *Arts & Crafts,* pp. 226–227

SWIRE HOUSE
Fashion: Bally Boutique, p. 110; Bottega Veneta, p. 111; Kenzo, p. 122; Tokio Kumagai, p. 122; Matsuda, pp. 122–123; Issey Miyake, p. 123; Joseph Ho, p. 125; Ragence Lam, pp. 125–126; Jenny Lewis, pp. 126–127; Walter Ma, p. 128; Camberley, p. 157; Bruno Magli, p. 234; Mayer Shoe Co., p. 195
Tailors: Art's, pp. 186–187; H. Baroman Ltd., p. 187
Antiques/Home Furnishings: Grenley's, p. 219

CHATER ROAD

PRINCE'S BUILDING
Fashion: Chanel, pp. 112–113; Christian Dior Monsieur, p. 113; Jean-Paul Gaultier, p. 115; Esprit, p. 120; Diane Freis, pp. 120–121; Daks, p. 114

QUEEN'S ROAD

PEDDER STREET

THE PEDDER BUILDING

QUEENSWAY

THE MALL PACIFIC PLACE

ICE HOUSE STREET

OBSERVATORY ROAD

MIDDLE ROAD

CARNARVON ROAD

HAIPHONG ROAD

ASHLEY ROAD

PRAT AVENUE

HANKOW ROAD

CHATHAM ROAD

MODY ROAD

Tsimshatsui East, Kowloon

GRANVILLE ROAD

MODY ROAD

Yaumatei, Kowloon

NATHAN ROAD

Lai Chi Kok, Kowloon

CHEUNG SHUN STREET

CHEUNG SHA WAN ROAD

WING HONG STREET

SHING YIP STREET

KWUN TONG ROAD

About the Authors

SUZY GERSHMAN is an author and journalist who also writes under her maiden name, Suzy Kalter. She has worked in the fiber and fashion industry since 1969 in both New York and Los Angeles and has held editorial positions at *California Apparel News, Mademoiselle, Gentleman's Quarterly*, and *People* magazine, where she was West Coast Style editor. She writes regularly for *Travel and Leisure*; her essays on retailing are text at the Harvard Business School. Mrs. Gershman lives in Connecticut with her husband, author Michael Gershman, and their son. Michael Gershman also contributes to the *Born to Shop* pages.

JUDITH THOMAS is a designer who began her career working in the creative and advertising departments of Estee Lauder and Helena Rubinstein in New York. Previously she was an actress in television commercials as well as on and off Broadway. In 1973 she moved to Los Angeles where she was an art director for various studios while studying for her ASID at UCLA. She later formed Panache and Associates, a commercial design firm. She is currently involved in developing and marketing new trends in building design for MPS Systems. Mrs. Thomas lives in Pennsylvania with her husband and two children.